A More Perfect Union

A More Perfect Union

Documents in U.S. History

Sixth Edition

Volume 1: To 1877

Paul F. Boller, Jr.

Professor Emeritus, Texas Christian University

Ronald Story

University of Massachusetts, Amherst

Houghton Mifflin Company

Boston   New York

Sponsoring Editor: Sally Constable
Development Editor: Lisa Kalner Williams
Editorial Assistant: Kisha Mitchell
Associate Project Editor: Teresa Huang
Editorial Assistant: Jake Perry
Senior Art and Design Coordinator: Jill Haber
Senior Photo Editor: Jennifer Meyer Dare
Senior Composition Buyer: Sarah Ambrose
Senior Manufacturing Coordinator: Priscilla J. Bailey
Senior Marketing Manager: Sandra McGuire
Marketing Associate: Ilana Gordon

Cover image: Original Design for the Great Seal of the United States, 1782. Jonathan Wallen/The National Archives, Washington, D.C. Background: The Declaration of Independence. Jonathan Wallen.

Printed in the U.S.A.

Library of Congress Catalog Card Number: 2004105785

ISBN: 0-618-43683-9

23456789-MVP-08   07   06   05

CONTENTS

Chapter Two

★─────────────────────

Breaking Away

★——————

CHAPTER THREE

Nationalists and Partisans

★————————————

CHAPTER FOUR

The Age of Reform

★————————————

CHAPTER SIX

The Agony of Reconstruction

PREFACE

Our two-volume reader, *A More Perfect Union: Documents in U.S. History*, presents students with the original words of speeches and testimony, political and legal writings, and literature that have reflected, precipitated, and implemented pivotal events of the past four centuries. The readings in Volume 1 cover the era from first settlement to Reconstruction. Volume 2 begins with the post–Civil War period and concludes with selections that relate to recent history. We are pleased with the reception that *A More Perfect Union* has received, and we have worked toward refining the contents of this new edition.

Changes to the Sixth Edition

More than a third of the material is new to this edition. New selections in Volume 1 include, for example, poems by Anne Bradstreet, a Great Awakening sermon by Jonathan Edwards, a resolution by Boston journeymen carpenters, and a fresh selection from *Uncle Tom's Cabin*. Among the new selections in Volume 2 are statements by Samuel Gompers on the rights of labor, Theodore Roosevelt on the Monroe Doctrine, and Senator Sam Ervin on Richard Nixon's impeachment proceedings, as well as labor organizing songs from the 1930s.

Goal and Format

The readings in these volumes represent a blend of social and political history, along with some cultural and economic trends, suitable for introductory courses in American history. We made our selections with three thoughts in mind. First, we looked for famous documents with a lustrous place in the American tradition—the Gettysburg Address, for example, or Franklin D. Roosevelt's First Inaugural Address. These we chose for their great mythic quality, as expressions of fundamental sentiments with which students should be familiar. Second, we looked for writings that caused something to happen or had an impact when they appeared. Examples include the Virginia slave statutes, the Emancipation Proclamation, and Earl Warren's opinion in *Brown* v. *Board of Education of Topeka*—all of them influential pieces, some of them famous as well. Third, we looked for documents that seem to reflect important attitudes or developments. Into this group fall the writings of Upton Sinclair on industrial Chicago and of Martin Luther King, Jr., on Vietnam. In this category, where the need for careful selection from a wide field was most apparent, we looked especially for thoughtful pieces with a measure of fame and influence. Horace Mann's statement on schools reflected common attitudes; it also caused something to happen and is a well-known reform statement. We have also tried to mix a few unusual items into the stew, as with the "Report of the Joint Committee on Reconstruction" and a statement by the Catholic bishops on parochial schools.

We have edited severely in places, mostly when the document is long or contains extraneous material or obscure references. We have also, in some cases, modernized spelling and punctuation.

Each document has a lengthy headnote that summarizes the relevant trends of the era, provides a specific setting for the document, and sketches the life of the author. In addition, "Questions to Consider" guide students through the prose and suggest ways of thinking about the selections.

Acknowledgements

We would like to thank the following people who reviewed the sixth edition manuscript for one or both volumes: Jonathan M. Atkins, Berry College; Lorri Glover, University of Tennessee; Carol Sue Humphrey, Oklahoma Baptist University; Steven E. Siry, Baldwin-Wallace College; and Andrew McMichael, Western Kentucky University.

We would also like to thank the following people who reviewed the manuscript in prior editions: John K. Alexander, University of Cincinnati; June G. Alexander, University of Cincinnati; Judith L. Demark, Northern Michigan University; Kurk Dorsey, University of New Hampshire; Paul G. Faler, University of Massachusetts at Boston; Harvey Green, Northeastern University; Richard H. Peterson, San Diego State University; Ben Rader, University of Nebraska at Lincoln; C. Elizabeth Raymond, University of Nevada–Reno; Thomas Templeton Taylor, Wittenberg University; and John Scott Wilson, University of South Carolina.

We owe a debt of gratitude to Kisha Mitchell, our editorial assistant, and to Teresa Huang, our associate project editor, for this edition. We also wish to express our appreciation to the editorial staff of Houghton Mifflin Company for their hard and conscientious work in producing these volumes.

P. F. B.
R. S.

A More Perfect Union

An Indian village in the early Virginia region. This engraving from a watercolor by the Englishman John White shows an Algonquian community with quonset-style huts, scenes of family and religious life, and plantings of corn on the right and tobacco on the left. A hunting party is at the top. White hoped to spur colonization by persuading European readers that the North Americans were settled and civilized rather than nomadic savages. (Miriam and Ira D. Wallach Division of Art, Prints and Photographs, The New York Public Library. Astor, Lenox and Tilden Foundations)

CHAPTER ONE

Planters and Puritans

1

CONTACT

Englishmen came to Virginia in 1607 with one overriding purpose: to find gold and find it quickly. If possible, they would achieve this goal by raiding Spanish treasure galleons; more likely, they would force the so-called Indians to mine it for them, as the Spaniards had in Mexico and Peru. "Our gilded refiners with their golden promises made all men their slaves in hope of recompense," complained Captain John Smith, the settlement's military leader and chronicler. "There was no talk, no hope, but dig gold, wash gold, refine gold, load gold."

Unfortunately for the English, the Chesapeake Bay region proved not only too distant from the Spanish Main for raiding but also barren of precious metal. The Virginia Company, which was organized militarily, was short of provisions and top-heavy with "gentlemen adventurers" and luxury craftsmen without the skill or will to grow crops. The company lost half its men within two years, and without help from the Native American population, the remainder would also have perished.

The Chesapeake region was inhabited mostly by Powhatans, a confederacy of ten thousand people in one hundred and thirty villages. Their shrewd leader, Chief Powhatan, bore the tribal name. Powhatan might easily have refused to help the hapless English. European-borne diseases had afflicted the tribal population even before these English arrived. European raiders, English and Spanish, had attacked and burned Powhatan villages. But there were also reasons to offer help. The Powhatans, reared in a collective, uncompetitive ethos, were generous—both among themselves and with nonthreatening neighbors, as the tiny English band probably appeared at first. Chief Powhatan was looking for allies in a territorial dispute with nonconfederacy tribes. The English, who carried edged metal weapons and primitive firearms, appeared likely recruits.

Reduced to eating "dogs, cats, rats, and mice" (and eventually cadavers and one another), the English should have received Powhatan's gifts of corn and meat with gratitude. But Captain Smith was an aggressive mercenary soldier who had once been enslaved by "infidel" Turks and was deeply suspicious of "infidel Indians," particularly given the defenseless state of the English settlement. He tended to see even acts of generosity as the mere treachery of "wild cruel Pagans."

Smith preferred to take by force what he needed rather than to receive it by gift. While engaged in raiding forays, he sometimes found himself trapped by Powhatan's forces. On one such occasion, Powhatan sought to demonstrate his authority by arranging a mock execution of Smith. He had Pocahantas, his young daughter, halt the proceedings by throwing herself upon the prisoner. Smith, perhaps understandably, misinterpreted the gesture as an expression of love for the English, thus supplying one of the earliest Anglo-American fables.

Powhatan delivered the address reprinted below during an encounter with Smith in the winter of 1608, when the English were again desperate for provisions. The speech first appeared in Smith's *A Map of Virginia, with a Description of the Countrey, the Commodities, People, Government, and Religion,* published in London in 1612. Transcribed into Elizabethan English by men barely familiar with Native American ways and language, the passage nevertheless seems a clear and straightforward rendering of Powhatan's concerns and hopes.

The chief, whom Smith estimated to be about sixty years old in 1607, was himself the son of a chief from south of the Chesapeake, possibly from Spanish Florida. When Powhatan saw the English continually raiding villages despite his overtures to John Smith, this accomplished statesman and stern ruler determined to starve the English into submission through intermittent war. His policy was partially successful. English weakness and the marriage of Pocahantas to settler John Rolfe in 1614 brought an uneasy truce that lasted until Powhatan's death in 1618. However, his successor, Opechankanough, saw the English as competitors for land rather than as raiders for food. In 1622 he launched an attack that killed a third of the settlers. The bankruptcy of the Virginia Company, the conversion of Virginia to a royal colony, and a rapid increase in European settlement soon followed. By 1669, when the first Virginia census was taken, the Powhatans themselves numbered barely 2,000.

Questions to Consider. Do Powhatan's opening remarks contain anything to substantiate his reputation for shrewd statecraft? According to Powhatan, why had his people refused to give corn to the English? What arguments did Powhatan use in trying to persuade the English not to wage war against him? What did he mean by the word that the English translated as *love?* Was Powhatan aware that Captain Smith was a much younger man? Why did Powhatan want John Smith and his men to come unarmed for talks? Why did the English fail to respond to so promising and open-handed an appeal?

★━━★━━★

Address to John Smith (1608)

POWHATAN

Captain Smith, some doubt I have of your coming hither, that makes me not so kindly seek to relieve you as I would; for many do inform me, your coming is not for trade, but to invade my people and possess my Country, who dare not come to bring you corn, seeing you thus armed with your men. To cheer [relieve] us of this fear, leave aboard your weapons, for here they are needless, we being all friends and forever Powhatans. . . .

Captain Smith, you may understand that I, having seen the death of all my people thrice, and not one living of those three generations but myself, I know the difference of peace and war better than any in my Country. But now I am old, and ere long must die. My brethren, namely Opichapam, Opechankanough, and Kekataugh, [and] my two sisters, and their two daughters, are distinctly each others' successors. I wish their experiences no less than mine, and your love to them, no less than mine to you: but this brute [noise] from Nansamund, that you are come to destroy my Country, so much affrighteth all my people, as they dare not visit you. What will it avail you to take that which perforce, you may quietly have with love, or to destroy them that provide you food? What can you get by war, when we can hide our provision and flee to the woods, whereby you must famish, by wronging us your friends? And why are you thus jealous of our love, seeing us unarmed, and both do, and are willing still to feed you with what you cannot get but by our labors?

Think you I am so simple not to know it is better to eat good meat, lie well, and sleep quietly with my women and children, laugh, and be merry with you, have copper, hatchets, or what I want being your friend; than be forced to flee from all, to lie cold in the woods, feed upon acorns, roots and such trash, and be so hunted by you that I can neither rest, eat nor sleep, but my tired men must watch, and if a twig but break, everyone cry, there comes Captain Smith: then must I flee I know not whither, and thus with miserable fear end my miserable life, leaving my pleasures to such youths as you, which through your rash unadvisedness, may quickly as miserably end, for want of that you never know how to find? Let this therefore assure you of our loves, and every year our friendly trade shall furnish you with corn; and now also, if you would come in friendly manner to see us, and not thus with your guns and swords as to invade your foes.

Edward Arber, ed., *Travels and Works of Captain John Smith* (Edinburgh, 1910), I: 132–136.

King Powhatan comands C:Smith to be slayne, his daughter Pokahontas beggs his life his thankfullnes and how h subiected 39 of their kings. reade his ty.

printed by Iames Reeve

Ceremonial execution of John Smith. In this drawing from John Smith's *History of Virginia,* Pocahontas, standing on the right, is pleading with her father, Powhatan, seated, wearing a crown, to spare Captain Smith's life. The ceremony may have been a mock execution that would have allowed Smith to become a surrogate father to Pocahontas and therefore eligible for membership in the Indian community. Powhatan and Pocahontas are disproportionately large because the English artist wanted to convey their importance, much as European artists frequently enlarged the figures of European monarchs. (Library of Congress)

2

FIRST PRIVILEGES

The first representative body in the New World was the Virginia Assembly, or House of Burgesses. This development came about when the directors of the Virginia Company, a joint-stock corporation of British investors, decided to allow more freedom in order to attract more colonists. The directors scrapped the colony's military and communal organization when the little settlement at Jamestown, established in 1607, failed to produce a profit and came close to collapsing due to disease and starvation. The company directors distributed land to the settlers, arranged to transport craftsmen and servants, as well as women, to the colony, and authorized the election of a general assembly to help govern the colony. On July 30, 1619, twenty-two burgesses, chosen by the settlers, met for the first time with the governor and the council, appointed by the company.

The document authorizing the House of Burgesses has been lost, but an "ordinance" of 1621 (reproduced below) is believed to reproduce the provisions of 1619. Largely the work of Sir Edwin Sandys, one of the leading directors of the Virginia Company, the ordinance provided for a Council of State, appointed by the company, as well as for an assembly elected by the people. The Virginia Assembly had the power to "make, ordain, and enact such general Laws and Orders, for the Behoof of the said Colony, and the good Government thereof, as shall, from time to time, appear necessary or requisite," subject to the company's approval. The new governmental arrangements, together with the discovery that tobacco could be a lucrative crop, soon made Virginia a thriving enterprise, and these arrangements were continued after Virginia became a royal colony in 1624.

Born in 1561, Sir Edwin Sandys was an English Member of Parliament and leader of the "joint stock" corporation that helped colonize and invest in Virginia. Ingenious and resourceful, Sandys himself never sailed to the New World, although members of his family did. But he was a dominant figure among the early absentee owners of Virginia, and breathed life and funds into a venture near failure by stressing settlement rather than trade. As it turned out, his enthusiasm led the company to overexpansion and, after the bitter Indian battles of 1622, to bankruptcy.

Questions to Consider. In examining the ordinance's description of the two councils for governing Virginia, it is helpful to consider the following questions: How large was the Council of State? How was it chosen? What responsibilities did it possess? How did the responsibilities of the General Assembly compare in importance with those of the Council of State? Who possessed the ultimate authority in Virginia?

★━━★━━★

The Virginia Ordinance of 1619

EDWIN SANDYS

An ordinance and Constitution of the Treasurer, Council, and Company in England, for a Council of State and General Assembly. . . .

To all People, to whom these Presents shall come, be seen, or heard the Treasurer, Council, and Company of Adventurers and Planters for the city of *London* for the first colony of *Virginia*, send Greeting. . . .

We . . . the said Treasurer, Council, and Company, by Authority directed to us from his Majesty under the Great Seal, upon mature Deliberation, do hereby order and declare, that, from henceforward, there shall be TWO SUPREME COUNCILS in *Virginia*, for the better Government of the said Colony aforesaid.

The one of which Councils, to be called THE COUNCIL OF STATE (and whose Office shall chiefly be assisting, with their Care, Advise, and Circumspection, to the said Governor) shall be chosen, nominated, placed and displaced, from time to time, by Us, the said Treasurer, Council, and Company, and our Successors: Which Council of State shall consist, for the present, only of these Persons, as are here inserted, *viz*. Sir *Francis Wyat*, Governor of *Virginia*, Captain *Francis West*, Sir *George Yeardley*, Knight, Sir *William Neuce*, Night Marshal of *Virginia*, Mr. *George Sandys*, Treasurer, Mr. *George Thorpe*, Deputy of the College, Captain *Thomas Neuce*, Deputy for the Company, Mr. *Pawlet*, Mr. *Leech*, Captain *Nathaniel Powel*, Mr. *Harwood*, Mr. *Samuel Macock*, Mr. *Christopher Davison*, Secretary, *Doctor Pots*, Physician to the Company, Mr. *Roger Smith*, Mr. *John Berkley*, Mr. *John Rolfe*, Mr. *Ralph Hamer*, Mr. *John Pountis*, Mr. *Michael Lapworth*. Which said Counsellors and Council we earnestly pray and desire, and in his Majesty's Name strictly charge and command, that (all Factions, Partialities, and sinister Respect laid aside) they bend their Care and Endeavors to assist the said Governor; first and principally in the Advancement of the Honour and Service of God, and the Enlargement of his

F. N. Thorpe, ed., *The Federal and State Constitutions* (7 v., Government Printing Office, Washington, D.C., 1909), VII: 3810–3812.

The first colonial legislature meets in Jamestown, Virginia. Here are members of the Virginia House of Burgesses, the first legislature in British North America in their best clothing, including the extravagant headwear of the era. The Burgesses (from "burger," or townsman) would have dressed this way to demonstrate that they were still English gentlemen despite being in Virginia. The broad-brimmed hats were not only fashionable but served as umbrellas to keep off the rain. The helmeted men at arms around the room were for effect, but also to ward off possible Indian attacks. (The Library of Virginia)

Kingdom amongst the Heathen People; and next, in erecting of the said Colony in due obedience to his Majesty, and all lawful Authority from his Majesty's Directions; and lastly, in maintaining the said People in Justice and *Christian* Conversation amongst themselves, and in Strength and Ability to withstand their Enemies. And this Council, to be always, or for the most Part, residing about or near the Governor.

The other Council, more generally to be called by the Governor, once yearly, and no oftener, but for very extraordinary and important occasions, shall consist, for the present, of the said Council of State, and of two Burgesses out of every Town, Hundred, or other particular Plantation, to be respectively chosen by the Inhabitants; Which Council shall be called THE GENERAL ASSEMBLY, wherein (as also in the said Council of State) all Matter shall be decided, determined, and ordered, by the greater Part of the Voices then present; reserving to the Governor always a Negative Voice. And this General Assembly shall have free Power to treat, consult, and conclude, as well of all emergent Occasions concerning the Public Weal of the said Colony and every Part thereof, as also to make, ordain, and enact such general Laws and Orders, for the Behoof of the said Colony, and the good Government thereof, as shall, from time to time, appear necessary or requisite. . . .

Whereas in all other Things, we require the said General Assembly, as also the said Council of State, to imitate and follow the Policy of the Form of Government—Laws, Customs, and Manner of Trial, and other administration of Justice, used in the Realm of *England,* as near as may be, even as ourselves, by his Majesty's Letters Patent, are required.

Provided, that no Law or Ordinance, made in the said General Assembly, shall be or continue in Force or Validity, unless the same shall be solemnly ratified and confirmed, in a General Quarter Court of the said Company here in England and so ratified, be returned to them under our Seal; It being our Intent to afford the like Measure also unto the said Colony, that after the Government of the said Colony shall once have been well framed, and settled accordingly, which is to be done by Us, as by Authority derived from his Majesty, and the same shall have been so by Us declared, no Orders of Court afterwards shall bind the said Colony, unless they be ratified in like Manner in the General Assemblies. IN WITNESS whereof we have here unto set our Common Seal, the 24th of *July* 1621, and in the Year of the Reign of our Sovereign Lord, JAMES, King of *England,* &c.

3

Pilgrims and Settlers

The Mayflower Compact, sometimes called the first American constitution, was the handiwork of "Separatists," a small group of religious extremists who had separated from the Church of England because they did not think it was "pure" enough in its religious observances. Like all Puritans ("purifiers"), the Separatists disliked the elaborate ceremonies of the Church of England, which smacked of vanity and superstition; they favored plain and simple church services centered on preaching and the Bible. They also rejected the hierarchical structure of the Church of England, with its archbishops and bishops, which seemed to block the relation between the individual and the Lord and therefore true faith and piety. For them the congregation, organized by devout people who had experienced conversion and with the power to choose its own ministers and deacons and adopt rules for governing the church, was the center of religious authority. Regarded with hostility by the British government and with suspicion by their neighbors, the Separatists left England in 1608 and formed a "community of saints" in Holland. But they did not feel at home among the Dutch, and so decided to move to the American wilderness.

In September 1620, thirty-five "Pilgrims" (called that because of their wanderings in search of a place to live) sailed for the New World on the *Mayflower*. They had received a grant from the Virginia Company, a joint-stock corporation of British investors, to establish a settlement in "northern Virginia" and financial aid from some London merchants. Sixty-seven additional emigrants, not all of them Puritans, were aboard the *Mayflower* to help make the colony profitable for the London investors. Arriving off Cape Cod in November, before landing, the Pilgrim leaders sought to retain their authority over the settlers and unify them for the difficult tasks lying ahead by drawing up the Mayflower Compact.

Although the compact professed allegiance to the king of England, it was actually an extension of the Separatists' church covenant to matters of civil government. Since the Pilgrims who settled at Plymouth never managed to obtain a royal charter for their colony, the Mayflower

Compact itself served as their constitution until Plymouth was absorbed by Massachusetts Bay Colony in 1691.

In 1630 a much larger group of Puritan settlers arrived from England, with greater financial backing and full leeway to dispose of the lands they were claiming for themselves. Land distribution was in fact the major task of the magistrates of the General Court, the central legislative body of this new Massachusetts Bay Colony, together with adjudicating land disputes and bitter Indian warfare that necessarily followed the process of granting and settling land.

In the summer of 1636 some 30 families petitioned for lands to found the town of Dedham, in the immediate vicinity of the colonial capital, Boston. They began, as most Puritan communities did, with a "covenant" setting out the basic principles that would govern their lives together. The Dedham covenant is significant not because Dedham became especially important in Massachusetts Bay history, but because it illustrates both the pattern of covenanting and petitioning that would shape New England for the next century and the complicated mix of idealism and self-interest that characterized early Puritanism.

Questions to Consider. What objectives other than religious ones did the Pilgrims set forth in the Mayflower Compact? Examine the list of people who signed it. What does this list reveal about the representation of the 102 settlers, their status, and their view of women? What does the Compact tell you about the Pilgrims' belief in self-government? Why do you think the Pilgrims had not bothered to prepare some plan of governance long before their arrival or even before leaving Europe?

In the case of Dedham, to what extent did the settlers' covenant seem to focus on community goals as opposed to individual goals? Did the founders appear to welcome new settlers? If so, what kind? Did this covenant provide for direct democracy or representative government? Did it seem to assume that the town would control its own affairs? According to the Dedham covenant, what was the ultimate purpose of the founding of the new town?

★═══★═══★

The Mayflower Compact (1620)

In the Name of God, Amen. We, whose names are underwritten, the Loyal Subjects of our dread Sovereign Lord King *James,* by the Grace of God, of *Great Britain, France,* and *Ireland,* King, *Defender of the Faith,* &c. Having undertaken for the Glory of God, and Advancement of the Christian Faith, and the Honour of our King and Country, a Voyage to plant the first colony in the northern Parts of Virginia; Do by these Presents, solemnly and mutually in the Presence of God and one another, covenant and combine ourselves together into a civil Body Politick, for our better Ordering and Preservation, and Furtherance of the Ends aforesaid; and by Virtue hereof do enact, constitute, and frame, such just and equal Laws, Ordinances, Acts, Constitutions, and Offices, from time to time, as shall be thought most meet and convenient for the general Good of the Colony; unto which we promise all due Submission and Obedience. In WITNESS whereof we have hereunto subscribed our names at *Cape Cod* the eleventh of *November,* in the Reign of our Sovereign Lord King *James* of *England, France,* and *Ireland,* the eighteenth and of *Scotland,* the fifty-fourth. *Anno Domini,* 1620.

Mr. John Carver	Mr. Stephen Hopkins
Mr. William Bradford	Digery Priest
Mr. Edward Winslow	Thomas Williams
Mr. William Brewster	Gilbert Winslow
Isaac Allerton	Edmund Margesson
Miles Standish	Peter Brown
John Alden	Richard Bitteridge
John Turner	George Soule
Francis Eaton	Edward Tilly
James Chilton	John Tilly
John Craxton	Francis Cooke
John Billington	Thomas Rogers
Joses Fletcher	Thomas Tinker
John Goodman	John Ridgate
Mr. Samuel Fuller	Edward Fuller
Mr. Christopher Martin	Richard Clark
Mr. William Mullins	Richard Gardiner
Mr. William White	Mr. John Allerton
Mr. Richard Warren	Thomas English
John Howland	Edward Doten
	Edward Liester

Benjamin Perley Poore, ed., *The Federal and State Constitutions, Colonial Charters, and Other Organic Laws of the United States* (2 v., Government Printing Office, Washington, D.C., 1878), I: 931.

Signing the Mayflower Compact. This nineteenth-century painting depicts the signing of the famous Compact as a solemn moment with light, presumably from God, flowing into the *Mayflower* just prior to landing. William Bradford offers the quill to other members of the voyage. The interior of the little ship and the passengers' raiment look neat and clean, which would hardly have been the case after so long and grueling a voyage. The dark edges of the picture highlight the lighting from above to give the central drama a feeling similar to the works of Rembrandt and other Dutch painters who inspired this picture. (Private Collection)

★━━★━━★

A Massachusetts Town Covenant (1636)

One: We whose names are hereunto subscribed do, in the fear and reverence of our Almighty God, mutually and severally promise amongst ourselves and to each other to profess and practice one truth according to that most perfect rule, the foundation whereof is everlasting love.

Two: That we shall by all means labor to keep off from us all such as are contrary minded, and receive only such unto us as may be probably of one heart with us, as that we either know or may well and truly be informed to

Don Gleason Hill, ed., *Early Records of the Town of Dedham,* vol. 3 (Dedham, Mass., 1896), 2–3.

walk in a peaceable conversation with all meekness of spirit, for the edification of each other in the knowledge and faith of the Lord Jesus, and the mutual encouragement unto all temporal comforts in all things, seeking the good of each other, out of which may be derived true peace.

Three: That if at any time differences shall rise between parties of our said town, that then such party or parties shall presently refer all such differences unto some one, two, or three others of our said society, to be fully accorded and determined without any further delay, if it possibly may be.

Four: That every man that now, or at any time hereafter, shall have lots in our said town shall pay his share in all such rates money and charges as shall be imposed on him rateably in proportion with other men, as also become freely subject unto all such orders and constitutions as shall be necessarily had or made, now or at any time hereafter from this day forward, as well for loving and comfortable society in our said town as also for the prosperous and thriving condition of our said fellowship, especially respecting the fear of God, in which we desire to begin and continue whatsoever we shall by His loving favor take into hand. . . .

4

The Underside of Privilege

In 1619 a Dutch trader brought twenty "Negars" from Africa and sold them in Jamestown. For a long time, however, black slavery, though common in Spanish and Portuguese colonies in the New World, was not important in Virginia. For many years white indentured servants from England performed most of the labor in the colony; after three decades there were still only about three hundred blacks in the English colonies. By the end of the seventeenth century, however, transporting Africans to America had become a profitable business for English and American merchants, and the slave trade had grown to enormous proportions.

In Virginia the planters used Africans as cheap labor on their plantations and also employed them as household servants, coachmen, porters, and skilled workers. Their status was indeterminate at first, and they may have been treated somewhat like indentured servants for some time. As tobacco became important, however, and the number of blacks working on plantations soared, the position of blacks declined rapidly. The Virginia Assembly began enacting laws governing their behavior and regulating their relations with whites. The statutes, some of which are reproduced here, do not show whether racial prejudice and discrimination preceded slavery, followed it, or, more likely, accompanied it. But they do dramatize the fact that in Virginia, as elsewhere, the expansion of freedom and self-government for European Americans could go hand in hand with the exploitation and oppression of African Americans.

Questions to Consider. How strictly did the Virginia lawmakers attempt to control the behavior of Africans in the colony? How severe were the punishments provided for offenders against the law? What penalties were provided for the "casual killing" of slaves? What appeared to be the greatest fear of the Virginia lawmakers?

First slaves arrive in Jamestown. This illustration by Howard Pyle from the late nineteenth century, though lacking drama, superbly captures the historical detail—the attire and armaments of the guards, for example, and the demoralized and subordinate condition of the slaves, who were at this time nearly all male like the English settlers. Potential buyers, eager for forced laborers to work the tobacco fields, approach on the right in search of the most workers for the least cost. The shift from buying European indentured servants to buying African slaves occurred gradually throughout the seventeenth century, as did the laws and rulings that controlled them. (Library of Congress)

★══★══★

Virginia Slavery Legislation (1630–1691)

[1630]   Hugh David to be soundly whipped, before an assembly of Negroes and others for abusing himself to the dishonor of God and shame of Christians, by defiling his body in lying with a negro; which fault he is to acknowledge next Sabbath day.

[1640]   Robert Sweet to do penance in church according to laws of England, for getting a negro woman with child and the woman whipt.

[1661]   *Be it enacted* That in case any English servant shall run away in company with any negroes who are incapable of making satisfaction by addition of time, *Be it enacted* that the English so running away in company with them shall serve for the time of the said negroes absence as they are to do for their own by a former act.

[1668]   Whereas some doubts, have arisen whether negro women set free were still to be accompted tithable according to a former act, *It is declared by this grand assembly* that negro women, though permitted to enjoy their Freedom yet ought not in all respects to be admitted to a full fruition of the exemptions and impunities of England, and are still liable to payment of taxes.

[1669]   Whereas the only law in force for the punishment of refractory servants resisting their master, mistress or overseer cannot be inflicted upon negroes, nor the obstinancy of many of them by other than violent means supprest, *Be it enacted and declared by this grand assembly,* if any slave resist his master (or other by his master's order correcting him) and by the extremity of the correction should chance to die, that his death shall not be accompted Felony, but the master (or that other person appointed by the master to punish him) be acquit from molestation, since it cannot be presumed that prepensed malice (which alone makes murder Felony) should induce any man to destroy his own estate.

[1680]   *It is hereby enacted by the authority aforesaid,* that from and after the publication of this law, it shall not be lawful for any negro or other slave to carry or arm himself with any club, staff, gun, sword, or any other weapon of defence or offence, nor to go to depart from his master's ground without a certificate from his master, mistress or overseer, and such permission not to be granted but upon particular and necessary occasions; and every negro or slave so offending not having a certificate as aforesaid shall be sent to the next constable, who is hereby enjoined and required to give the said negro twenty lashes on his bare back well laid on, and so sent home to his said master, mistress or overseer. *And it is further enacted by the authority aforesaid* that if any negro or other slave shall presume to lift up his hand in opposition

William Hening, ed., *The Laws of Virginia, 1619–1792* (13 v., Samuel Pleasants, Richmond, 1809–1823).

against any Christian, shall for every such offense, upon due proof made thereof by the oath of the party before a magistrate, have and receive thirty lashes on his bare back well laid on.

[1691]   *It is hereby enacted,* that in all such cases upon intelligence of any such negroes, mulattoes, or other slaves lying out, two of their majesties' justices of the peace of that county, whereof one to be of the quorum, where such negroes, mulattoes or other slave shall be, shall be impowered and commanded, and are hereby impowered and commanded, to issue out their warrants directed to the sheriff of the same county to apprehend such negroes, mulattoes, and other slaves, which said sheriff is hereby likewise required upon all such occasions to raise such and so many forces from time to time as he shall think convenient and necessary for the effectual apprehending such negroes, mulattoes and other slaves, and in case any negroes, mulattoes or other slave or slaves lying out as aforesaid shall resist, run away, or refuse to deliver and surrender him or themselves to any person or persons that shall be by lawful authority employed to apprehend and take such negroes, mulattoes or other slaves that in such cases it shall and may be lawful for such person and persons to kill and destroy such negroes, mulattoes, and other slave or slaves by gun or any other ways whatsoever.

5

CHURCH VERSUS STATE

Massachusetts Bay Colony was not a theocracy; ministers, though important there, could not serve as magistrates, nor could magistrates be ministers. Yet in Massachusetts the Puritans made the Congregational church the official state church, supported it by taxation, and prohibited people who did not share their views from worshipping as they pleased in the colony. In 1631, a devout young Puritan preacher named Roger Williams arrived in Boston and from almost the beginning began challenging the Puritan establishment. Williams favored separation of church and state; he thought religion was corrupted when it got involved in politics. He also championed religious liberty; authentic religion, he insisted, flourishes only when people can practice it freely without government coercion.

To the consternation of John Winthrop and other Massachusetts leaders, Williams began attracting support for his views among some of the people in the colony. In 1635 they put him on trial, convicted him of spreading "dangerous opinions," and banished him from the colony. In January 1636 Williams and some of his followers fled into the wilderness. They made their way southward and finally reached the shores of Narragansett Bay, where they founded Providence Plantation. In 1640 the inhabitants of Providence drew up a "Plantation Agreement" for governing their town, emphasizing "liberty of conscience" and the settlement of disputes by peaceful arbitration. Eventually Providence joined with other settlements in the area to form the colony of Rhode Island, for which Williams secured a charter in 1644. Williams wrote many eloquent tracts setting forth his views on religious liberty and freedom of conscience; and in Rhode Island, where he held office for many years, there was religious freedom for Catholics and Jews as well as for Protestants of all denominations. In 1644 he published a book presenting his opinions entitled *The Bloody Tenent (Tenet) of Persecution for the Cause of Conscience,* the conclusion of which appears below.

Williams, the son of a tailor, was born in London around 1603. He studied theology at Cambridge University and served as chaplain to a

Puritan noble before coming to America. In Massachusetts he angered the authorities by both his political and his religious heresies. Not only did he espouse a democratic form of government ("The sovereign, original, and foundation of civil powers lies in the people"), he also insisted that the colonists were not entitled to the land on which they settled until they bought it from the Indians. In Rhode Island Williams purchased land from the Indians; he also made a study of their language and published a book about it. And he engaged Massachusetts's John Cotton in a lively controversy about religious liberty. When Cotton blasted Williams's *The Bloody Tenent of Persecution for the Cause of Conscience* with a book entitled *The Bloody Tenent Washed and Made White in the Blood of the Lamb* (1647), Williams responded with *The Bloody Tenent Yet More Bloody by Mr. Cotton's Endeavor to Wash it White in the Blood of the Lamb* (1652). Williams's fight against religious repression continued until his death in 1683.

Questions to Consider. Two questions come at once to mind in reading the following summary of the major points made in Williams's book. First, what were his main arguments against religious uniformity? Second, how far did his toleration of religious diversity extend? Can it be said that Williams's toleration of differing religious beliefs and practices grew out of a lukewarm faith? Do you agree that a close connection between church and state would likely lead to "hypocrisy" and "destruction"? Why did Williams caution against trying to convert non-Christians such as Jews?

★━━━━★━━━━★

The Bloody Tenent of Persecution (1644)

ROGER WILLIAMS

First, that the blood of so many hundred thousand souls of Protestants and Papists, spilt in the wars of present and former ages, for their respective consciences, is not required nor accepted by Jesus Christ the Prince of Peace.

Secondly, pregnant scriptures and arguments are throughout the work proposed against the doctrine of persecution for cause of conscience.

Thirdly, satisfactory answers are given to scriptures, and objections produced by Mr. Calvin, Beza [French theologian, 1519–1605], Mr. Cotton, and the ministers of the New English churches and others former and later, tending to prove the doctrine of persecution for cause of conscience.

Roger Williams, *The Bloody Tenent of Persecution* (London?, 1644), 3–4.

Roger Williams with the Narragansetts. Expelled from Massachusetts Bay for challenging the Puritan magistrates and ministers, Roger Williams sought refuge in the country of the Narragansett Indians, later to become Rhode Island. Appalled by what he considered the Narragansetts' un-Christian superstition, Williams nevertheless appreciated their generosity, considered them full of natural kindness and decency, and consistently urged European colonists to adopt a policy of accommodation and fair dealing with the Native communities. He was seldom heeded. (Rhode Island Historical Society)

Fourthly, the doctrine of persecution for cause of conscience is proved guilty of all the blood of the souls crying for vengeance under the altar.

Fifthly, all civil states with their officers of justice in their respective constitutions and administrations are proved essentially civil, and therefore not judges, governors or defenders of the spiritual or Christian state and worship.

Sixthly, it is the will and command of God that (since the coming of his Son the Lord Jesus) a permission of the most paganish, Jewish, Turkish, or anti-Christian consciences and worships, be granted to all men in all nations and countries: and they are only to be fought against with that sword which is only (in soul matters) able to conquer, to wit, the sword of God's spirit, the Word of God.

Seventhly, the state of the land of Israel, the kings and people thereof in peace and war, is proved figurative and ceremonial, and no pattern nor precedent for any kingdom or civil state in the world to follow.

Eighthly, God requireth not an uniformity of religion to be enacted and enforced in any civil state; which enforced uniformity (sooner or later) is the greatest occasion of civil war, ravishing of conscience, persecution of Christ Jesus in his servants, and of the hypocrisy and destruction of millions of souls.

Ninthly, in holding an enforced uniformity of religion in a civil state, we must necessarily disclaim our desires and hopes of the Jews' conversion to Christ.

Tenthly, an enforced uniformity of religion throughout a nation or civil state confounds the civil and religious, denies the principles of Christianity and civility, and that Jesus Christ is come in the flesh.

Eleventhly, the permission of other consciences and worships than a state professeth only can (according to God) procure a firm and lasting peace (good assurance being taken according to the wisdom of the civil state for uniformity of civil obedience from all sorts).

Twelfthly, lastly, true civility and Christianity may both flourish in a state or kingdom, notwithstanding the permission of divers and contrary consciences, either of Jew or Gentile.

6

THE HAND OF EMPIRE

The Navigation Acts, passed by the British Parliament over the span of a century, reflected the goals of mercantilism: to advance the interests of English merchants, shippers, shipbuilders, and producers and to make England, not other parts of the empire, wealthy. In this system the colonies would produce raw materials. England would ship, process, and market those materials and then sell manufactured goods back to the colonies.

There were, to be sure, some benefits for Americans. The English government paid bounties to producers of naval stores and indigo in America, for example, and saw to it that American tobacco had a preferential position in England. The British navy, moreover, protected the colonies as well as the mother country, and Britain clearly had a long-term interest in making the entire British Empire prosperous. Inevitably, however, given the realities of British political power, the system usually promoted the interests of businesses in Britain, not the colonies. Even among the British colonies, it was usually India and the Caribbean sugar islands, where profits were incredibly high, that got favored treatment, and not the North American mainland.

The first Act (1660) became the foundation for the entire trade and navigation system. As cracks appeared and the American economy changed, many other acts followed. Thus the Staple Act (1663) decreed that European products should pass through English ports before being shipped to the American colonies. When New England shippers defied this rule by smuggling goods into more profitable European ports, Parliament responded with the Act of 1672 to plug the illicit trade. The important Act of 1696 tried to reassert control by establishing a fully developed customs system in America (giving customs officers enormous powers to search and punish) and by declaring colonial laws contrary to the Act "illegal and void."

The 1733 "Sugar" (or Molasses) Act was ineffectual largely because Americans quickly elevated bribery and smuggling to an art form. Other measures tried to keep Americans from making beaver hats, a lucrative business, or starting their own banks. The 1764 Act tightened sugar controls and restricted the manufacture of iron products, thereby further injuring American industry. By now, moreover, Britain was carrying a huge war debt from its conquest of France in the Seven Years' ("French and Indian") War. It seemed only fair that the Americans, who benefitted from the English victory, should pay their share of the costs by means of customs duties.

But the Americans resisted. They refused, in the name of liberty, to submit to any authority not of their own making. Parliament claimed the right to regulate trade and raise revenue. Americans evaded, challenged, and defied, arguing that with Parliament free to tax trade, there could be "no Liberty, no Happiness, no Security." The 1764 Act seemed the culmination of a mercantile system designed to coerce the colonies. The Navigation Acts looked like a "conspiracy" to "tyrannize" them. A habit and a vocabulary of opposition arose in America that set Parliament and the colonists on a collision course.

Questions to Consider.   To what extent did the changing provisions of the Navigation Acts reflect changes in the colonial economies? What British economic interests did the different Acts appear to be protecting? How important were the sheer difficulties of enforcement in prompting the various Acts? What caused the Navigation Acts, which were imperial regulatory measures, to become a hot political issue?

★━━★━━★

The Navigation Acts (1660–1764)

1660

For the increase of Shipping and encouragement of the Navigation of this Nation, wherein under the good providence and protection of God the Wealth, Safety and Strength of this Kingdom is so much concerned, Be it Enacted . . . That . . . from thence forward no Goods or Commodities whatsoever shall be Imported into or Exported out of any Lands, Islands, Plantations or Territories to his Majesty belonging or in his possession or which may hereafter belong unto or be in the possession of His Majesty His Heirs and Successors in Asia, Africa, or America in any other Ship or Ships, Vessel or Vessels whatsoever but in such Ships or Vessels as do truly and without fraud belong only to the people of England or Ireland, . . . or are of the built of, and belonging to any of the said Lands, Islands, Plantations or Territories

Danby Pickering, *The Statutes at Large from the Magna Carta to the End of the Eleventh Parliament* (J. Bentham, Cambridge, 1806).

as the Proprietors and right Owners thereof and whereof the Master and three fourths of the Mariners at least are English under the penalty of the Forfeiture and Loss of all the Goods and Commodities which shall be Imported into, or Exported out of, any of the aforesaid places in any other Ship or Vessel, as also of the Ship or Vessel with all its Guns, Furniture, Tackle, Ammunition and Apparel. . . .

1672

[W]hereas by . . . [the Navigation Act of 1660] . . . , and by several other Laws passed since that time it is permitted to ship, carry, convey and transport Sugar, Tobacco, Cotton-wool, Indigo, Ginger, Fustic and all other Dyeing wood of the Growth, Production and Manufacture of any of your Majesties Plantations in America, Asia or Africa from the places of their Growth, Production and Manufacture to any other of your Majesties Plantations in those Parts (Tangier only excepted) and that without paying of Customs for the same either at lading or unlading of the said Commodities by means whereof the Trade and Navigation in those Commodities from one Plantation to another is greatly increased, and the Inhabitants of diverse of those Colonies not contenting themselves with being supplied with those Commodities for their own use free from all Customs (while the Subjects of this your Kingdom of England have paid great Customs and Impositions for what of them has been spent here) but contrary to the express Letter of the aforesaid Laws have brought into diverse parts of Europe great quantities thereof, and do also daily vend great quantities thereof to the shipping of other Nations who bring them into diverse parts of Europe to the great hurt and diminution of your Majesties Customs and of the Trade and Navigation of this your Kingdom; For the prevention thereof . . . be it enacted . . . That . . . If any Ship or Vessel which by Law may trade in any of your Majesties Plantations shall come to any of them to ship and take on board any of the aforesaid Commodities, and that Bond shall not be first given with one sufficient Surety to bring the same to England or Wales . . . and to no other place, and there to unload and put the same on shore (the danger of the Seas only excepted) that there shall be . . . paid to your Majesty . . . for so much of the said Commodities as shall be laded and put on board such Ship or Vessel these following Rates and Duties. . . .

1696

[F]or the more effectual preventing of Frauds and regulating Abuses in the Plantation Trade in America Be it further enacted . . . That all Ships coming into or going out of any of the said Plantations and lading or unlading any Goods or Commodities whether the same be His Majesties Ships of War or Merchants Ships and the Masters and Commanders thereof and their Ladings shall be subject and liable to the same Rules, Visitations, Searches,

Penalties, and Forfeitures as to the entering, lading or discharging their respective Ships and Ladings as Ships and their Ladings and the Commanders and Masters of Ships are subject and liable unto in this Kingdom . . . And that the Officers for collecting and managing His Majesties Revenue and inspecting the Plantation Trade in any of the said Plantations shall have the same Powers and Authorities for visiting and searching of Ships and taking their Entries and for seizing and securing or bringing on Shore any of the Goods prohibited to be imported or exported into or out of any of the said Plantations or for which any Duties are payable or ought to have been paid by any of the before mentioned Acts as are provided for the Officers of the Customs in England . . . and also to enter Houses or Warehouses to search for and seize any such Goods. . . .

And . . . That all laws, by-laws, usages or customs, at this time, or which hereafter shall be in practice . . . in any of the said Plantations, which are in any wise repugnant to the before mentioned laws, or any of them, so far as they do relate to the said Plantations, . . . or which are any ways repugnant to this present Act, or to any other law hereafter to be made in this Kingdom, so far as such law shall relate to and mention the said Plantations, are illegal, null and void. . . .

1733

WHEREAS the welfare and prosperity of your Majesty's sugar colonies in America are of the greatest consequence and importance to the trade, navigation and strength of this kingdom: and whereas the planters of the said sugar colonies have of late years fallen under such great discouragements, that they are unable to improve or carry on the sugar trade upon an equal footing with the foreign sugar colonies, without some advantage and relief be given to them from Great Britain: . . . be it enacted . . . , That . . . there shall be raised, levied, collected and paid, unto and for the use of his Majesty . . . , upon all rum or spirits of the produce or manufacture of any of the colonies or plantations in America, not in the possession or under the dominion of his Majesty . . . , which at any time or times within or during the continuance of this act, shall be imported or brought into any of the colonies or plantations in America, which now are or hereafter may be in the possession or under the dominion of his Majesty. . . , the sum of nine pence, money of Great Britain, . . . for every gallon thereof, and after that rate for any greater or lesser quantity: and upon all molasses or syrups of such foreign produce or manufacture as aforesaid, which shall be imported or brought into any of the said colonies or plantations . . . , the sum of six pence of like money for every gallon thereof . . . ; and upon all sugars and paneles of such foreign growth, produce or manufacture as aforesaid, which shall be imported into any of the said colonies or plantations . . . , a duty after the rate of five shillings of like money, for every hundred weight. . . .

1764

WHEREAS it is expedient that new provisions and regulations should be established for improving the revenue of this Kingdom, and for extending and securing the navigation and commerce between Great Britain and your Majesty's dominions in America, which, by the peace, have been so happily enlarged: and whereas it is just and necessary, that a revenue be raised, in your Majesty's said dominions in America, for defraying the expenses of defending, protecting and securing the same; . . . be it enacted . . . , That there shall be raised, levied, collected, and paid, unto his Majesty . . . , for and upon all white or clayed sugars of the produce or manufacture of any colony or plantation in America, not under the dominion of his Majesty . . . ; for and upon indigo, and coffee of foreign produce or manufacture; for and upon all wines (except French wine;) for and upon all wrought silks, bengals, and stuffs, mixed with silk or herba, of the manufacture of Persia, China, or East India, and all calico painted, dyed, printed, or stained there; and for and upon all foreign linen cloth called Cambrick and French Lawns, which shall be imported or brought into any colony or plantation in America, which now is, or hereafter may be, under the dominion of his Majesty . . . , the several rates and duties following; . . .

And be it further enacted . . . , That . . . no rum or spirits of the produce or manufacture of any of the colonies or plantations in America, not in the possession or under the dominion of his Majesty. . . , shall be imported or brought into any of the colonies or plantations in America which now are, or hereafter may be, in the possession or under the dominion of his Majesty . . . , upon forfeiture of all such rum or spirits, together with the ship or vessel in which the same shall be imported, with the tackle, apparel, and furniture thereof. . . .

And it is hereby further enacted . . . , That . . . no iron, nor any sort of wood, commonly called Lumber, as specified in an act passed in the eighth year of the reign of King George the First, entitled, An act for giving further encouragement for the importation of naval stores, and for other purposes therein mentioned, of the growth, production, or manufacture, of any British colony or plantation in America, shall be there loaded on board any ship or vessel to be carried from thence, until sufficient bond shall be given, with one surety besides the master of the vessel, to the collector or other principal officer of the customs at the loading port, in a penalty of double the value of the goods, with condition, that the said goods shall not be landed in any part of Europe except Great Britain.

7

A New England Woman

Though not enjoying equality of condition or rights with men, New England women were in some respects better off than women in Europe or the Southern colonies. This was due partly to religious ideals, partly to the conditions of settlement. Unable to hold office or vote in town or congregation, they were nevertheless fully eligible for membership ("sainthood") in the Puritan churches and exerted much indirect influence over church and village affairs, including the hiring and dismissal of ministers and the location and building of new meeting houses. Because New Englanders saw the family as a bulwark of piety and social stability, women enjoyed both protections (against severe domestic abuse, for example) and rights (to divorce in some circumstances) that women elsewhere did not have. Their elevated status permitted them to stand in for their husbands in trade or farming when men were away at war, a fairly common occurrence. Women also commonly handled a family's daily financial affairs and indeed wore the first "pockets," pouches tied by a string around the waist outside the dress to carry money and other small items.

Because Puritans were expected to study the Bible, a much higher percentage of New England women could read and write than in England or Virginia. Writing therefore became a means of self-expression for female New Englanders. Women were supposed to be deferential and modest—"Patience" and "Charity" were popular Puritan names— so their writing, like their speaking, was inevitably more private than public. Running a large household, moreover, absorbed nearly all of everyone's time and energy. Even so, many women chose to write as an outlet for their creativity beyond quilting, knitting, and gardening.

Some of this writing took the form of poetry. This in itself was remarkable, since Elizabethan court adventurers such as Sir Walter Raleigh had made versifying one of the great masculine skills, comparable to wielding a sword or commanding fleets. Thus poetry was mostly a preserve of men, and of "he-men" at that. Even in Puritan New England, which frowned on lusty courtier behavior, the bestselling work was a long poem by Michael Wigglesworth entitled *The Day of Doom.*

Yet by far the finest poet of early New England was a woman, Anne Bradstreet. Born in 1612 in England, Bradstreet married at age sixteen and two years later came to Massachusetts Bay with her father and husband, both of whom became governors of the colony. In time stolen from her duties as household manager, wife of a public official, and mother of eight children, she began to write religious verse of such quality that her brother-in-law took it to England without her knowledge, where it was published in 1650 to considerable acclaim. The author, because she was a woman, had to remain "anonymous," but her identity was soon known, especially in New England, where her countrymen not only read her work but celebrated her in verses of their own. Her later poems, less moralistic and more personal and immediate, were not published until the nineteenth century. The following two poems are from this period.

Questions to Consider. In the first poem, "To my Dear and Loving Husband," did Bradstreet consider herself a Puritan wife or simply a wife? Does the poem seem "worldly," or was it also religious? Puritans are supposed to have been sexually repressed and dreary. Does Bradstreet's poem reinforce or contradict this reputation? In the second poem, "As Weary Pilgrim," what is the main message Bradstreet was trying to convey? How far into the poem do you have to read to detect the religious dimension of her message? What did she mean in the line, "It is the bed Christ did perfume"? Who was the "Dear Bridegroom" of the last line? What were the common features, if any, of the two poems?

Two Poems (ca. 1660)

ANNE BRADSTREET

To my Dear and Loving Husband

If ever two were one, then surely we.
If ever man were loved by wife, then thee;
If ever wife was happy in a man,
Compare with me, ye women, if you can.
I prize thy love more than whole mines of gold,

John Harvard Ellis, ed., *The Works of Anne Bradstreet in Prose and Verse* (Charleston, 1867), 85–101.

Or all the riches that the East doth hold.
My love is such that rivers cannot quench,
Nor ought but love from thee give recompense.
Thy love is such I can no way repay;
The heavens reward thee manifold, I pray.
Then while we live, in love let's so persevere,
That when we live no more, we may live ever.

As Weary Pilgrim

As weary pilgrim, now at rest,
   Hugs with delight his silent nest,
His wasted limbs, now lie full soft,
   That miry steps, have trodden oft;
Blesses himself, to think upon
   His dangers past, and travails done:
The burning sun no more shall heat,
   Nor stormy rains, on him shall beat.
The briars and thorns no more shall scratch,
   Nor hungry wolves at him shall catch;
He erring paths no more shall tread,
   Nor wild fruits eat, instead of bread;
For waters cold he doth not long,
   For thirst no more shall parch his tongue;
No rugged stones his feet shall gall,
   Nor stumps nor rocks cause him to fall;
All cares and fears, he bids farewell
   And means in safety now to dwell.
A pilgrim I, on earth, perplext,
   With sins, with cares and sorrows vext,
By age and pains brought to decay
   And my clay house mould'ring away.
Oh, how I long to be at rest
   And soar on high among the blest.
This body shall in silence sleep;
   Mine eyes no more shall ever weep;
No fainting fits shall me assail
   Nor grinding pains; my body frail
With cares and fears ne'er cumbered be,
   Nor losses know, nor sorrows see.
What though my flesh shall there consume?
   It is the bed Christ did perfume;
And when a few years shall be gone,
   This mortal shall be clothed upon.
A corrupt carcass down it lies,
   A glorious body it shall rise.
In weakness and dishonor sown,
   In power 'tis raised by Christ alone,

Then soul and body shall unite
   And of their maker have the sight;
Such lasting joys shall there behold
   As ear ne'er heard nor tongue e'er told.
Lord make me ready for that day,
   Then come, Dear Bridegroom, come away.

A liberty pole. A liberty pole is raised in celebration of the Declaration of Independence. (Library of Congress)

CHAPTER TWO

Breaking Away

8

Diversity and Abundance

Driven out of Scotland by the wars of British succession, the Ulster Scots were initially lured to northern Ireland by James I's promises of good land. But the Ulstermen, as they came to call themselves, became victims of severe political and economic oppression at the hands of both Crown and Parliament—the great poet John Milton referred to them as "blockish Presbyterians" from a "barbarous nook of Ireland," and they soon fled Ireland in search of economic opportunity and freedom in America. Unwelcome in seventeenth-century Puritan towns, when the Scotch-Irish (as Americans called them) learned that Pennsylvania would accommodate them, they poured into the backcountry in great waves in the 1700s.

By the time of the American Revolution, the Scotch-Irish numbered more than a quarter of a million, and Pennsylvania had become the most cosmopolitan colony. To the distress of politicians who feared that "if they continue to come, they will make themselves proprietors of the province," the Scotch-Irish flouted all rules of settlement, squatting on virtually any "spot of vacant ground." Contemptuous even of legal requirements to show title, they asserted that it was "against the laws of God and nature that so much land should lie idle while so many Christians wanted it to labor on and raise their bread." They used virtually the same reasoning the Puritans had when they took over Indian lands in the fertile Connecticut Valley.

Like the Puritans, the Scotch-Irish were Calvinists, but while the Puritans migrated to New England to create a "holy commonwealth," the Scotch-Irish came to Pennsylvania because its rich farmland provided a way to make a living, and a good one. The Scotch-Irish looked at life through a markedly different lens, one that reflected expanding opportunities, as in this anonymous Pennsylvania poem of 1730:

> Stretched on the bank of Delaware's rapid stream
> Stands Philadelphia, not unknown to fame.
> Here the tall vessels safe at anchor ride,
> And Europe's wealth flows in with every tide.

The Scotch-Irish viewpoint was utilitarian and practical. The earliest Puritans labored for the glory of God. The Scotch-Irish labored for themselves and their families.

In the beginning of the eighteenth century, settlers in search of economic prospects ventured inland, away from the tidewater and the reassuring smell of the sea; as the frontier moved gradually westward, they were exposed to new vistas. The Scotch-Irish also carried religious convictions into the Pennsylvania frontier, but as the following document suggests, things of the spirit were somehow less newsworthy than the soil and its "extraordinary increase."

Robert Parke arrived in Pennsylvania from northern Ireland in about 1723 when good land was still cheap, and he and his family were fortunate to have funds sufficient to see them through the first difficult year. Enough money remained to allow them to acquire a sizable and fruitful piece of property. Parke wrote the following letter to his sister back in Ireland.

Questions to Consider. To what extent was this a strictly practical document? How did Parke relate to his children? How would you describe his feelings for the land? Is there evidence that Parke had a personality suited for life in a demanding environment? Was he a religious man?

★━━★━━★

Letter from Pennsylvania (1725)

ROBERT PARKE

Thee writes in thy letter that there was a talk went back to Ireland that we were not satisfied in coming here, which was utterly false. Now, let this suffice to convince you. In the first place he that carried back this story was an idle fellow, and one of our shipmates, but not thinking this country suitable to his idleness, went back with [Captain] Cowman again. He is sort of a lawyer, or rather a liar, as I may term him; therefore, I would not have you give credit to such false reports for the future, for there is not one of the family but what likes the country very well and would, if we were in Ireland again, come here directly, it being the best country for working folk and tradesmen of any in the world. But for drunkards and idlers, they cannot live well anywhere. . . . Land is of all prices, even from ten pounds to one hundred pounds a hundred [acres], according to the goodness or else the situation thereof, and grows dearer every year by reason of vast quantities of

Charles A. Hanna, *The Scotch-Irish* (New York and London, 1902), II: 64–67.

Small farm and roads, southern Pennsylvania. Eighteenth-century Pennsylvania was one of the most productive agricultural areas on earth. The soil was rich, the timber mostly cleared by now, and the roads to market towns and Atlantic ports comparatively well laid out and maintained. Family labor was the norm rather than slave labor, although the farmers also employed indentured servants on seven-year contracts late into the century. Children were expected to labor in the fields, and women as necessary. The figure carrying wood in the center of the picture is a woman. One attraction of Pennsylvania farming was that the land was fruitful enough, if worked properly, to support large families. (Library of Congress)

people that come here yearly from several parts of the world. Therefore, thee and thy family or any that I wish well, I would desire to make what speed you can to come here, the sooner the better.

We have traveled over a pretty deal of this country to seek land and though we met with many fine tracts of land here and there in the country, yet my father being curious and somewhat hard to please did not buy any land until the second day of tenth month last, and then he bought a tract of land consisting of five hundred acres for which he gave 350 pounds. It is excellent good land but none cleared, except about twenty acres, with a small log house and orchard planted. We are going to clear some of it directly, for our next summer's fallow. We might have bought land much cheaper but not so much to our satisfaction. We stayed in Chester three months and then we rented a place one mile from Chester with a good brick house and 200 acres of land for——pounds a year, where we continue till next May. We have sowed about 200 acres of wheat and seven acres of rye this season. We sowed but a bushel on an acre. . . .

I am grown an experienced plowman and my brother Abell is learning. Jonathan and thy son John drives for us. He is grown a lusty fellow since thou saw him. We have the finest plows here that can be. We plowed up our summer's fallows in May and June with a yoke of oxen and two horses and they go with as much ease as double the number in Ireland. We sow our wheat with two horses. A boy of twelve or fourteen years old can hold plow here; a man commonly holds and drives himself. They plow an acre, nay, some plows two acres a day.

They sow wheat and rye in August and September. We have had a crop of oats, barley, and very good flax and hemp, Indian corn and buckwheat all of our own sowing and planting this last summer. We also planted a bushel of white potatoes which cost us five shillings and we had ten or twelve bushels' increase. This country yields extraordinary increase of all sorts of grain likewise. . . .

This country abounds in fruit, scarce an house but has an apple, peach, and cherry orchard. As for chestnuts, walnuts, and hazelnuts, strawberries, billberries, and mulberries, they grow wild in the woods and fields in vast quantities.

They also make great preparations against harvest. Both roast and boiled [meats], cakes and tarts and rum, stand at the land's end, so that they may eat and drink at pleasure. A reaper has two shillings and threepence a day, a mower has two shillings and sixpence and a pint of rum, besides meat and drink of the best, for no workman works without their victuals in the bargain throughout the country.

As to what thee writ about the governor's opening letters, it is utterly false and nothing but a lie, and anyone except bound servants[1] may go out of the country when they will and servants when they serve their time may come away if they please. But it is rare any are such fools to leave the country except men's business require it. They pay nine pounds for their passage (of this money) to go to Ireland.

There is two fairs yearly and two markets weekly in Philadelphia; also two fairs yearly in Chester and likewise in Newcastle, but they sell no cattle nor horses, no living creatures, but altogether merchants' goods, as hats, linen and woolen cloth, handkerchiefs, knives, scissors, tapes and threads, buckles, ribbons, and all sorts of necessaries fit for our wooden country, and here all young men and women that wants wives or husbands may be supplied. Let this suffice for our fairs. As to [religious] meetings, they are so plenty one may ride to their choice. . . .

Dear sister, I desire thee may tell my old friend Samuel Thornton that he could give so much credit to my words and find no "ifs" nor "ands" in my letter, that in plain terms he could not do better than to come here, for both his and his wife's trade are very good here. The best way for him to do is to pay what money he can conveniently spare at that side and engage himself to pay the rest at this side, and when he comes here, if he can get no friend to lay down the money for him, when it comes to the worst, he may hire out two or three children.

---

1. **Bound servants:** Indentured servants, who agreed to work without rights or wages for a specified number of years in exchange for having their passage paid from Europe to America. The right to their labor could be sold from one owner to another.—*Eds.*

9

SELF-IMPROVEMENT

Benjamin Franklin was amazingly versatile. He was at various times printer, journalist, editor, educator, satirist, reformer, scientist, inventor, political activist, and diplomat. He was also a successful businessman. His printing business did so well that he was able to retire from active work while in his forties and devote the rest of his life to public service, humanitarian causes, and science and invention. His most famous and rewarding publication was *Poor Richard's Almanack*, which he published annually from 1733 to 1758. In addition to weather and astronomical information, Franklin's *Almanack* also printed mottoes and proverbs touting the virtues of diligence, temperance, moderation, and thrift. "Keep thy shop and thy shop will keep thee," advised Franklin. "Early to bed, and early to rise, makes a man healthy, wealthy, and wise." God, after all, "helps them that help themselves."

Franklin filled his *Almanack* with self-help proverbs because they were popular. But he also believed they worked. He himself had risen from the obscurity of working-class Boston to become a notable Pennsylvanian through self-discipline and improvement—by training himself to think clearly, speak correctly, and write elegantly and to labor diligently in his print shop.

Franklin believed the self-help maxims would work for communities as well as for individuals. He was the quintessential community organizer and was responsible for the establishment of Philadelphia's first public library and its first fire company. Among his other accomplishments were an academy that became the University of Pennsylvania and the first scientific society and the first hospital in British North America.

Perhaps Franklin's earliest civic initiative was an improvement society, the "Junto," whose members met each Friday to discuss some point of morals, politics, or science. The society's members, mostly young craftsmen, discussed each of the following twenty-four "standing queries" at every Junto meeting, with "a pause between each while one might fill and drink a glass of wine." Discussion must have been sober enough, however. From the Junto came numerous spin-off improvement societies, the library and other public projects, and, eventually, much of the civic leadership of eighteenth-century Pennsylvania.

Born in Boston in 1706, the son of a candlemaker, Benjamin Franklin was apprenticed at the age of twelve to his brother, a printer. At seventeen, having mastered the trade, Franklin ran away to Philadelphia and soon established a thriving printing establishment of his own. Not only did he become famous as a writer and publisher, he also represented the colonies in England from 1757 to 1775 and served as minister to France during the war for independence. For his pioneering work in the field of electricity, he was as famous in Europe as in America. In his *Autobiography,* which he wrote for his son in 1777, he dwelt on his early years, to make it, he said, "of more general use to young readers, as exemplifying strongly the effects of prudent and imprudent conduct in the commencement of a life of business." He remained active until his death in 1790, becoming president of the executive council of Pennsylvania at the age of seventy-nine and representing his state in the Constitutional Convention, which met in Philadelphia in 1787.

Questions to Consider. Why might young male workers who enjoyed a good time have wanted to discuss "queries" of this kind at their meetings? Do the twenty-four queries seem to have been drawn up in any particular order? Which query strikes you as most interesting, surprising, or absurd? Do organizations like the Junto exist today? Would the queries have to be amended to be useful today? What sort of society were the Junto members hoping to create? Was this a good way to create it?

★━━━★━━━★

The Junto Queries (1729)

BENJAMIN FRANKLIN

Have you read over these queries this morning, in order to consider what you might have to offer the Junto[1] touching any one of them viz:?

1. Have you met with anything in the author you last read, remarkable, or suitable to be communicated to the Junto, particularly in history, morality, poetry, physic, travels, mechanic arts, or other parts of knowledge?

---

1. **Junto:** A group of persons joined for a common purpose.

John Bigelow, ed., *The Complete Works of Benjamin Franklin* (G. P. Putnam & Sons, New York and London, 1887), I: 319–322.

Lessons in labor for young and old—Poor Richard illustrated. Benjamin Franklin taught the virtues of thrift and diligence in his *Poor Richard's Almanack,* a bestseller of the colonial era. This drawing, from *Bowles' Moral Pictures,* a later version of the *Almanack,* shows sowing, plowing, and sheep-shearing on a prosperous-looking farm, probably in the middle colonies. The sower looks cheerful—as do the chickens! The slogan in the white band circling the drawing is typical of Franklin in contrasting sluggards with hard workers who will make a good cash crop, corn; and also in suggesting, somewhat ominously, that you'd better work hard while you can because you might not be able to later. (Library of Congress)

2. What new story have you lately heard agreeable for telling in conversation?

3. Hath any citizen in your knowledge failed in his business lately, and what have you heard of the cause?

4. Have you lately heard of any citizen's thriving well, and by what means?

5. Have you lately heard how any present rich man, here or elsewhere, got his estate?

6. Do you know of a fellow-citizen, who has lately done a worthy action, deserving praise and imitation; or who has lately committed an error, proper for us to be warned against and avoid?

7. What unhappy effects of intemperance have you lately observed or heard; of imprudence, of passion, or of any other vice or folly?

8. What happy effects of temperance, prudence, of moderation, or of any other virtue?

9. Have you or any of your acquaintance been lately sick or wounded? If so, what remedies were used, and what were their effects?

10. Whom do you know that are shortly going on voyages or journeys, if one should have occasion to send by them?

11. Do you think of anything at present, in which the Junto may be serviceable to *mankind*, to their country, to their friends, or to themselves?

12. Hath any deserving stranger arrived in town since last meeting, that you have heard of?; and what have you heard or observed of his character or merits?; and whether, think you, it lies in the power of the Junto to oblige him, or encourage him as he deserves?

13. Do you know of any deserving young beginner lately set up, whom it lies in the power of the Junto anyway to encourage?

14. Have you lately observed any defect in the laws of your *country*, of which it would be proper to move the legislature for an amendment?; or do you know of any beneficial law that is wanting?

15. Have you lately observed any encroachment on the just liberties of the people?

16. Hath anybody attacked your reputation lately?; and what can the Junto do towards securing it?

17. Is there any man whose friendship you want, and which the Junto, or any of them, can procure for you?

18. Have you lately heard any member's character attacked, and how have you defended it?

19. Hath any man injured you, from whom it is in the power of the Junto to procure redress?

20. In what manner can the Junto or any of them, assist you in any of your honorable designs?

21. Have you any weighty affair on hand in which you think the advice of the Junto may be of service?

22. What benefits have you lately received from any man not present?

23. Is there any difficulty in matters of opinion, of justice, and injustice, which you would gladly have discussed at this time?

24. Do you see anything amiss in the present customs or proceedings of the Junto, which might be amended?

10

A RIGHT TO CRITICIZE

In 1735 came the first great battle over freedom of the press in America. Two years earlier, John Peter Zenger, publisher of the outspoken *New-York Weekly Journal,* began printing articles satirizing corruption and highhandedness in the administration of William Cosby, the new royal governor of New York, and he also distributed song sheets praising those who would "boldly despise the haughty knaves who keep us in awe." In 1734 Cosby arranged for Zenger to be arrested, charged with seditious libel, and thrown in prison. He also ordered copies of the *New-York Weekly Journal* burned in public. When Zenger's case came before the court in 1735, Andrew Hamilton, a prominent Philadelphian who was the most skillful lawyer in America, agreed to defend him. According to English law, a printed attack on a public official, even if true, was considered libelous; and the judge ruled that the fact that Zenger had criticized the New York governor was enough to convict him. But Hamilton argued that no one should be punished for telling the truth; Zenger, he pointed out, had told the truth and should not be convicted of libel. In "a free government," he insisted, the rulers should "not be able to stop the people's mouths when they feel themselves oppressed." Liberty, he added, is the "only bulwark against lawless power." Hamilton was so eloquent in his plea that in the end the jury voted "not guilty" and spectators in the courtroom cheered the verdict.

After his release, Zenger printed a complete account of the trial in his paper (some of which appears below) and also arranged to have it printed separately as a pamphlet. The report of the trial aroused great interest in Britain as well as in America and went through many editions. Hamilton's plea to the jury on behalf of "speaking and writing the truth" was one of the landmarks in the struggle for a free press in America. Though other royal judges did not accept the principle enunciated by Hamilton, the decision in the Zenger case did set an important precedent against judicial tyranny in libel suits. Gouverneur Morris, a statesman and diplomat from New York, called it "the morning star of that liberty which subsequently revolutionized America."

Zenger did not speak on his own behalf during the trial. But he had planned, if found guilty, to make a speech reminding the jurors that he and his parents had "fled from a country where oppression, tyranny, and arbitrary power had ruined almost all the people." Zenger, who was born in Germany in 1697, came to America, along with many other German immigrants, when he was twelve years old and was indentured to William Bradford, "the pioneer printer of the middle colonies." In 1726 he set up a printing shop of his own, publishing tracts and pamphlets mainly of a religious nature, and in 1730 he published the first arithmetic text in New York. A few years after his famous trial he became public printer for the colony of New York and a little later for New Jersey as well. He died in 1746.

Andrew Hamilton, a well-known Philadelphia lawyer who waived his fee in the Zenger case, was born in Scotland in 1676. Trained in the law in Britain, Hamilton came to Virginia in about 1700, worked as a schoolmaster and plantation steward, and married a wealthy widow who introduced him to important imperial officials. He moved to Philadelphia in 1716, became attorney-general of Pennsylvania within a year while maintaining a private legal practice, and served as speaker of the Pennsylvania assembly from 1729 to 1739. He referred in an assembly speech to "liberty, the love of which as it first drew me to, so it constantly prevailed on me to reside in this Province." His performance in the Zenger trial made Hamilton famous on both sides of the Atlantic. He was also an amateur architect, helping design and construct the provincial state house that would soon become Independence Hall. He died in Philadelphia in 1741.

Questions to Consider. In the following exchange between the prosecuting attorney and Hamilton, Zenger's lawyer, why did Hamilton place such emphasis on the word *false?* What complaint did he make about his effort to present evidence to the court on behalf of his client? What did he mean by saying that "the suppression of evidence ought always to be taken for the strongest evidence"? Why did he think Zenger's case was so important? Do you consider his final appeal to the jury a convincing one?

★━━★━━★

John Peter Zenger's Libel Trial (1735)

Mr. Attorney. . . . The case before the court is whether Mr. Zenger is guilty of libeling His Excellency the Governor of New York, and indeed the whole administration of the government. Mr. Hamilton has confessed the printing and publishing, and I think nothing is plainer than that the words in the information [indictment] are scandalous, and tend to sedition, and to disquiet the minds of the people of this province. And if such papers are not libels, I think it may be said there can be no such thing as a libel.

Mr. Hamilton. May it please Your Honor, I cannot agree with Mr. Attorney. For though I freely acknowledge that there are such things as libels, yet I must insist, at the same time, that what my client is charged with is not a libel. And I observed just now that Mr. Attorney, in defining a libel, made use of the words "scandalous, seditious, and tend to disquiet the people." But (whether with design or not I will not say) he omitted the word "false."

Mr. Attorney. I think I did not omit the word "false." But it has been said already that it may be a libel, notwithstanding it may be true.

Mr. Hamilton. In this I must still differ with Mr. Attorney; for I depend upon it, we are to be tried upon this information now before the court and jury, and to which we have pleaded not guilty, and by it we are charged with printing and publishing a certain false, malicious, seditious, and scandalous libel. This word "false" must have some meaning, or else how came it there? . . .

Mr. Chief Justice. You cannot be admitted, Mr. Hamilton, to give the truth of a libel in evidence. A libel is not to be justified; for it is nevertheless a libel that it is true. . . .

Mr. Hamilton. I thank Your Honor. Then, gentlemen of the jury, it is to you we must now appeal, for witnesses, to the truth of the facts we have offered, and are denied the liberty to prove. And let it not seem strange that I apply myself to you in this manner. I am warranted so to do both by law and reason.

The law supposes you to be summoned out of the neighborhood where the fact [crime] is alleged to be committed; and the reason of your being taken out of the neighborhood is because you are supposed to have the best knowledge of the fact that is to be tried. And were you to find a verdict against my client, you must take upon you to say the papers referred to in the information, and which we acknowledge we printed and published, are false, scandalous, and seditious. But of this I can have no apprehension. You are citizens of New York; you are really what the law supposes you to be, honest and lawful men. And, according to my brief, the facts which we offer to prove were not committed in a corner; they are notoriously known to be true; and therefore in your justice lies our safety. And as we are denied the liberty of giving evidence to prove the truth of what we have published, I will beg leave to lay it down, as a standing rule in such cases, that the suppressing of evidence ought always to be taken for the strongest evidence; and I hope it will have weight with you. . . .

I hope to be pardoned, sir, for my zeal upon this occasion. It is an old and wise caution that when our neighbor's house is on fire, we ought to take care of our own. For though, blessed be God, I live in a government [Penn-

J. P. Zenger, *The Tryal of J. P. Z. of New York* (London, 1738), 10–17.

The trial of John Peter Zenger. This tapestry depicts the New York courtroom in August 1735, when a jury acquitted the printer of a charge of libel. Crown officers and attorneys wore white-powdered wigs, as officials did in England, to emphasize their authority. Since imperial bureaucrats such as these not only were distant geographically from the real center of British power in London but also had to deal with obstreperous colonials such as Zenger, they may have taken even more care than their counterparts at home to keep their wigs white and imposing as symbols of British authority. (The Metropolitan Museum of Art, A Bicentennial Gift to America from a Grateful Armenian-American People, 1978)

sylvania] where liberty is well understood, and freely enjoyed, yet experience has shown us all (I'm sure it has to me) that a bad precedent in one government is soon set up for an authority in another. And therefore I cannot but think it mine, and every honest man's duty, that (while we pay all due obedience to men in authority) we ought at the same time to be upon our guard against power, wherever we apprehend that it may affect ourselves or our fellow subjects.

I am truly very unequal to such an undertaking on many accounts. And you see I labor under the weight of many years, and am borne down with great infirmities of body. Yet old and weak as I am, I should think it my duty, if required, to go to the utmost part of the land, where my service could be of any use, in assist—to quench the flame of prosecutions upon informations, set on foot by the government, to deprive a people of the right of remonstrating (and complaining too) of the arbitrary attempts of men in power. Men who injure and oppress the people under their administration provoke them to cry out and complain; and then make that very complaint the foundation for new oppressions and prosecutions. I wish I could say there were no instances of this kind.

But to conclude. The question before the court and you, gentlemen of the jury, is not of small nor private concern. It is not the cause of a poor printer, nor of New York alone, which you are now trying. No! It may, in its consequence, affect every freeman that lives under a British government on the main[land] of America. It is the best cause. It is the cause of liberty. And I make no doubt but your upright conduct, this day, will not only entitle you to the love and esteem of your fellow citizens; but every man who prefers freedom to a life of slavery will bless and honor you, as men who have baffled the attempt of tyranny, and, by an impartial and uncorrupt verdict, have laid a noble foundation for securing to ourselves, our posterity, and our neighbors, that to which nature and the laws of our country have given us a right—the liberty both of exposing and opposing arbitrary power (in these parts of the world, at least) by speaking and writing truth. . . .

11

THE GREAT AWAKENING

In the early eighteenth century, as the population of the colonies grew and Americans developed a thriving trade with other parts of the world, they became more "worldly"—less spiritual and church-centered, less concerned with piety and community, more materialistic, acquisitive, and individualistic. This was a far cry from the Calvinist "Christian Commonwealth" of the earliest settlers, and it represented a challenge to Protestant ministers of the Gospel, who preached emotional sermons throughout the colonies urging their listeners to search their souls for evidence of Christ's saving grace and to live the saintly lives that would demonstrate true salvation. Otherwise they might not only lose the overwhelming joys of heaven but tumble into the eternal agonies of hell.

The so-called "Great Awakening" seems to have started among Presbyterian preachers in New Jersey and Pennsylvania. By the 1730s there was a quickening of religious fervor among Baptists and Congregationalists. Stoked by the labors of traveling itinerants such as the English Methodist George Whitfield, who moved from parish to parish and colony to colony, this fervor burst a few years later into the passionate full-scale "revivalism" that typified much of American Protestantism ever after.

The Great Awakening burned itself out by mid-century. Its demands for strict piety and chronic anxiety were too great to sustain for long. But it left a substantial legacy in its wake, including a willingness to criticize conservative ministers, especially Anglicans; more missionary activity, especially among Indians; attention to the needs of women, young people, and others who responded powerfully to the revivalist preachers; and scattered frontier colleges to train future evangelists. The Awakening was vivid proof that a major social movement could span colonial boundaries, and that there was a hunger for something beyond self-indulgence and materialism—if not the church, then something.

Jonathan Edwards was one of the transcendent figures of the Great Awakening. Born in Connecticut in 1703, Edwards studied at Yale before going to Northampton, a prosperous river town in western Massachusetts, to take over the pulpit that his grandfather had filled for several decades. There he became perhaps the greatest theologian in American history, producing works that explored the nature of the sanctified life and tried to reconcile doctrines such as original sin and freedom of the will to modern physics and psychology. There, too, he preached some of the best-known Awakening sermons, including his two masterpieces, "Heaven Is a World of Love," one of his most popular, and "Sinners in the Hands of an Angry God," which became a model for generations of evangelists. Together they represent the twin halves of Awakening preaching: the call to unity with Christ and the warning that complacency might lead to eternal damnation. In 1750 Edwards was forced out of his pulpit for criticizing his congregation too severely. He died of smallpox in 1758, just before becoming president of the College of New Jersey (now Princeton).

The following brief excerpt from "Heaven Is a World of Love"—which stretched in its original form over six hours and three Sundays—omits scriptural citations and references.

Questions to Consider. What, for Edwards, were the specific features of heaven that would make it so wonderful? According to Edwards, what specific attitudes and conditions kept people from experiencing heavenly joy here on earth? Why did Edwards say that in heaven, "All shall have propriety [property] in one another," and that they shall "have the possession of all things"? If heaven is perfect love, how might Jonathan Edwards have defined hell? Do you find Edwards's vision of a perfect society compelling? Why might colonists find such a sermon exciting enough to foster revivalism?

★━━━★━━━★

Heaven Is a World of Love (1738)

JONATHAN EDWARDS

There are none but lovely objects in heaven. There is no odious or polluted person or thing to be seen there. There is nothing wicked and unholy. There is nothing which is deformed either in natural or moral deformity. Everything which is to be beheld there is amiable. The God, who dwells and gloriously manifests himself there, is infinitely lovely. There is to be seen a glorious heavenly Father, a glorious Redeemer; there is to be felt and possessed a glorious Sanctifier. All the persons who belong to that blessed society are lovely. The Father of the family is so, and so are all his children. The Head of the body is so, and so are all the members. Concerning the angels, there are none who are unlovely. There are no evil angels suffered to infest heaven as they do this world. They are not suffered to come near, but are kept at a distance with a great

Jonathan Edwards, *Ethical Writings,* ed. Paul Ramsey (Yale University Press, New Haven and London, 1989), 370–397.

Jonathan Edwards. The only known portrait of Jonathan Edwards, painted around 1750, shows him in his full ministerial garb— wig, white collar, and dark robe. Edwards, with open eyes, pursed mouth, long nose, and high forehead, turns slightly to gaze at the viewer. The effect is often felt to be severe, as with other ministe- rial portraits of the age. One reason may be that Edwards was not striving to be likeable the way modern men might. God did not put ministers of the Gospel on the earth to be liked. But in fact, the picture shows a soft face, with warmth in the eyes and a hint of a smile at the corners of the mouth—a fairly accurate depiction of the historical Edwards. (Yale University Art Gallery, Bequest of Eugene Phelps Edwards)

gulf between them. In the church of saints there are no unlovely persons; there are no false professors, none who pretend to be saints, who are persons of an unchristian, hateful spirit and behavior, as is often the case in this world. There is no one object there to give offense, or at any time to give any occasion for any passion or motion of hatred; but every object shall draw forth love. . . .

That God who so fully manifests himself there is perfect with an absolute and infinite perfection. That Son of God who is the brightness of his Father's glory appears there in his glory, without that veil of outward meanness in which he appeared in this world, as a root out of dry ground destitute of outward glory. There the Holy Spirit shall be poured forth with perfect sweetness, as a pure river of water of life, clear as crystal. . . . And every member of that glorious society shall be without blemish of sin or imprudence or any kind of failure. The whole church shall then be presented to Christ as a bride clothed in fine linen, clean and white, without spot or wrinkle. . . .

. . . There is no enemy of God in heaven, but all love him as his children. They all are united with one mind to breathe forth their whole souls in love to their eternal Father, and to Jesus Christ, their common Head. Christ loves all his saints in heaven. His love flows out to his whole church there, and to every individual member of it; and they all with one heart and one soul, without any schism in the body, love their common Redeemer. Every heart is wedded to this spiritual husband. All rejoice in him, the angels concurring. And the angels and saints all love one another. All that glorious society are sincerely united. There is no secret or open enemy among them; not one heart but is full of love, nor one person who is not beloved. As they are all lovely, so all see each other's loveliness with answerable delight and complacence. Everyone there loves every other inhabitant of heaven whom he sees, and so he is mutually beloved by everyone. . . .

They shall have nothing within themselves to clog them in the exercises and expressions of love. In this world they find much to hinder them. They have a great deal of dullness and heaviness. They carry about with them a heavy moulded body, a lump of flesh and blood which is not fitted to be an organ for a soul inflamed with high exercises of divine love, but is found a great clog to the soul, so that they cannot express their love to God as they would. They cannot be so active and lively in it as they desire. . . . Love disposes them to praise, but their tongues are not obedient; they want words to express the ardor of their souls, and cannot order their speech by reason of darkness. And oftentimes for want of expressions they are forced to content themselves with groans that cannot be uttered. But in heaven they shall have no such hindrance. They will have no dullness or unwieldiness, no corruption of heart to fight against divine love and hinder suitable expressions, no clog of a heavy lump of clay, or an unfit organ for an inward heavenly flame. They shall have no difficulty in expressing all their love. Their souls, which are like a flame of fire with love, shall not be like a fire pent up but shall be perfectly at liberty. The soul which is winged with love shall have no weight tied to the feet to hinder its flight. There shall be no want of strength or activity, nor any want of words to praise the object of their love. They shall find nothing to hinder them in praising or seeing God, just as their love inclines. Love naturally desires to express itself; and in heaven the love of the saints shall be at liberty to express itself as it desires, either towards God or one another. . . .

There shall be nothing external to keep them at a distance or hinder the most perfect enjoyment of each other's love. There shall be no separation wall to keep them asunder. They shall not be hindered from the full and constant enjoyment of each other's love by distance of habitation, for they shall be together as one family in their heavenly Father's house. There shall be no want of full acquaintance to hinder the greatest possible intimacy; much less shall there be any misunderstanding between them, or wrong construction of things which are said or done; no disunion through difference of tempers and manners, or through different circumstances, or various opinions, or various interests or alliances; for they shall all be united in the same interest, and all alike allied or related to the same God, and the same Savior, and all employed in the same business, serving and glorifying the same God.

They shall all be united together in a very near relation. Love seeks a near relation to the object beloved. And in heaven all shall be nearly related. They shall be nearly allied to God, the supreme object of their love; for they shall all be his children. And all shall be nearly related to Christ; for he shall be the Head of the whole society, and husband of the whole church of saints. All together shall constitute his spouse, and they shall be related one to another as brethren. It will all be one society, yea, one family. . . .

All shall have *propriety* one in another. Love seeks to have the beloved its own. . . . And in heaven all shall not only be related one to another, but they shall be each other's. The saints shall be God's. He brings them hence to him in glory, as that part of the creation which he has chosen for his peculiar treasure. And on the other hand God shall be theirs. He made over himself to them in an everlasting covenant in this world, and now they shall be in full possession of him as their portion. And so the saints shall be Christ's, for he has bought them with a price, and he shall be *theirs;* for he who gave himself *for* them, will have given himself *to* them. Christ and the saints will have given themselves, the one to the other. . . .

They shall enjoy each other's love in perfect and undisturbed prosperity. What oftentimes diminishes the pleasure and sweetness of earthly friendship is that though they live in love, yet they live in poverty, and meet with great difficulties and sore afflictions whereby they are grieved for themselves, and for one another. For love and friendship in such cases, though in some respects lightens each other's burdens, yet in other respects adds to persons' afflictions, because it makes them sharers in others' afflictions. So that they have not only their afflictions to bear, but also those of their afflicted friends. But there shall be no adversity in heaven to give occasion for a pitiful grief of spirit, or to molest those heavenly friends in the enjoyment of each other's friendship. But they shall enjoy one another's love in the greatest prosperity, in glorious riches, having the possession of all things.

All things in that world shall conspire to promote their love, and give advantage for mutual enjoyment. There shall be none there to tempt them to hatred, no busy adversary to make misrepresentations or create misunderstandings. Everyone and everything there shall conspire to promote love, and promote the enjoyment of each other's love. . . .

. . . All their love is holy, humble, and perfectly Christian, without the least impurity or carnality; where love is always mutual, where the love of the beloved is answerable to the love of the lovers; where there is no hypocrisy or dissembling, but perfect simplicity and sincerity; where there is no treachery, unfaithfulness or inconstancy, nor any such thing as jealousy. And no clog or hindrance to the exercises and expressions of love, nor imprudence or indecency in the manner of expressing love, no instance of folly or indiscretion in any word or deed; where there is no separation wall, no misunderstanding or strangeness, but full acquaintance and perfect intimacy in all; no division through different opinions or interests, where all that glorious loving society shall be most nearly and divinely related, and all shall be one another's, having given themselves one to another. And all shall enjoy one another in perfect prosperity, riches, and honor, without any sickness, pain, or persecution, or any enemy to molest them, any talebearer, or busybody to create jealousies and misunderstandings.

And all this in a garden of love, the Paradise of God, where everything has a cast of holy love, and everything conspires to promote and stir up love, and nothing to interrupt its exercises; where everything is fitted by an all-wise God for the enjoyment of love under the greatest advantages. And all this shall be without any fading of the beauty of the objects beloved, or any decaying of love in the lover, and any satiety in the faculty which enjoys love. O! what tranquility may we conclude there is in such a world as this! Who can express the sweetness of this peace? . . .

And lastly. They shall know that they shall forever be continued in the perfect enjoyment of each other's love. They shall know that God and Christ will be forever, and that their love will be continued and be fully manifested forever, and that all their beloved fellow saints shall live forever in glory with the same love in their hearts. And they shall know that they themselves shall ever live to love God, and love the saints, and enjoy their love. They shall be in no fear of any end of this happiness, nor shall they be in any fear or danger of any abatement of it through a weariness of the exercises and expressions of love, or cloyed with the enjoyment of it, or the beloved objects becoming old or decayed, or stale or tasteless. All things shall flourish there in an eternal youth. . . .

. . . We all hope to have a part in heaven, that world of love of which we have heard, and that in a little time. Surely then we should endeavor to use the same temper of mind. Here let several things be considered as motives.

This is the way to be like the inhabitants of heaven. You have heard how they love one another; and therefore they, and they only, are conformed to them who live in love in this world. In this way you will be like them in excellence and loveliness, for their holiness and loveliness consists in being of such an excellent spirit. And this will be the way to make you like them in happiness and comfort. For this happiness and joy and rest lies in loving the inhabitants of that world. And by living in love in this world the saints partake of a like sort of inward peace and sweetness. It is in this way that you are to have the foretastes of heavenly pleasures and delights. . . .

By living a life of love, you will be in the way to heaven. As heaven is a world of love, so the way to heaven is the way of love. This will best prepare you for heaven, and make you meet for an inheritance with the saints in that land of light and love. And if ever you arrive at heaven, faith and love must be the wings which must carry you there.

12

A RIGHT TO PRIVACY

The British controlled their colonies chiefly in two ways: through the regulation of trade and investment, as with the Navigation Acts; and by appointing, in most colonies, a royal governor with varying powers, including the power to arrange naval contracts, make land grants, raise militia, and influence local legislatures. As long as things went reasonably well, as they did for much of the eighteenth century, London ruled lightly—permitting, for example, modest smuggling and illicit manufacturing despite the prohibitions of the Navigation Acts. All this changed with the coming of the Seven Years' War with France (1756–1763), which damaged Britain's economy, strained its finances, and made tax collections, including customs duties from the colonies, imperative. The Navigation Acts would therefore be enforced.

Smugglers in seaports such as Philadelphia, Salem, New Haven, and especially Boston bore the brunt of the new policy. But a serious problem soon arose—namely, that local constables failed to search out smugglers and local juries failed to convict them. The British responded by using their own imperial officers to investigate possible smugglers and their naval vice-admiralty courts to try them. Accordingly, in 1760 British officials in Boston announced that the long-neglected provisions of the Sugar Act of 1733 would be enforced, and they issued writs of assistance, or general search warrants, allowing enforcement officers to search any house for smuggled goods.

Responsibility for implementing this new policy lay with James Otis, a 35-year-old lawyer then serving as the king's advocate general of the vice-admiralty court. Rather than supervise the orders, Otis resigned his position and in fact argued against them in court when the first case came to trial in 1761. Otis understood the economics of the situation— that the policy would produce not only higher imperial tax collections but also higher prices for sugar and molasses, key materials in the manufacture of rum, a New England trade staple that hundreds of people depended on for their living.

But as the following excerpt from his main argument makes clear, Otis chose not to argue on practical economic grounds. He argued rather on the much broader grounds of legal and political principle—that the writs of assistance constituted a terrible threat to individual liberty, which guaranteed reasonable sanctuary from snooping officials whatever the urgency of the threat. John Adams, who attended the proceedings and heard Otis speak, called him "a flame of fire" who thus mounted the first act of opposition to the "arbitrary claims" of Great Britain. "American independence," Adams later wrote, "was there and then born; the seeds of patriots and heroes were then and there sown." Otis lost his case, as it turned out. But the authorities soon withdrew the hated writs.

Born into a well-to-do West Barnstable, Massachusetts, family in 1725, James Otis graduated from Harvard and practiced law in Boston before agreeing to serve as a British official. Renowned for his elo-quence and passion—"No taxation without representation!" was an Otis slogan—he was elected to the legislature after the writs of assis-tance case and nearly became Speaker of the House, only to have the royal governor overturn his selection. He wrote extensively on the rights of the British colonies and served in the intercolonial Stamp Act Congress. Although never an advocate of a complete break with Britain, Otis would almost certainly have become a leading figure of the Rev-olutionary era except that a scuffle with a Crown officer in 1769 left him with a severe head injury and chronic mental illness, essentially ending his career. He was struck and killed by lightning in Andover, Massachusetts, in 1783.

Questions to Consider. What specific reasons did Otis give for oppos-ing such writs? Which of his arguments strike you as most relevant and persuasive? Did Otis exaggerate his case for effect? If so, why? What famous phrase appears in this speech, and what famous "privilege" did Otis say would be annihilated by the issuing of the writs? Does Otis sound like he was a revolutionary or a loyalist? Does he anywhere appear to have made implied threats? Do his arguments still hold sway today, in an age of espionage, terrorism, and sophisticated electronic surveillance?

★━━★━━★

No Writs of Assistance (1761)

JAMES OTIS

May it please your honors, I was desired by one of the court to look into the books, and consider the question now before them concerning writs of assis-tance. I have, accordingly, considered it, and now appear not only in obedi-ence to your order, but likewise in behalf of the inhabitants of this town, who

C. F. Adams, ed., *The Works of John Adams* (Boston, 1850–1856), II: 522–523.

have presented another petition, and out of regard to the liberties of the subject. And I take this opportunity to declare that, whether under a fee or not (for in such a cause as this I despise a fee), I will to my dying day oppose with all the powers and faculties God has given me all such instruments of slavery, on the one hand, and villainy, on the other, as this writ of assistance is.

It appears to me the worst instrument of arbitrary power, the most destructive of English liberty and the fundamental principles of law, that ever was found in an English lawbook. I must, therefore, beg your honors' patience and attention to the whole range of an argument, that may, perhaps, appear uncommon in many things. . . . I shall not think much of my pains in this cause, as I engaged in it from principle. I was solicited to argue this cause as Advocate General; and because I would not, I have been charged with desertion from my office. To this charge I can give a very sufficient answer. I renounced that office, and I argue this cause from the same principle; and I argue it with the greater pleasure, as it is in favor of British liberty, at a time when we hear the greatest monarch upon earth declaring from his throne that he glories in the name of Briton, and that the privileges of his people are dearer to him than the most valuable prerogatives of his crown; and as it is in opposition to a kind of power the exercise of which, in former periods of history, cost one king of England his head and another his throne. . . .

Your honors will find in the old books concerning the office of a justice of the peace precedents of general warrants to search suspected houses. But in more modern books you will find only special warrants to search such and such houses, specially named, in which the complainant has before sworn that he suspects his goods are concealed; and will find it adjudged that special warrants only are legal. In the same manner I rely on it that the writ prayed for in this petition, being general, is illegal. It is a power that places the liberty of every man in the hands of every petty officer. I say I admit that special writs of assistance, to search special places, may be granted to certain persons on oath; but I deny that the writ now prayed for can be granted, for I beg leave to make some observations on the writ itself, before I proceed to other acts of Parliament. In the first place, the writ is universal, being directed "to all and singular justices, sheriffs, constables, and all other officers and subjects"; so that, in short, it is directed to every subject in the king's dominions. Everyone with this writ may be a tyrant; if this commission be legal, a tyrant in a legal manner, also, may control, imprison, or murder anyone within the realm. In the next place, it is perpetual; there is no return. A man is accountable to no person for his doings. Every man may reign secure in his petty tyranny, and spread terror and desolation around him, until the trump of the archangel shall excite different emotions in his soul. In the third place, a person with this writ, in the daytime, may enter all houses, shops, etc., at will, and command all to assist him. Fourthly, by this writ, not only deputies, etc., but even their menial servants, are allowed to lord it over us. What is this but to have the curse of Canaan with a witness on us; to be the servant of servants, the most despicable of God's creation? Now, one of the most essential branches of English liberty is the freedom of one's house. A man's house is his castle; and whilst he is quiet, he is as well guarded as a prince in his castle. This writ, if it should be declared legal, would totally annihilate this privilege. Customhouse officers may enter our houses when they please; we are commanded to permit their entry. Their menial servants may enter, may break locks, bars, and everything in their way; and whether they break through malice or revenge, no man, no court, can inquire. Bare suspicion without oath is sufficient. This wanton exercise of this power is not a chimerical suggestion of a heated brain. I will mention some facts. Mr. Pew had one of these writs, and when Mr. Ware succeeded him, he indorsed this writ over to Mr. Ware; so that these writs are negotiable from one officer to another; and so your honors have no opportunity of judging the persons to whom this vast power is delegated. Another instance is this: Mr. Justice Walley had called this same Mr. Ware before him, by a constable, to answer for a breach of the Sabbath Day Acts, or that of profane swearing. As soon as he had finished, Mr. Ware asked him if he had done. He replied: "Yes." "Well, then," said Mr. Ware, "I will show you a little of my power. I command you to permit me to search your house for uncustomed goods"; and went on to search the house from the garret to the cellar, and then served the constable in the same manner! But to show another absurdity in this writ, if it should be established, I insist upon it that every person, by the 14th of Charles II, has this power as well as the customhouse officers. The words are: "It shall be lawful for any person or persons authorized," etc. What a scene does this open! Every man prompted by revenge, ill humor, or wantonness to inspect the inside of his neighbor's house may get a writ of assistance. Others will ask it from self-defense; one arbitrary exertion will provoke another, until society be involved in tumult and in blood. . . .

13

Ideology and Agitation

On December 18, 1776, George Washington wrote his brother discouragingly: "Between you and me, I think our affairs are in a very bad situation. . . . If every nerve is not strained up to the utmost to recruit the new army with all possible expedition, I think the game is up." A few days later Thomas Paine published the first number of *The Crisis*, a pamphlet calling attention to the heartbreaking difficulties the Americans faced in their struggle with Britain and appealing for renewed dedication to the Revolutionary cause. Paine said he wrote in "a passion of patriotism." His essay quickly "rallied and reanimated" the people, according to one observer, and before long "hope succeeded to despair, cheerfulness to gloom, and firmness to irresolution." In twelve more issues of *The Crisis* Paine continued his impassioned fight against apathy, indifference, and defeatism in American ranks. He wrote additional numbers about American problems after the Yorktown victory in 1781.

Paine, a British corset maker and excise officer, was an ardent supporter of the American cause from almost the beginning. Shortly after arriving in Philadelphia in November 1774, he became editor of the *Pennsylvania Magazine,* discovered he had great gifts as a journalist, and in January 1776 published a little pamphlet entitled *Common Sense,* urging Americans to convert their resistance to British oppression into a fight for national independence. Before long thousands of copies of his pamphlet were circulating in the colonies and Washington arranged to have passages from it read to his troops. The first bestseller in American history, *Common Sense* persuaded many Americans who were wavering that separation from Britain was both possible and desirable.

Paine pioneered a new kind of journalism. He avoided the elegant and ornate kind of writing fashionable in aristocratic circles and wrote simply, naturally, and forcefully. He used homely metaphors, introduced everyday words and phrases into his essays, translated foreign phrases for his readers, interspersed his logical arguments with lively anecdotes, and brought a sense of immediacy to his writings by including personal, on-the-spot reports. He was, in short, writing for the plain people from whom he himself had come. His influence on the thinking of countless people was enormous.

Paine, born in England of Quaker parents in 1737, lived in obscurity until he came to America in 1774. He became editor of the *Pennsylvania Magazine* and quickly identified himself with the American cause. After the American Revolution he went to France, supported the revolution that broke out there in 1789, and published *The Rights of Man* (1791–1792), a work defending the principles of the French Revolution. He also wrote *The Age of Reason* (1793–1795), criticizing both atheism and orthodox Christianity and calling for a religion based on reason. Though sympathetic to the French Revolution, Paine opposed the execution of King Louis XVI and was appalled by the Reign of Terror that accompanied the Revolution. In the end he was thrown in prison and sentenced to the guillotine; but he was saved by the intervention of the American minister in France, James Monroe. In 1802 he returned to America; but his attacks on George Washington while in France and his religious radicalism made him an outcast. He died in New York, lonely, poverty-stricken, and largely forgotten, in 1809.

Questions to Consider. Paine is eminently quotable. Do you find any passages in the essay below that seem especially eloquent? Do you think Paine's appeal rests on substance as well as style? How did he attempt to whip up enthusiasm for the American cause despite reverses on the battlefield? Do you think his handling of Tories, that is, Americans who were sympathetic to Britain, was effective? Do you think he was just to the Loyalists, to King George III, and to General William Howe? Were his appeals to God likely to impress religious people in America? What parts of the essay do you think George Washington chose to have read to his troops?

★━━★━━★

The Crisis, Number One (1776)

THOMAS PAINE

These are the times that try men's souls. The summer soldier and the sunshine patriot will, in this crisis, shrink from the service of his country; but he that stands it NOW, deserves the love and thanks of man and woman. Tyranny, like hell, is not easily conquered; yet we have this consolation with us, that the harder the conflict, the more glorious the triumph. What we obtain

Daniel E. Wheeler, ed., *Life and Writings of Thomas Paine* (10 v., V. Parke and Co., New York, 1915), III: 1–16.

The destruction of the statue of King George in New York City, July 9, 1776. The statue stood in Bowling Green at the tip of Manhattan Island. Soldiers and artisans, provoked by the words of anti-British firebrands such as Tom Paine and Patrick Henry, did most of the damage, after a public reading of the Declaration of Independence. In this imaginative engraving, a well-dressed woman, possibly of Tory sympathies, watches this violent mob behavior in apparent alarm. (Chicago Historical Society)

too cheap, we esteem too lightly: 'Tis dearness only that gives every thing its value. Heaven knows how to put a proper price upon its goods; and it would be strange indeed, if so celestial an article as FREEDOM should not be highly rated. Britain, with an army to enforce her tyranny, has declared that she has a right (*not only to* TAX) but "*to* BIND *us in* ALL CASES WHATSOEVER," and if being *bound in that manner,* is not slavery, then is there not such a thing as slavery upon earth. Even the expression is impious, for so unlimited a power can belong only to GOD. . . .

I have as little superstition in me as any man living, but my secret opinion has ever been, and still is, that God Almighty will not give up a people to military destruction, or leave them unsupportedly to perish, who had so earnestly and so repeatedly sought to avoid the calamities of war, by every decent method which wisdom could invent. Neither have I so much of the infidel in me, as to suppose that HE has relinquished the government of the world, and given us up to the care of devils; and as I do not, I cannot see on what grounds the king of Britain can look up to Heaven for help against us:

A common murderer, a highwayman, or a house-breaker has as good a pretence as he. . . .

I shall not now attempt to give all the particulars of our retreat to the Delaware; suffice it for the present to say, that both officers and men, though greatly harassed and fatigued, frequently without rest, covering, or provision, the inevitable consequences of a long retreat, bore it with a manly and a martial spirit. All their wishes were one, which was, that the country would turn out and help them to drive the enemy back. Voltaire has remarked that King William never appeared to full advantage but in difficulties and in action; the same remark may be made on George Washington, for the character fits him. There is a natural firmness in some minds which cannot be unlocked by trifles, but which, when unlocked, discovers a cabinet of fortitude; and I reckon it among those kind of public blessings, which we do not immediately see, that GOD hath blest him with uninterrupted health, and given him a mind that can even flourish upon care.

I shall conclude this paper with some miscellaneous remarks on the state of our affairs; and shall begin with asking the following question, Why is it that the enemy have left the New-England provinces, and made these middle ones the seat of war? The answer is easy: New-England is not infested with tories, and we are. I have been tender in raising the cry against these men, and used numberless arguments to shew them their danger, but it will not do to sacrifice a world to either their folly or their baseness. The period is now arrived, in which either they or we must change our sentiments, or one or both must fall. And what is a tory? Good GOD! what is he? I should not be afraid to go with an hundred whigs against a thousand tories, were they to attempt to get into arms. Every tory is a coward, for a servile, slavish, self-interested fear is the foundation of toryism; and a man under such influence, though he may be cruel, never can be brave. . . .

I once felt all that kind of anger, which a man ought to feel, against the mean principles that are held by the tories: A noted one, who kept a tavern at Amboy, was standing at his door, with as pretty a child in his hand, about eight or nine years old, as most I ever saw, and after speaking his mind as freely as he thought was prudent, finished with this unfatherly expression, *"Well! give me peace in my day."* Not a man lives on the continent but fully believes that a separation must some time or other finally take place, and a generous parent should have said, *"If there must be trouble, let it be in my day that my child may have peace"* and this single reflection, well applied, is sufficient to awaken every man to duty. Not a place upon earth might be so happy as America. Her situation is remote from all the wrangling world, and she has nothing to do but to trade with them. A man may easily distinguish in himself between temper and principle, and I am as confident, as I am that GOD governs the world, that America will never be happy till she gets clear of foreign dominion. Wars, without ceasing, will break out till that period arrives, and the continent must in the end be conqueror; for though the flame of liberty may sometimes cease to shine, the coal never can expire. . . .

Not all the treasures of the world, so far as I believe, could have induced me to support an offensive war, for I think it murder; but if a thief break into my house, burn and destroy my property, and kill or threaten to kill me, or those that are in it, and to *"bind me in all cases whatsoever,"* to his absolute will, am I to suffer it? What signifies it to me, whether he who does it, is a king or a common man; my countryman or not my countryman? whether it is done by an individual villain, or an army of them? If we reason to the root of things we shall find no difference; neither can any just cause be assigned why we should punish in the one case and pardon in the other. Let them call me rebel, and welcome. I feel no concern from it; but I should suffer the misery of devils, were I to make a whore of my soul by swearing allegiance to one whose character is that of a sottish, stupid, stubborn, worthless, brutish man. I conceive likewise a horrid idea in receiving mercy from a being, who at the last day shall be shrieking to the rocks and mountains to cover him, and fleeing with terror from the orphan, the widow, and the slain of America.

There are cases which cannot be overdone by language, and this is one. There are persons too who see not the full extent of the evil which threatens them, they solace themselves with hopes that the enemy, if they succeed, will be merciful. It is the madness of folly to expect mercy from those who have refused to do justice; and even mercy, where conquest is the object, is only a trick of war: The cunning of the fox is as murderous as the violence of the wolf; and we ought to guard equally against both. [General William] Howe's first object is partly by threats and partly by promise, to terrify or seduce the people to deliver up their arms, and receive mercy. The ministry recommended the same plan to [General Thomas] Gage, and this is what the tories call making their peace: *"a peace which passeth all understanding"* indeed! A peace which would be the immediate forerunner of a worse ruin than any we have yet thought of. Ye men of Pennsylvania, do reason upon these things! Were the back counties to give up their arms, they would fall an easy prey to the Indians, who are all alarmed. This perhaps is what some tories would not be sorry for. Were the home counties to deliver up their arms, they would be exposed to the resentment of the back counties, who would then have it in their power to chastise their defection at pleasure. And were any one state to give up its arms, THAT state must be garrisoned by all Howe's army of Britons and Hessians to preserve it from the anger of the rest. Mutual fear is a principal link in the chain of mutual love, and woe be to that state that breaks the compact. Howe is mercifully inviting you to barbarous destruction, and men must be either rogues or fools that will not see it. I dwell not upon the powers of imagination; I bring reason to your ears; and in language as plain as A, B, C, hold up truth to your eyes.

I thank GOD that I fear not. I see no real cause for fear. I know our situation well, and can see the way out of it. While our army was collected, Howe dared not risk a battle, and it is no credit to him that he decamped from the White Plains, and waited a mean opportunity to ravage the defenceless Jerseys; but it is great credit to us, that, with a handful of men, we sustained an orderly retreat for near an hundred miles, brought off our ammunition, all our field-pieces, the greatest part of our stores, and had four rivers to pass. None can say that our retreat was precipitate, for we were near three weeks in performing it, that the country might have time to come in. Twice we marched back to meet the enemy and remained out till dark. The sign of fear was not seen in our camp, and had not some of the cowardly and disaffected inhabitants spread false alarms through the country, the Jerseys had never been ravaged. Once more we are again collected and collecting; our new army at both ends of the continent is recruiting fast, and we shall be able to open the next campaign with sixty thousand men, well armed and cloathed. This is our situation, and who will may know it. By perseverance and fortitude we have the prospect of a glorious issue; by cowardice and submission, the sad choice of a variety of evils—a ravaged country—a depopulated city—habitations without safety, and slavery without hope—our homes turned into barracks and bawdy-houses for Hessians, and a future race to provide for whose fathers we shall doubt of. Look on this picture and weep over it! and if there yet remains one thoughtless wretch who believes it not, let him suffer it unlamented.

14

A REPUBLICAN ARMY

The Americans could not have won the War for Independence without the Continental Army. Valuable as the militia was, only the army could mount planned campaigns, hold British regulars at bay, shield militia from counterattack, and force a British capitulation. Building a regular army was the most crucial task of the Continental Congress, which appointed its general officers and requisitioned money from the states to pay the bills. George Washington became the "father of his country" because he forged an army, held it together in defeat and turmoil, and in 1781 finally led it, with French allies, to victory at Yorktown.

But the mere existence of a "standing army" of this kind raised serious issues for Revolutionary and early Constitutional leaders. They knew, from the behavior of the Redcoats in earlier years, how destructive of life and liberty an army could be, and the brutal violence of the British during the Revolution only confirmed this view. Even more, they knew from their reading of history that armies could take over governments and establish tyrannies, as in ancient Rome or Sparta, and they had read deeply in contemporary English constitutional theory, which assumed that an army had to remain small, tightly disciplined, and under civilian control in order to preserve parliamentary government. The English deployed their army abroad, not at home.

In any case, years of hard fighting had strained the American economy, making it difficult to persuade state governments to raise tax revenues to pay for the army, especially considering that a major reason for the war in the first place was excessive taxation. But these considerations did not mollify the officers of the army, who received little pay for their services—George Washington received none at all—yet had to remain in the field with their troops well after Yorktown because a formal peace treaty was not signed until the fall of 1783. Matters came to a head in March 1783 when Washington got wind of a movement among the officers to threaten Congress into paying deferred salaries or the army would retire to some "unsettled country," presumably beyond the Appalachians, leaving the country to fend for itself. Seeing this for what it was, the gravest possible threat to republican government, Washington gave the following speech to his assembled officers.

Some believe that in thus thwarting the so-called Newburgh Conspiracy, Washington averted a military coup that would have ended the American experiment in self-government before it had begun. Given the frequency of military coups in the next two centuries, particularly among the new nations of Latin America, Asia, and Africa, this may have been Washington's most crucial contribution to the evolution of American democracy. This issue continued to play itself out in the early days of the nation in contradictory ways. The framers of the Constitution, for instance, wanted a stronger central government so as to sustain a military establishment if need be. On the other hand, the drafters of the Bill of Rights later sought to guarantee the right to a citizens' militia partly in order to avoid the need for a large standing army that might trample liberty. The debate that continues to this day over the meaning of the Second Amendment echoes nearly all of these early concerns. The issue of civilian control over the military would also arise again, during the Civil War and the Korean conflict.

George Washington was born in 1732 to a moderately prosperous Virginia planter. After sporadic schooling, Washington inherited an estate at Mount Vernon, which he made his main residence, and expanded his holdings of land and slaves through marriage to Martha Custis, a rich widow. His military experience came in the Seven Years' War, when he commanded forces along the frontier. This plus his wealth and standing, his early support for the independence movement, and especially his natural leadership abilities made him a logical choice for commander in chief, a post he filled with remarkable distinction until late 1783, when he returned to Virginia to try to repair his suffering estates. He became the first president in 1789, served two terms, then declined a third on somewhat the same grounds outlined in his Newburgh speech—that it would be bad for the country. Although increasingly sympathetic to Alexander Hamilton and the Strong Nationalists over the small-government Jeffersonians, Washington provided an example of restraint in his conduct that served later generations well. He died at Mount Vernon in 1799.

Questions to Consider. What were Washington's chief arguments against the plotters? Which arguments seem designed to appeal to military men, and which to patriots? Do they all seem equally valid? To what extent did he appeal to the officers' republican idealism? How important was his own personal record and honor to the argument? Would the argument have succeeded if someone besides Washington—a civilian member of Congress, perhaps—had made it?

■═■═■

The Newburgh Address (1783)

GEORGE WASHINGTON

An attempt has been made to convene you together; how inconsistent with the rules of propriety, how unmilitary, and how subversive of all order and discipline, let the good sense of the army decide. . . .

I have thought it incumbent on me to observe to you, to show upon what principles I opposed the irregular and hasty meeting which was proposed to have been held on Tuesday last—and not because I wanted a disposition to give you every opportunity consistent with your own honor, and the dignity of the army, to make known your grievances. If my conduct heretofore has not evinced to you that I have been a faithful friend to the army, my declaration of it at this time would be equally unavailing and improper. But as I was among the first who embarked in the cause of our common country. As I have never left your side one moment, but when called from you on public duty. As I have been the constant companion and witness of your distresses, and not among the last to feel and acknowledge your merits. As I have ever considered my own military reputation as inseparably connected with that of the army. As my heart has ever expanded with joy, when I have heard its praises, and my indignation has arisen, when the mouth of detraction has been opened against it, it can scarcely be supposed, at this late stage of the war, that I am indifferent to its interests.

But how are they to be promoted? The way is plain, says the anonymous addresser. If war continues, remove into the unsettled country, there establish yourselves, and leave an ungrateful country to defend itself. But who are they to defend? Our wives, our children, our farms, and other property which we leave behind us. Or, in this state of hostile separation, are we to take the two first (the latter cannot be removed) to perish in a wilderness, with hunger, cold, and nakedness? If peace takes place, never sheathe your swords, says he, until you have obtained full and ample justice; this dreadful alternative, of either deserting our country in the extremest hour of her distress or turning our arms against it (which is the apparent object, unless Congress can be compelled into instant compliance), has something so shocking in it that humanity revolts at the idea. My God! What can this writer have in view, by recommending such measures? Can he be a friend to the army? Can he be a friend to this country? Rather, is he not an insidious foe? Some emissary, perhaps, from New York, plotting the ruin of both, by sowing the seeds of discord and separation between the civil and military powers of the continent? . . .

W. C. Ford et al., eds., *Journals of the Continental Congress* XXIV: 295–297.

I cannot, in justice to my own belief, and what I have great reason to conceive is the intention of Congress, conclude this address, without giving it as my decided opinion, that that honorable body entertains exalted sentiments of the services of the army; and, from a full conviction of its merits and sufferings, will do it complete justice. That their endeavors to discover and establish funds for this purpose have been unwearied, and will not cease till they have succeeded, I have not a doubt. But, like all other large bodies, where there is a variety of different interests to reconcile, their deliberations are slow. Why, then, should we distrust them? And, in consequence of that distrust, adopt measures which may cast a shade over that glory which has been so justly acquired; and tarnish the reputation of an army which is celebrated through all Europe, for its fortitude and patriotism? . . .

For myself, . . . a grateful sense of the confidence you have ever placed in me, a recollection of the cheerful assistance and prompt obedience I have experienced from you, under every vicissitude of fortune, and the sincere affection I feel for an army I have so long had the honor to command will oblige me to declare, in this public and solemn manner, that, in the attainment of complete justice for all your toils and dangers, and in the gratification of every wish, so far as may be done consistently with the great duty I owe my country and those powers we are bound to respect, you may freely command my services to the utmost of my abilities. . . .

. . . Let me entreat you, gentlemen, on your part, not to take any measures which, viewed in the calm light of reason, will lessen the dignity and sully the glory you have hitherto maintained; let me request you to rely on the plighted faith of your country, and place a full confidence in the purity of the intentions of Congress; that, previous to your dissolution as an army, they will cause all your accounts to be fairly liquidated. . . . And let me conjure you, in the name of our common country, as you value your own sacred honor, as you respect the rights of humanity, and as you regard the military and national character of America, to express your utmost horror and detestation of the man who wishes, under any specious pretenses, to overturn the liberties of our country, and who wickedly attempts to open the floodgates of civil discord and deluge our rising empire in blood.

By thus determining and thus acting, you will pursue the plain and direct road to the attainment of your wishes. You will defeat the insidious designs of our enemies, who are compelled to resort from open force to secret artifice. You will give one more distinguished proof of unexampled patriotism and patient virtue, rising superior to the pressure of the most complicated sufferings. And you will, by the dignity of your conduct, afford occasion for posterity to say, when speaking of the glorious example you have exhibited to mankind, "Had this day been wanting, the world had never seen the last stage of perfection to which human nature is capable of attaining."

15

Securing Liberty

In May 1787 delegates from every state except Rhode Island met in Philadelphia to revise the Articles of Confederation. But they disregarded their instructions; by mid-September they had drawn up an entirely new frame of government for the nation that had achieved its independence in 1783. The Constitutional Convention was a distinguished gathering; the states sent their ablest men to Philadelphia. George Washington was there; so were Benjamin Franklin, Alexander Hamilton, and James Madison. For many weeks the delegates labored mightily to construct a constitution that would "form a more perfect union" without jeopardizing liberty. In September they completed their work and submitted the Constitution to the states for ratification. At once a great debate commenced. In countless essays, editorials, pamphlets, and handbills the American people discussed the merits and defects of the new instrument of government offered for their consideration. The most famous of all the commentaries on the Constitution appeared in *The Federalist.*

The Federalist Papers consist of eighty-five essays appearing in various New York newspapers between October 1787 and August 1788. Hamilton, who had taken part in the Constitutional Convention, wrote the major portion of them; but James Madison, whose diligence in Philadelphia won him the nickname "Father of the Constitution," wrote a sizable number as well. John Jay, author of the New York State Constitution of 1777, also wrote a few. The essays, which were soon published in book form, discussed the weakness of the Confederation, the powers assigned to the federal government in the new Constitution and the organization of these powers into legislative, executive, and judicial branches of government, and the safeguards that were built into the Constitution to prevent oppression. Thomas Jefferson, who was in Paris at the time as minister to France, wrote to say he read the *Papers* with "care, pleasure, and improvement" and called them the "best commentary on the principles of government which was ever written."

The immediate impact of *The Federalist Papers* was probably not great. Some of the states had completed ratification before many of the essays were published. But the essays may have helped persuade New York and Virginia to ratify the Constitution, and their long-range influence has been profound. Since their first appearance the *Papers* have become a classic of political science. Scholars, legislators, judges, and Supreme Court justices have looked to them time and again for clues to understanding the Constitution that was accepted by the states in 1788. After the Declaration of Independence and the Constitution they are the nation's most important political statement. *The Federalist,* Number Ten, written by Madison, is perhaps the most famous. In it, Madison points out the inevitability of conflicts of interest (particularly economic interest) in free societies and insists that representative government can keep these conflicts from getting out of hand and endangering both private rights and the public good.

James Madison, son of a Virginia planter, was born in Port Conway, Virginia, in 1751, and attended the College of New Jersey (now Princeton). In 1776 he helped frame Virginia's constitution and declaration of rights. Between 1780 and 1783 he was a member of the Continental Congress; after the Revolution he served in Virginia's House of Delegates, where he sponsored legislation to disestablish the Anglican church and provide for religious freedom. As a member of Virginia's delegation to the Philadelphia convention in 1787 he played a major role in shaping the Constitution; his notes on the debates are our main source for information about what was discussed. As a member of the First Congress under Washington he sponsored legislation establishing the State, Treasury, and War Departments and also introduced the first ten amendments to the Constitution (the Bill of Rights) into the House of Representatives. For eight years he served as Thomas Jefferson's secretary of state and succeeded him as president in 1809. His own presidency was a stormy one. Though a man of peace, he presided over the controversial War of 1812 with Britain ("Mr. Madison's War"), which ended with a treaty settling none of the outstanding disputes between the two countries. While he was president, the Republican Party gradually accepted the economic program once sponsored by Hamilton and opposed by Jefferson: a second Bank of the United States, a protective tariff, and a large funded debt. In 1817, Madison retired to his estate at Montpelier to manage his farm, pursue his studies, advise James Monroe, his successor in the White House, and warn against disunion. He died in 1836 at the age of eighty-five.

Questions to Consider. In the extract from *The Federalist,* Number Ten, presented below, Madison began by singling out factions as the chief problem confronting free nations like the United States. How did he define *faction?* He said there are two ways to prevent factions from forming. What are they? Why did he reject both of them? What did he mean by saying that the "latent causes of faction" are found in human nature? Do you think he was right in his statement that "the most common and durable source of factions has been the various and unequal distribution of property"? What examples did he give of various propertied interests? Did Madison think a "pure democracy" could handle the "mischief of faction"? How did he distinguish a republic from a democracy? Why did he think a republican form of government, such as outlined in the U.S. Constitution, could deal effectively with the problem of factions?

★━━★━━★

The Federalist, **Number Ten** **(1787)**

JAMES MADISON

Among the numerous advantages promised by a well-constructed Union, none deserves to be more accurately developed than its tendency to break and control the violence of faction. The friend of popular governments never finds himself so much alarmed for their character and fate as when he contemplates their propensity to this dangerous vice. He will not fail, therefore, to set a due value on any plan which, without violating the principles to which he is attached, provides a proper cure for it. . . .

By a faction I understand a number of citizens, whether amounting to a majority or minority of the whole, who are united and actuated by some common impulse of passion, or of interest, adverse to the rights of other citizens, or to the permanent and aggregate interests of the community.

There are two methods of curing the mischiefs of faction: the one, by removing its causes; the other, by controlling its effects.

There are again two methods of removing the causes of faction: the one, by destroying the liberty which is essential to its existence; the other, by giving to every citizen the same opinions, the same passions, and the same interests.

It could never be more truly said than of the first remedy that it was worse than the disease. Liberty is to faction what air is to fire, an aliment without which it instantly expires. But it could not be a less folly to abolish liberty, which is essential to political life, because it nourishes faction than it would be to wish the annihilation of air, which is essential to animal life, because it imparts to fire its destructive agency.

The second expedient is as impracticable as the first would be unwise. As long as the reason of man continues fallible, and he is at liberty to exercise it, different opinions will be formed. As long as the connection subsists between his reason and his self-love, his opinions and his passions will have a reciprocal influence on each other; and the former will be objects to which the latter will attach themselves. The diversity in the faculties of men, from which

The Federalist (Colonial Press, New York, 1901), 44–52.

A miniature of James Madison in 1783 at the age of thirty-two. A small, shy, often sickly Virginia planter and lawyer, Madison commissioned this portrait from Charles Willson Peale—one of the earliest outstanding American artists—as a gift to his fiancée, Kitty Floyd of New York, whom he had met through his friend Thomas Jefferson. Kitty, alas, jilted Madison in favor of one William Clarkson, who "hung round Kitty at the harpsichord." Madison recovered sufficiently to become a chief draftsman of the Constitution and eventually president of the United States and to marry a young Philadelphia widow, Dolley Todd, who would become perhaps the most famous of First Ladies. (Library of Congress)

the rights of property originate, is not less an insuperable obstacle to a uniformity of interests. The protection of these faculties is the first object of government. From the protection of different and unequal faculties of acquiring property, the possession of different degrees and kinds of property immediately results; and from the influence of these on the sentiments and views of the respective proprietors ensues a division of the society into different interests and parties.

The latent causes of faction are thus sown in the nature of man; and we see them everywhere brought into different degrees of activity, according to the different circumstances of civil society. A zeal for different opinions concerning religion, concerning government, and many other points, as well of speculation as of practice; an attachment to different leaders ambitiously contending for pre-eminence and power; or to persons of other descriptions whose fortunes have been interesting to the human passions, have, in turn, divided mankind into parties, inflamed them with mutual animosity, and rendered them much more disposed to vex and oppress each other than to co-operate for their common good. So strong is this propensity of mankind to fall into mutual animosities that where no substantial occasion presents itself the most frivolous and fanciful distinctions have been sufficient to kindle their unfriendly passions and excite their most violent conflicts. But the most common and durable source of factions has been the various and unequal distribution of property. Those who hold and those who are without property have ever formed distinct interests in society. Those who are creditors, and those who are debtors, fall under a like discrimination. A landed interest, a manufacturing interest, a mercantile interest, a moneyed interest, with many lesser interests, grow up of necessity in civilized nations, and divide them into different classes, actuated by different sentiments and views. . . .

Shall domestic manufacturers be encouraged, and in what degree, by restrictions on foreign manufacturers? are questions which would be differently decided by the landed and the manufacturing classes, and probably by neither with a sole regard to justice and the public good. The apportionment of taxes on the various descriptions of property is an act which seems to require the most exact impartiality; yet there is, perhaps, no legislative act in which greater opportunity and temptation are given to a predominant party to trample on the rules of justice. Every shilling with which they overburden the inferior number is a shilling saved to their own pockets.

It is in vain to say that enlightened statesmen will be able to adjust these clashing interests and render them all subservient to the public good. Enlightened statesmen will not always be at the helm. Nor, in many cases, can such an adjustment be made at all without taking into view indirect and remote considerations, which will rarely prevail over the immediate interest which one party may find in disregarding the rights of another or the good of the whole.

The inference to which we are brought is that the *causes* of faction cannot be removed and that relief is only to be sought in the means of controlling its *effects.*

If a faction consists of less than a majority, relief is supplied by the republican principle, which enables the majority to defeat its sinister views by regular vote. It may clog the administration, it may convulse the society; but it will be unable to execute and mask its violence under the forms of the Constitution. When a majority is included in a faction, the form of popular government, on the other hand, enables it to sacrifice to its ruling passion or interest both the public good and the rights of other citizens. To secure the public good and private rights against the danger of such a faction, and at the same time to preserve the spirit and the form of popular government, is then the great object to which our inquiries are directed. . . .

By what means is this object attainable? Evidently by one of two only. Either the existence of the same passion or interest in a majority at the same time must be prevented, or the majority, having such coexistent passion or interest, must be rendered, by their number and local situation, unable to concert and carry into effect schemes of oppression. . . .

[A] pure democracy, by which I mean a society consisting of a small number of citizens, who assemble and administer the government in person, can admit of no cure for the mischiefs of faction. A common passion or interest will, in almost every case, be felt by a majority of the whole; a communication and concert results from the form of government itself; and there is nothing to check the inducements to sacrifice the weaker party or an obnoxious individual. Hence it is that such democracies have ever been spectacles of turbulence and contention; have ever been found incompatible with personal security or the rights of property; and have in general been as short in their lives as they have been violent in their deaths. . . .

A republic, by which I mean a government in which the scheme of representation takes place, opens a different prospect and promises the cure for which we are seeking. Let us examine the points in which it varies from pure democracy, and we shall comprehend both the nature of the cure and the efficacy which it must derive from the Union.

The two great points of difference between a democracy and a republic are: first, the delegation of the government, in the latter, to a small number of citizens elected by the rest; secondly, the greater number of citizens and greater sphere of country over which the latter may be extended.

The effect of the first difference is, on the one hand, to refine and enlarge the public views by passing them through the medium of a chosen body of citizens, whose wisdom may best discern the true interest of their country and whose patriotism and love of justice will be least likely to sacrifice it to temporary or partial considerations. Under such a regulation it may well happen that the public voice, pronounced by the representatives of the people, will be more consonant to the public good than if pronounced by the people themselves, convened for the purpose. On the other hand, the effect may be inverted. Men of factious tempers, of local prejudices, or of sinister designs, may, by intrigue, by corruption, or by other means, first obtain the suffrages, and then betray the interests of the people. . . .

In the first place it is to be remarked that however small the republic may be the representatives must be raised to a certain number in order to guard against the cabals of a few; and that however large it may be they must be limited to a certain number in order to guard against the confusion of a multitude. . . .

In the next place, as each representative will be chosen by a greater number of citizens in the large than in the small republic, it will be more difficult for unworthy candidates to practise with success the vicious arts by which elections are too often carried; and the suffrages of the people being more free, will be more likely to center on men who possess the most attractive merit and the most diffusive and established characters. . . .

The other point of difference is the greater number of citizens and extent of territory which may be brought within the compass of republican than of democratic government; and it is this circumstance principally which renders factious combinations less to be dreaded in the former than in the latter. The smaller the society, the fewer probably will be the distinct parties and interests composing it; the fewer the distinct parties and interests, the more frequently will a majority be found of the same party; and the smaller the number of individuals composing a majority, and the smaller the compass within which they are placed, the more easily will they concert and execute their plans of oppression. Extend the sphere and you take in a greater variety of parties and interests. . . .

The influence of factious leaders may kindle a flame within their particular States but will be unable to spread a general conflagration through the other States. A religious sect may degenerate into a political faction in a part of the Confederacy; but the variety of sects dispersed over the entire face of it must secure the national councils against any danger from that source. A rage for paper money, for an abolition of debts, for an equal division of property, or for any other improper or wicked project, will be less apt to pervade the whole body of the Union than a particular member of it, in the same proportion as such a malady is more likely to taint a particular county or district than an entire State.

In the extent and proper structure of the Union, therefore, we behold a republican remedy for the diseases most incident to republican government.

A political campaign of the Jacksonian era. (Franklin D. Roosevelt Library)

CHAPTER THREE

Nationalists and Partisans

16

CHURCH AND STATE

Finding a role for religion in the new republic was a major preoccupation for the leaders of the Revolutionary era. Their solution was to take religion out of the political and governmental arena to the extent possible.

Most of the great figures of this generation—Benjamin Franklin, Thomas Jefferson, Thomas Paine, and James Madison, among others—were Enlightenment rationalists. Their religion, to the extent they had any, was "deism," belief in a Supreme Being or Primary Cause (deity) who created the universe but then left it alone to operate in more or less clockwork fashion according to natural law. Some attended religious services as a matter of habit and good form. Few believed in the claims of supernatural revelation, or that Jesus was divine rather than mortal, or that the Bible rather than reason was the best source of truth. Thus Ethan Allen, one of the most famous of Revolutionary leaders, entitled his major work *Reason, the Ultimate Oracle of Man,* while the members of the Continental Congress who adopted the Declaration of Independence were perfectly comfortable referring to "Nature and Nature's God," a standard deist construction.

They were therefore not inclined, as a matter of principle, to allow religion a role in governmental affairs. Equally important, they tended to privilege individual human reason and individual autonomy unfettered by state restrictions. Their familiarity with the long history of oppression in Catholic Europe and Anglican Britain made it difficult to imagine either a religious establishment or even significant religious involvement in government that would not stifle freedom of thought. Furthermore, they feared religious passion as a source of enormous social instability and bloody conflict, as the history of Europe again showed.

Many Americans, to be sure, were still true believers, but they belonged to numerous denominations—Catholic, Quaker, even Jewish, as well as Baptist and other evangelical sects. Tax support for one denomination inevitably angered the others. Anglicanism (now Episcopalianism), the faith of the recent foe, Britain, and long established in some places, was a particular source of irritation and anxiety. Deism may have been one source of antiestablishment sentiment. Diversity was another.

Nowhere was the effort to deal with the issues of church and government more important or difficult than in Virginia, the largest state and the birthplace of so many prominent men. In 1777 Thomas Jefferson, fresh from drafting the Declaration of Independence and now a member of the Virginia legislature, wrote a bill to establish religious freedom in Virginia. It failed, but the issue surfaced again in the 1780s. With Jefferson temporarily in France, his protégé, James Madison, led the fight, putting together a coalition of freethinkers, tax cutters, and minority religious denominations that finally enacted the law in 1786. Jefferson considered this act one of the three most important accomplishments of his career, along with the writing of the Declaration and the founding of the University of Virginia.

Thomas Jefferson was born in 1743 on his father's Virginia plantation. He attended William and Mary College, studied law, and was elected to the legislature in 1769. He would eventually serve as governor, minister to France, secretary of state, and, from 1801 to 1809, president. Architect, naturalist, connoisseur, gentleman farmer, avid reader in seven languages, first rector of the University of Virginia, first president of the American Philosophical Society, and promoter of the Bill of Rights, Jefferson was the quintessential Enlightenment man. Yet while he worked to halt the Atlantic slave trade and fretted over the morality of human ownership, he owned even more slaves than Washington, and despite his commitment to the principles of liberty and self-government, he freed only a few of them before his death at his Monticello home on July 4, 1826—precisely fifty years after the adoption of his beloved Declaration of Independence.

Questions to Consider. Most of the Act for Establishing Religious Freedom in Virginia is a preamble and explanation of the reasons for passage of the bill. Why did Jefferson feel obligated to provide so lengthy an explanation for his bill? Which of his arguments seem strongest? Did he intend to protect the liberty of nonbelievers as well as believers? Why did he say (paragraph one) that presumptuous rulers have imposed "false religions over the greatest parts of the world"? Was he right (paragraph four) that government officials should never have the power to determine religious matters because they cannot avoid judging according to their own prejudices? Jefferson later wrote to a constituent that there should be "a wall between church and state." Did this statute build such a wall? Are you surprised that some of Virginia's evangelical denominations supported this effort to insulate the state from religious influence?

★══★══★

An Act for Establishing Religious Freedom
(1786)

THOMAS JEFFERSON

Well aware that Almighty God hath created the mind free; that all attempts to influence it by temporal punishments or burdens, or by civil incapacitations, tend only to beget habits of hypocrisy and meanness, and are a departure from the plan of the Holy Author of our religion, who being Lord both of body and mind, yet chose not to propagate it by coercions on either, as was in his Almighty power to do; that the impious presumption of legislators and rulers, civil as well as ecclesiastical, who, being themselves but fallible and uninspired men have assumed dominion over the faith of others, setting up their own opinions and modes of thinking as the only true and infallible, and as such endeavoring to impose them on others, hath established and maintained false religions over the greatest part of the world, and through all time. . . .

. . . That to compel a man to furnish contributions of money for the propagation of opinions which he disbelieves, is sinful and tyrannical; that even the forcing him to support this or that teacher of his own religious persuasion, is depriving him of the comfortable liberty of giving his contributions to the particular pastor whose morals he would make his pattern, and whose powers he feels most persuasive to righteousness, and is withdrawing from the ministry those temporal rewards, which proceeding from an approbation of their personal conduct, are an additional incitement to earnest and unremitting labors for the instruction of mankind. . . .

. . . That our civil rights have no dependence on our religious opinions, more than our opinions in physics or geometry; that, therefore, the proscribing any citizen as unworthy the public confidence by laying upon him an incapacity of being called to the offices of trust and emolument, unless he profess or renounce this or that religious opinion, is depriving him injuriously of those privileges and advantages to which in common with his fellow citizens he has a natural right; that it tends also to corrupt the principles of that very religion it is meant to encourage, by bribing, with a monopoly of worldly honors and emoluments, those who will externally profess and conform to it; that though indeed these are criminal who do not withstand such temptation, yet neither are those innocent who lay the bait in their way. . . .

. . . That to suffer the civil magistrate to intrude his powers into the field of opinion and to restrain the profession or propagation of principles, on the supposition of their ill tendency, is a dangerous fallacy, which at once de-

W. W. Hening, ed., *Statutes at Large of Virginia* XII: 84–85.

stroys all religious liberty, because he being of course judge of that tendency, will make his opinions the rule of judgment, and approve or condemn the sentiments of others only as they shall square with or differ from his own; that it is time enough for the rightful purposes of civil government, for its offices to interfere when principles break out into overt acts against peace and good order. . . .

. . . And finally, that truth is great and will prevail if left to herself, that she is the proper and sufficient antagonist to error, and has nothing to fear from the conflict, unless by human interposition disarmed of her natural weapons, free argument and debate, errors ceasing to be dangerous when it is permitted freely to contradict them.

Be it therefore enacted by the General Assembly, That no man shall be compelled to frequent or support any religious worship, place or ministry whatsoever, nor shall be enforced, restrained, molested, or burthened in his body or goods, nor shall otherwise suffer on account of his religious opinions or belief; but that all men shall be free to profess, and by argument to maintain, their opinions in matters of religion, and that the same shall in nowise diminish, enlarge, or affect their civil capacities.

And though we well know this Assembly, elected by the people for the ordinary purposes of legislation only, have no power to restrain the acts of succeeding assemblies, constituted with the powers equal to our own, and that therefore to declare this act irrevocable, would be of no effect in law, yet we are free to declare, and do declare, that the rights hereby asserted are of the natural rights of mankind, and that if any act shall be hereafter passed to repeal the present or to narrow its operation, such act will be an infringement of natural right.

17

MOVING WEST

The existence of vast tracts of land between the Appalachian Mountains and the Mississippi River was enormously important in the late eighteenth century. Great Britain fought and defeated France in the Seven Years' War partly to control this territory. London then tried to keep Americans from settling there out of fear that they would anger the Indian nations in the area and be harder to control so far from the seacoast. This in turn incensed the Americans, who had every intention of expanding westward. Not only did settlers cross into the region despite British law, but investors, including George Washington, bought acreage there on a speculative basis. The Americans needed to control the territory in order to guarantee their personal land titles as well as to quicken the pace of settlement and protect the western claims of the various colonies, and they went to war partly to establish that control.

So winning the Revolution not only meant doubling the size of the new country. It also meant shaping the future of this immense western area—determining its relationship to the original states, disposing of the acreage in an appropriate way, and imposing social and political arrangements. This was of some urgency since there were already tens of thousands of settlers, many of them (as in the unauthorized state of "Franklin" in the southern Appalachians) starting to clamor for their own country or even a link to Spanish Louisiana. As a result, Congress passed three acts in 1784, 1785, and 1787; key portions of these Northwest Ordinances are excerpted below. Because Congress authorized southern states with western claims to organize the lands south of the Ohio River, the ordinances ended up dealing almost entirely with the northern part of the region, comprising the future states of Ohio, Indiana, Illinois, Michigan, and Wisconsin.

The Ordinance of 1784, the shortest of the three but possibly the most important in asserting that the new lands would become full-fledged states with representative governments, was drafted by Thomas Jefferson, whose hopes and assumptions pervaded all of the ordinances. Jefferson's original plan included the clause, "That after the year 1800 there shall be neither slavery nor involuntary servitude in any of the

[new] states." Congress deleted this clause by a vote of 7–6; every Southern state opposed it, including Jefferson's own Virginia. The 1787 Ordinance did contain this proviso, however (along with a companion clause requiring the return of runaway slaves). This clause proved fateful because most Northern states, suffused with the egalitarian ideology of the Revolution, had already written state constitutions that abolished slavery either then or in the future. The antislavery clause of the 1787 Ordinance extended this pattern. The South would therefore develop on a basis of human bondage. Thanks to Thomas Jefferson, among others, the North, including its new states, would not.

Questions to Consider. In legislation, the "devil" is usually in the details. Seldom have the details of legislative measures revealed the circumstances and expectations of a new country the way the Northwest Ordinances did. In the 1784 Ordinance, for example, what form of territorial government might Congress have anticipated besides statehood? What factors made eventual statehood seem the best way to proceed? Why was Congress careful to assert here (and in 1787) that the new states would "forever remain a part" of the United States and subject to its laws? What clause tried to reassure the new states of equal treatment?

In 1785, why did Congress provide for a "right angle" system of land surveying and sale? What aspects of political organization and land distribution did this system facilitate? Why was public schooling considered so important that Congress required land to be set aside for it? Given the state of the American economy at the time, do you think the purpose of education was to promote economic opportunity or good citizenship? For what other public purposes was land set aside in this and the other two ordinances?

In 1787, the number of inhabitants required to form a state rose from that in 1784, while the number of permissible states fell. Why might this have happened? What specific liberties did the 1787 Ordinance guarantee? Why did Congress insist that the future state governments be "republican"? What other governments might have emerged? Did the ordinance provide for universal voting rights? Why did Congress mention the Mississippi and Saint Lawrence river systems and the importance of dealing fairly with the Indians?

★━━★━━★

The Northwest Ordinances (1784–1787)

1784

Resolved, that so much of the territory ceded or to be ceded by individual states to the United States as is already purchased or shall be purchased of the Indian inhabitants & offered for sale by Congress, shall be divided into distinct states. . . .

That when any such State shall have acquired twenty thousand inhabitants, on giving due proof thereof to Congress, they shall receive from them authority with appointment of time and place to call a convention of representatives to establish a permanent Constitution and Government for themselves. Provided that both the temporary and permanent governments be established on these principles as their basis.

First. That they shall forever remain a part of this confederacy of the United States of America. Second. That they shall be subject to the articles of Confederation in all those cases in which the original states shall be so subject. . . . Third. That they shall in no case interfere with the primary disposal of the soil by the United States. . . .

Seventh. That the lands of non-resident proprietors shall in no case, be taxed higher than those of residents . . . before the admission thereof to a vote by its delegates in Congress.

That whensoever any of the said states shall have, of free inhabitants, as many as shall then be in any one the least numerous of the thirteen Original states, such State shall be admitted by its delegates into the Congress of the United States on an equal footing with the said original states. . . .

1785

A surveyor from each state shall be appointed by Congress or a Committee of the States. . . .

The Surveyors, as they are respectively qualified, shall proceed to divide the said territory into townships of six miles square, by lines running due north and south, and others crossing these at right angles, as near as may be, unless where the boundaries of the late Indian purchases may render the same impracticable. . . .

The plats of the townships respectively, shall be marked by subdivisions into lots of one mile square, or 640 acres. . . .

And the geographer shall make . . . returns, from time to time, of every seven ranges as they may be surveyed. The Secretary of War shall have recourse thereto, and shall take by lot therefrom, a number of townships . . . as will be equal to one seventh part of the whole of such seven ranges, . . . for the use of the late Continental army. . . .

There shall be reserved for the United States out of every township the four lots, being numbered 8,11,26,29, and out of every fractional part of a township, so many lots of the same numbers as shall be found thereon, for future sale. There shall be reserved the lot No. 16, of every township, for the maintenance of public schools within the said township.

1787

There shall be appointed, from time to time, by Congress, a governor, whose commission shall continue in force for the term of three years, unless sooner revoked by Congress; he shall reside in the district, and have a freehold estate therein, in one thousand acres of land, while in the exercise of his office. . . .

So soon as there shall be five thousand free male inhabitants, of full age, in the district, upon giving proof thereof to the governor, they shall receive authority, with time and place, to elect representatives from their counties or townships, to represent them in the general assembly. . . . *Provided*, That no person be eligible or qualified to act as a representative unless he shall have been a citizen of one of the United States three years, and be a resident in the district, or unless he shall have resided in the district three years; and, in either case, shall likewise hold in his own right, in fee-simple, two hundred acres of land within the same: *Provided also*, That a freehold in fifty acres of land in the district, having been a citizen of one of the states, and being resident in the district, or the like freehold and two years' residence in the district, shall be necessary to qualify a man as an elector of a representative. . . .

It is hereby ordained and declared, by the authority aforesaid, that the following articles shall be considered as articles of compact between the original states and the people and states in the said territory, and forever remain unalterable, unless by common consent:

Article I

No person, demeaning himself in a peaceable and orderly manner, shall ever be molested on account of his mode of worship, or religious sentiments, in the said territory.

Article II

The inhabitants of the said territory shall always be entitled to the benefits of the writs of habeas corpus and of the trial by jury, of a proportionate representation of the people in the legislature, and of judicial proceedings according to the course of the common law. . . .

Article III

Religion, morality, and knowledge being necessary to good government and the happiness of mankind, schools and the means of education shall forever be encouraged. The utmost good faith shall always be observed toward the Indians; their lands and property shall never be taken from them without their consent; and in their property, rights, and liberty they never shall be invaded or disturbed unless in just and lawful wars authorized by Congress; but laws founded in justice and humanity shall, from time to time, be made, for preventing wrongs being done to them and for preserving peace and friendship with them.

Article IV

The said territory, and the states which may be formed therein, shall forever remain a part of the confederacy of the United States of America. . . . No tax shall be imposed on lands the property of the United States; and in no case shall nonresident proprietors be taxed higher than residents. The navigable waters leading into the Mississippi and Saint Lawrence, and the carrying places between the same, shall be common highways, and forever free. . . .

Article V

There shall be formed in the said territory not less than three nor more than five states. . . . And whenever any of the said states shall have sixty thousand free inhabitants therein, such state shall be admitted by its delegates into the Congress of the United States, on an equal footing with the original states, in all respects whatever; and shall be at liberty to form a permanent constitution and state government: *Provided,* The constitution and goverment, so to be formed, shall be republican. . . .

Article VI

There shall be neither slavery nor involuntary servitude in the said territory, otherwise than for the punishment of crimes, whereof the party shall have been duly convicted: *Provided always,* That any person escaping into the same, from whom labor or service is lawfully claimed in any one of the original states, such fugitive may be lawfully reclaimed, and conveyed to the person claiming his or her labor or service as aforesaid. . . .

18

An Industrial Vision

Under the new Constitution, Congress had the power to tax, borrow, and regulate trade and money. But the president was also important; he could recommend to Congress "such measures" as he thought "necessary and expedient." While George Washington was president, he established many precedents of economic policy and behavior. Probably the most important recommendations made during his presidency came from Secretary of the Treasury Alexander Hamilton. Hamilton's four reports to Congress on economic and financial policies were crucial in shaping the development of the new nation. In them Hamilton sought to make the Constitution's promise of a "more perfect Union" a reality by recommending governmental policies that fostered private enterprise and economic growth.

Hamilton's first three reports had to do with funding the national debt and creating a national bank. Hamilton wanted the federal government to take over the old Revolutionary debt as well as the debts incurred by the states during the Revolution, convert them into bonds, and pay for the interest on the bonds by levying excise taxes on distilled spirits and by imposing customs duties on such imports as tea, coffee, and wine. Congress adopted his funding proposals; it also accepted his plan for a large national bank that could make loans to businesses and issue currency backed by federal bonds. Hamilton's fourth report, "On Manufactures," urged a system of import taxes ("protective tariffs"), better roads and harbors ("internal improvements"), and subsidies ("bounties") in order to spur manufacturing.

Hamilton's four reports, with their emphasis on national rather than state power, on industry rather than agriculture, and on public spending to promote private enterprise, had a tremendous political impact. First, they triggered the birth of the earliest formal party system: Hamiltonian Federalists urging passage of the program and Democratic Republicans, followers of Secretary of State Thomas Jefferson, trying to modify or block it. Second, the reports helped establish the questions of governmental power and the nature of the economy as basic issues of political debate over the next half-century. Finally, Hamilton's reports became a veritable fountainhead for Americans concerned with the enhancement of capitalism and national power. Hamiltonian conservatives did not want an uninvolved government; they wanted to forge a partnership between government and business in which federal policies would actively promote business enterprise.

Congress did not immediately adopt Hamilton's recommendations for manufacturing. Protective tariffs, internal improvements, and bounties came much later and were adopted in a piecemeal fashion. Still, "On Manufactures" is important in its preview of the future. Hamilton was perceptive in foreseeing that America's destiny was an industrial one. Long after he had passed from the scene, industrialism did overtake and surpass agriculture (with the encouragement of the states as well as of the federal government) as the driving force of the American economy.

Hamilton himself was concerned more with the political implications of his reports than with their economic effects. His major aim was to strengthen the Union. This strong nationalism probably came from Hamilton's lack of state loyalties. He was born in 1755 in the West Indies (Hamilton claimed 1757). Orphaned at the age of thirteen, he was sent by relatives to the colony of New York in 1772. After preliminary study in New Jersey, he entered King's College (now Columbia University). When war with Britain broke out, he joined the army; in 1777 George Washington made him his aide-de-camp and personal secretary. After the Revolution he studied law, married well, rose rapidly in New York society, and became a dominant force in the Washington administration and the Federalist party. Overbearing and ambitious as well as bright and energetic, he proceeded to alienate important party leaders such as John Adams, and his career declined steadily after Washington left office. In 1804, Vice-President Aaron Burr, a long-time political adversary who had just been defeated in the election for governor of New York, demanded a duel of honor with Hamilton because of some alleged derogatory remarks. On July 11, Burr shot Hamilton at their meeting in a field near Weehawken, New Jersey. He died the following day.

Questions to Consider. Hamilton argued for manufacturing on the grounds that it would attract immigrants and employ women and children. What does this prediction tell us about the availability and condition of labor in early America and about the attitudes of American leaders toward the work force? Hamilton argued not just for the specialization of labor but even more for the easier application of machinery that would result from labor specialization. What two models did he suggest for combining machinery and labor, and what does his simultaneous use of these two very different models indicate about the state of American industry at the time he was writing? Hamilton thought the spirit of capitalist enterprise must be fostered by government. Why, if this spirit was so prevalent, did Hamilton feel the need for special measures to promote it? How compatible was Hamilton's economic nationalism with Madison's political federalism?

★═══★═══★

On Manufactures (1791)

ALEXANDER HAMILTON

It is now proper to proceed a step further, and to enumerate the principal circumstances, from which it may be inferred that manufacturing establishments not only occasion an augmentation of the produce and revenue of the society, but that they contribute essentially to rendering them greater than they could possibly be without such establishments.

Each of these circumstances has a considerable influence upon the total mass of industrious effort in a community; together, they add to it a degree of energy and effect which is not easily conceived. . . .

1. As to the Division of Labor

It has justly been observed, that there is scarcely any thing of greater moment in the economy of a nation than the proper division of labor. The separation of occupations causes each to be carried to a much greater perfection than it could possibly acquire if they were blended. This arises principally from three circumstances:

1st. The greater skill and dexterity naturally resulting from a constant and undivided application to a single object. It is evident that these properties must increase in proportion to the separation and simplification of objects, and the steadiness of the attention devoted to each; and must be less in proportion to the complication of objects, and the number among which the attention is distracted.

2nd. The economy of time, by avoiding the loss of it, incident to a frequent transition from one operation to another of a different nature. This depends on various circumstances: the transition itself, the orderly disposition of the implements, machines, and materials employed in the operation to be relinquished, the preparatory steps to the commencement of a new one, the interruption of the impulse which the mind of the workman acquires from being engaged in a particular operation, the distractions, hesitations, and reluctances which attend the passage from one kind of business to another.

Henry Cabot Lodge, ed., *The Works of Alexander Hamilton* (12 v., G. P. Putnam's Sons, New York, 1904), IV: 70–198.

Americans, Encourage the Manufactories of your Country, if you wish for its prosperity.

An artisan urges manufactures. Alexander Hamilton drew support for his efforts to promote manufacturing from small operations such as the Boston wallpaper shop of Ebenezer Clough. This is the top of Clough's letterhead, which touts his own wares ("a great variety of Paper Hangings") and calls upon his countrymen to achieve prosperity through manufacturing. As the illustrations in the letterhead show, "manufacturing" meant "made by hand" rather than the giant factory system that characterized U.S. industry from the Civil War era until the late twentieth century. (Courtesy, American Antiquarian Society)

3rd. An extension of the use of machinery. A man occupied on a single object will have it more in his power, and will be more naturally led to exert his imagination, in devising methods to facilitate and abridge labor, than if he were perplexed by a variety of independent and dissimilar operations. Besides this, the fabrication of machines, in numerous instances, becoming itself a distinct trade, the artist who follows it has all the advantages which have been enumerated, for improvement in his particular art; and, in both ways, the invention and application of machinery are extended. . . .

2. As to an Extension of the Use of Machinery, A Point Which, Though Partly Anticipated, Requires to Be Placed in One or Two Additional Lights

The employment of machinery forms an item of great importance in the general mass of national industry. It is an artificial force brought in aid of the natural force of man; and, to all the purposes of labor, is an increase of hands, an accession of strength, unencumbered too by the expense of maintaining the laborer. . . .

The cotton mill, invented in England, within the last twenty years, is a signal illustration of the general proposition which has been just advanced. In consequence of it, all the different processes for spinning cotton are performed by means of machines, which are put in motion by water, and attended chiefly by women and children—and by a smaller number of persons, in the whole, than are requisite in the ordinary mode of spinning. And it is an advantage of great moment, that the operations of this mill continue with convenience during the night as well as through the day. The prodigious effect of such a machine is easily conceived. To this invention is to be attributed, essentially, the immense progress, which has been so suddenly made in Great Britain, in the various fabrics of cotton.

3. As to the Additional Employment of Classes of the Community Not Originally Engaged in the Particular Business

This is not among the least valuable of the means by which manufacturing institutions contribute to augment the general stock of industry and production. In places where those institutions prevail, besides the persons regularly engaged in them, they afford occasional and extra employment to industrious individuals and families, who are willing to devote the leisure resulting from the intermissions of their ordinary pursuits to collateral labours, as a resource for multiplying their acquisitions or their enjoyments. The husbandman himself experiences a new source of profit and support from the increased industry of his wife and daughters, invited and stimulated by the demands of the neighboring manufactories.

Besides this advantage of occasional employment to classes having different occupations, there is another, of a nature allied to it, and of a similar tendency. This is the employment of persons who would otherwise be idle, and in many cases a burthen on the community, either from the bias of temper, habit, infirmity of body, or some other cause, indisposing or disqualifying them for the toils of the country. It is worthy of particular remark that, in general, women and children are rendered more useful, and the latter more early useful by manufacturing establishments, than they would otherwise be. Of the number of persons employed in the cotton manufactories of Great Britain, it is computed that four sevenths nearly are women and children, of whom the greatest proportion are children, and many of them of a very tender age. . . .

4. As to the Promoting of Emigration from Foreign Countries

Men reluctantly quit one course of occupation and livelihood for another, unless invited to it by very apparent and proximate advantages. Many who would go from one country to another, if they had a prospect of continuing with more benefit the callings to which they have been educated, will often not be tempted to change their situation by the hope of doing better in some other way. Manufacturers who, listening to the powerful invitations of a better price for their fabrics, or their labor, of greater cheapness of provisions and raw materials, of an exemption from the chief part of the taxes, burthens and restraints, which they endure in the Old World, of greater personal independence and consequence, under the operation of a more equal government, and of what is far more precious than mere religious toleration, a perfect equality of religious privileges, would probably flock from Europe to the United States to pursue their own trades or professions, if they were once made sensible of the advantages they would enjoy, and were inspired with an assurance of encouragement and employment, will with difficulty, be induced to transplant themselves, with a view to becoming cultivators of Land.

If it be true, then, that it is in the interest of the United States to open every possible avenue to immigration from abroad, it affords a weighty argument for the encouragement of manufactures; which, for the reasons just assigned, will have the strongest tendency to multiply the inducements to it. . . .

5. As to the Furnishing Greater Scope for the Diversity of Talents and Dispositions, Which Discriminate Men from Each Other

This is a much more powerful means of augmenting the fund of national industry, than may at first sight appear. It is a just observation, that minds of the strongest and most active powers for their proper objects, fall below mediocrity, and labor without effect, if confined to uncongenial pursuits. And it is thence to be inferred, that the results of human exertion may be immensely increased by diversifying its objects. When all the different kinds of industry obtain in a community, each individual can find his proper element, and can call into activity the whole vigor of his nature. And the community is benefited by the services of its respective members, in the manner in which each can serve it with most effect.

If there be any thing in a remark often to be met with, namely, that there is, in the genius of the people of this country, a peculiar aptitude for mechanic improvements, it would operate as a forcible reason for giving opportunities to the exercise of that species of talent, by the propagation of manufactures.

6. As to the Affording a More Ample and Various Field for Enterprise

. . . To cherish and stimulate the activity of the human mind, by multiplying the objects of enterprise, is not among the least considerable of the expedients by which the wealth of a nation may be promoted. Even things in themselves not positively advantageous sometimes become so, by their tendency to provoke exertion. Every new scene which is opened to the busy nature of man to rouse and exert itself, is the addition of a new energy to the general stock of effort.

The spirit of enterprise, useful and prolific as it is, must necessarily be contracted or expanded, in proportion to the simplicity or variety of the occupations and productions which are to be found in a society. It must be less in a nation of mere cultivators, than in a nation of cultivators and merchants; less in a nation of cultivators and merchants, than in a nation of cultivators, artificers and merchants.

19

SEDITION OR DISSENT

Driven by differences in policy, philosophy, and personality, American politics became formal party politics for the first time in the 1790s, with incendiary consequences. The "Federalists" lined up behind Alexander Hamilton's program: a significant national debt with higher taxes to pay the interest on it, a huge federally-chartered Bank of the United States, protective tariffs to foster manufacturing, and major federal transportation projects. Federalists, including both Washington and his successor as president, John Adams, wanted a more powerful federal judiciary and military. They were generally pro-British—and therefore anti–Revolutionary France—in foreign policy. And they distrusted, even feared, the impulses of the "populace" as opposed to the wealthy and well-educated, whom they assumed to be the country's natural leaders. Hamilton called the common people a "great beast." Other Federalists tended to agree.

All this generated much opposition, led by Vice-President Thomas Jefferson and his allies, the so-called Republicans or Democrats. Jefferson opposed nearly everything the Federalists stood for, and he was as suspicious of their "monarchical" intentions as they were of his irresponsible radicalism. The Jeffersonian press, urged on by Jefferson himself, was particularly aggressive in calling for "resistance" to the corrupt, pro-British, monarchical Federalist cabal. This mattered, since by 1800 there were over two hundred newspapers that together reached a third of the eligible voters. Meanwhile, a host of radical immigrants from England, Ireland, and France was now streaming into the country. Nearly all of them supported the hated Jefferson, heaped scorn on John Adams, and demanded American intervention on behalf of Revolutionary France, which Federalists thought would be a disaster.

In Federalist eyes, something clearly had to be done if the United States were to avoid the kind of bloody mob revolt that had convulsed France. In 1798 the Federalist-controlled Congress tripled the regular army to ten thousand men. In case of war, the army would automatically expand to fifty thousand, but the real target was potential radical mobs, not a foreign power. Even more ominously, the Federalists rammed through Congress the Alien and Sedition Acts. The first authorized the president to expel, without proof, "dangerous" foreign residents; the second forbade anyone, even citizens, to "oppose any measure or measures of the United States" or bring the president "into contempt of disrepute." The intent was clear. "It is patriotism," according to a Federalist newspaper, "to write in favor of our government—it is sedition to write against it." Within a few months four of the five largest Jeffersonian papers were under charges of sedition. By mid-1800, amid a hot presidential campaign, ten people had been convicted, including a sitting Vermont congressman.

Nothing else ever angered Thomas Jefferson so much. "I am unalterably opposed," he had written, "to every form of tyranny over the mind of man," and these acts surely smacked of tyranny. But it was not clear how to respond. The Federalists controlled all three branches of the central government, so neither constitutional checks and balances nor the Bill of Rights seemed reliable. Neither did elections, since if dissent was going to be suppressed how could there be free elections? The question of how to rule on problems of constitutionality had not yet been resolved in favor of the Supreme Court, so there seemed only one recourse—the states. Jefferson therefore drafted a resolution for the Kentucky legislature, which his supporters controlled. James Madison, his lieutenant, did the same in Virginia. The final portion of the Kentucky Resolutions, containing Jefferson's essential arguments, follows below.

In a further show of resolve, the governors of Kentucky and Virginia mobilized their militia; entire units of young men carrying long rifles signed petitions denouncing this attack on freedom of expression. In the event, the elections went forward, and the backlash over the Alien and Sedition Acts helped make Jefferson president. One of his first actions was to persuade the new Democratic–Republican Congress to repeal them.

Questions to Consider. Why, according to the resolutions, did the Alien and Sedition Acts worry Jefferson so much? What common constitutional recourse did they threaten to prevent? Was Jefferson right to be so concerned? Are there any interests besides those of freedom of dissent that would justify this kind of states rights view? To what extent did the rhetoric of the Kentucky Resolutions resemble the rhetoric of, for example, James Otis and Tom Paine in the Revolutionary era? In 1798 Jefferson wrote: "Party division is necessary to induce each to watch & relate to the people the proceedings of the other. . . . A little patience and we shall see the reign of witches pass over and the people recovering their true sight." What was Jefferson's point here? Who were the "witches"?

★▬▬★▬▬★

The Kentucky Resolutions of 1798

THOMAS JEFFERSON

Resolved, That a committee of conference and correspondence be appointed . . . to communicate . . . to the legislatures of the several States; to assure them this commonwealth continues in the same esteem of their friendship and union which it has manifested from that moment at which a common danger first suggested a common union: that it considers union, for specified national purposes, and particularly to those specified in their late federal compact, to be friendly to the peace, happiness and prosperity of all the States; that faithful to that compact, according to the plain intent and meaning in which it was understood and acceded to by the several parties, it is sincerely anxious for its preservation: that it does also believe, that to take from the States all the powers of self-government and transfer them to a general and consolidated government . . . is not for the peace, happiness or prosperity of these States. . . .

. . . And that therefore this commonwealth is determined . . . to submit to undelegated, and consequently unlimited powers in no man, or body of men on earth: that in cases of an abuse of the delegated powers, the members of the General Government, being chosen by the people, a change by the people would be the constitutional remedy; but, where powers are assumed which have not been delegated, a nullification of the act is the rightful remedy: that every State has a natural right in cases not within the compact . . . to nullify of their own authority all assumptions of power by others within their limits: that without this right, they would be under the dominion, absolute and unlimited, of whatsoever might exercise this right of judgment for them: that nevertheless, this commonwealth, from motives of regard and respect for its co-States, has wished to communicate with them on the subject: that with them alone it is proper to communicate, they alone being parties to the compact, and solely authorized to judge in the last resort of the powers exercised under it, Congress being not a party, but merely the creature of the compact. . . .

That if the acts before specified should stand, these conclusions would flow from them:

- That the General Government may place any act they think proper on the list of crimes, and punish it themselves whether enumerated or not enumerated by the Constitution as cognizable by them.
- That they may transfer its cognizance to the President, or any other

N. S. Shaler, *Kentucky* (Houghton Mifflin, Boston, 1885), 410–412.

person, who may himself be the accuser, counsel, judge and jury, whose *suspicions* may be the evidence, his *order* the sentence, his *officer* the executioner, and his breast the sole record of the transaction.

- That a very numerous and valuable description of the inhabitants of these States being, by this precedent, reduced, as outlaws, to the absolute dominion of one man, and the barrier of the Constitution thus swept away from us all, no rampart now remains against the passions and the powers of a majority in Congress to protect from a like exportation, or other more grievous punishment, the minority of the same body, the legislatures, judges, governors, and counsellors of the States, nor their other peaceable inhabitants, who may venture to reclaim the consitutional rights and liberties of the States and people, or who for other causes, good or bad, may be obnoxious to the views, or marked by the suspicions of the President, or be thought dangerous to his or their election, or other interests, public or personal.
- That the friendless alien has indeed been selected as the safest subject of a first experiment; but the citizen will soon follow, or rather, has already followed, for already has a sedition act marked him as its prey.
- That these and successive acts of the same character, unless arrested at the threshold, necessarily drive these States into revolution and blood, and will furnish new calumnies against republican government, and new pretexts for those who wish it to be believed that man cannot be governed but by a rod of iron.
- That it would be a dangerous delusion were a confidence in the men of our choice to silence our fears for the safety of our rights: that confidence is everywhere the parent of despotism—free government is founded in jealousy, and not in confidence; it is jealousy and not confidence which prescribes limited constitutions, to bind down those whom we are obliged to trust with power: our Constitution has accordingly fixed the limits to which, and no further, our confidence may go.
- And let the honest advocate of confidence read the alien and sedition acts, and say if the Constitution has not been wise in fixing limits to the government it created, and whether we should be wise in destroying those limits. Let him say what the government is, if it be not a tyranny, which the men of our choice have conferred on our President, and the President of our choice has assented to, and accepted over the friendly strangers to whom the mild spirit of our country and its laws have pledged hospitality and protection: that the men of our choice have more respected the bare *suspicions* of the President, than the solid right of innocence, the claims of justification, the sacred force of truth, and the forms and substance of law and justice. In questions of power, then, let no more be heard of confidence in man, but bind him down from mischief by the chains of the Constitution.

20

THE CONSTITUTION CONSTRUED

Marbury v. *Madison* was the first case in which the Supreme Court exercised the right of "judicial review" over laws passed by Congress. In February 1803, Chief Justice John Marshall, a staunch Federalist, speaking for the majority of justices on the Supreme Court, announced his opinion in the case. William Marbury had been appointed justice of the peace for the District of Columbia by John Adams in the last hours of his administration. But because Marbury was a Federalist, James Madison, Jefferson's secretary of state, withheld the commission from him. Marbury appealed to the Supreme Court for a writ of mandamus, that is, a court order compelling Madison to deliver the commission.

Marshall did not believe that Madison was justified in denying Marbury his commission as justice of the peace. But in his opinion he declared that the Supreme Court could not force Madison to deliver the commission. The Constitution, he said, in defining the original jurisdiction of the Supreme Court, did not include the issue of writs to executive officers. Nonetheless, section 13 of the Judiciary Act of 1789 did give the Supreme Court the power to issue such writs, and it was under this law that Marbury had applied to the Court. Marshall, however, declared that section 13 of the Judiciary Act was unconstitutional and that therefore the Court could not render judgment. He then went on to assert the right of the Supreme Court to pass on the constitutionality of laws passed by Congress. "It is a proposition too plain to be contested," he declared, "that the constitution controls any legislative act repugnant to it" and that "a legislative act contrary to the constitution is not law." He added, "It is emphatically the province and duty of the judicial department to say what the law is." And he concluded that "a law repugnant to the constitution is void, and that courts, as well as other departments, are bound by that instrument." By claiming for the Court the duty of deciding whether acts of Congress were constitutional, Marshall upheld the prestige of the judiciary, even though he was unable to do anything for Marbury. But it was not until the *Dred Scott* case, more than half a century later, that the Supreme Court invalidated a congressional act for the second time.

Born in 1755 to well-to-do Virginians, John Marshall received little formal schooling. He studied law, however, and eventually became active in state politics. His service in the army during the American Revolution helped develop his nationalistic outlook. A distant cousin of Thomas Jefferson but a devoted Federalist nonetheless, Marshall served on a commission to France in 1797 and was elected to Congress in 1799. In 1801 President John Adams named him to the U.S. Supreme Court, where he served as chief justice for the next thirty-four years. Among his notable decisions besides *Marbury* v. *Madison* were *Mc-Culloch* v. *Maryland* (1819), which protected federal agencies such as the Bank of the United States from state taxes; *Dartmouth College* v. *Woodward* (1819), which upheld the sanctity of contracts; and *Gibbons* v. *Ogden* (1824), which established federal authority over interstate and foreign commerce. In these and other cases Marshall sought to protect the rights of property, increase the power of the federal government, and raise the prestige of the federal judiciary. Personally convivial, gossipy, courtly with women, and generally reveling in the social life of the slaveholding gentry, Marshall in public remained a figure of controversy throughout his career. He died in Philadelphia in 1835.

Questions to Consider. Why, according to Chief Justice Marshall, should the Constitution and its principles be considered permanent? How important was it to Marshall's argument that the U.S. Constitution was written? What alternative did he have in mind, and why did he feel compelled to assert the special character of a written document? Why did he single out the legislative branch as opposed to the executive (or judiciary) as the chief danger to the permanence of the Constitution and its principles? On what grounds, according to Marshall, did the judiciary become the final arbiter of constitutional quarrels with the right to annul legislation? Why was Marshall's decision seen as a victory for the Federalist party?

★━━★━━★

Marbury v. Madison (1803)

JOHN MARSHALL

The question whether an act repugnant to the constitution can become the law of the land is a question deeply interesting to the United States; but, happily not of an intricacy proportioned to its interest. It seems only necessary to

1 *Craven* 137 (1803).

recognize certain principles supposed to have been long and well established, to decide it.

That the people have an original right to establish for their future government such principles as, in their opinion, shall most conduce to their own happiness, is the basis on which the whole American fabric has been erected. The exercise of this original right is a very great exertion, nor can it nor ought it to be frequently repeated. The principles therefore so established are deemed fundamental. And as the authority from which they proceed is supreme and can seldom act, they are designed to be permanent.

This original and supreme will organizes the government, and assigns to different departments their respective powers. It may either stop here or establish certain limits not to be transcended by those departments.

The government of the United States is of the latter description. The powers of the legislature are defined and limited; and that those limits may not be mistaken or forgotten, the constitution is written. To what purpose are powers limited, and to what purpose is that limitation committed to writing, if these limits may, at any time, be passed by those intended to be restrained? The distinction between a government with limited and unlimited powers is abolished if those limits do not confine the persons on whom they are imposed and if acts prohibited and acts allowed are of equal obligation. It is a proposition too plain to be contested, that the constitution controls any legislative act repugnant to it; or the legislature may alter the constitution by an ordinary act.

Between these alternatives there is no middle ground. The constitution is either a superior paramount law, unchangeable by ordinary means, or it is on a level with ordinary legislative acts, and, like other acts, is alterable when the legislature shall please to alter it.

If the former part of the alternative be true, then a legislative act contrary to the constitution is not law; if the latter part be true, then written constitutions are absurd attempts, on the part of the people, to limit a power in its own nature illimitable.

Certainly all those who have framed written constitutions contemplate them as forming the fundamental and paramount law of the nation, and consequently the theory of every such government must be that an act of the legislature repugnant to the constitution is void.

This theory is essentially attached to a written constitution, and is consequently to be considered, by this court, as one of the fundamental principles of our society. It is not, therefore, to be lost sight of in the further consideration of this subject.

If an act of the legislature repugnant to the constitution is void, does it, notwithstanding its invalidity, bind the courts and oblige them to give it effect? Or, in other words, though it be not law, does it constitute a rule as operative as if it was a law? This would be to overthrow in fact what was established in theory, and would seem, at first view, an absurdity too gross to be insisted on. It shall, however, receive a more attentive consideration.

It is emphatically the province and duty of the judicial department to say what the law is. Those who apply the rule to particular cases must of necessity expound and interpret that rule. If two laws conflict with each other, the courts must decide on the operation of each.

So if a law be in opposition to the constitution; if both the law and the constitution apply to a particular case, so that the court must either decide that case conformably to the law, disregarding the constitution, or conformably to the constitution, disregarding the law, the court must determine which of these conflicting rules governs the case. This is of the very essence of judicial duty.

If, then, the courts are to regard the constitution, and the constitution is superior to any ordinary act of the legislature, the constitution, and not such ordinary act, must govern the case to which they both apply.

Those, then, who controvert the principle that the constitution is to be considered in court as a paramount law, are reduced to the necessity of maintaining that courts must close their eyes on the constitution and see only the law.

This doctrine would subvert the very foundation of all written constitutions. It would declare that an act which, according to the principles and theory of our government, is entirely void, is yet, in practice, completely obligatory. It would declare that if the legislature shall do what is expressly forbidden, such act, notwithstanding the express prohibition, is in reality effectual. It would be giving to the legislature a practical and real omnipotence with the same breath which professes to restrict their powers within narrow limits. It is prescribing limits and declaring that those limits may be passed at pleasure.

That it thus reduces to nothing what we have deemed the greatest improvement on political institutions, a written constitution, would of itself be sufficient, in America, where written constitutions have been viewed with so much reverence, for rejecting the construction. But the peculiar expressions of the constitution of the United States furnish additional arguments in favor of its rejection.

The judicial power of the United States is extended to all cases arising under the constitution.

Could it be the intention of those who gave this power to say that in using it the constitution should not be looked into? That a case arising under the constitution should be decided without examining the instrument under which it arises?

This is too extravagant to be maintained.

In some cases, then, the constitution must be looked into by the judges. And if they can open it at all, what part of it are they forbidden to read or to obey?

There are many other parts of the constitution which serve to illustrate this subject.

It is declared that "no tax or duty shall be laid on articles exported from any state." Suppose a duty on the export of cotton, of tobacco, or of flour, and a suit instituted to recover it, ought judgment to be rendered in such a case? Ought the judges to close their eyes on the constitution, and only see the law?

The constitution declares "that no bill of attainder or *ex post facto* law shall be passed." If, however, such a bill should be passed, and a person should be prosecuted under it, must the court condemn to death those victims whom the constitution endeavors to preserve?

"No person," says the constitution, "shall be convicted of treason unless on the testimony of two witnesses to the same overt act, or on confession in open court."

Here the language of the constitution is addressed especially to the courts. It prescribes, directly for them, a rule of evidence not to be departed from. If the legislature should change that rule, and declare one witness, or a confession out of court, sufficient for conviction, must the constitutional principle yield to the legislative act?

From these, and many other selections which might be made, it is apparent that the framers of the constitution contemplated that instrument as a rule for the government of *courts,* as well as of the legislature. Why otherwise does it direct the judges to take an oath to support it? This oath certainly applies in an especial manner to their conduct in their official character. How immoral to impose it on them if they were to be used as the instruments, and the knowing instruments, for violating what they swear to support!

The oath of office, too, imposed by the legislature, is completely demonstrative of the legislative opinion on this subject. It is in these words: "I do solemnly swear that I will administer justice without respect to persons, and do equal right to the poor and to the rich; and that I will faithfully and impartially discharge all the duties incumbent on me as ———, according to the best of my abilities and understanding, agreeably to *the constitution* and laws of the United States." Why does a judge swear to discharge his duties agreeably to the constitution of the United States, if that constitution forms no rule for his government—if it is closed upon him, and cannot be inspected by him?

If such be the real state of things, this is worse than solemn mockery. To prescribe, or to take this oath, becomes equally a crime.

It is also not entirely unworthy of observation, that in declaring what shall be the *supreme* law of the land, the constitution itself is first mentioned, and not the laws of the United States generally, but those only which shall be made in *pursuance* of the constitution, have that rank.

Thus, the particular phraseology of the constitution of the United States confirms and strengthens the principle, supposed to be essential to all written constitutions, that a law repugnant to the constitution is void, and that courts, as well as other departments, are bound by that instrument.

21

THE SECTIONAL SPECTER

The first great sectional struggle in the United States (after the Missouri crisis over slavery) was over the tariff. Northern industrialists favored high tariffs to protect their products from foreign competition. But the South was an agricultural region, and Southerners complained that protective tariffs raised the price of manufactured goods and prevented them from importing low-priced goods from abroad. On May 20, 1828, Congress passed a tariff bill with rates so high that South Carolina's John C. Calhoun (vice-president at the time) called it a "Tariff of Abominations." He presented a lengthy statement of the Southern position on tariffs in which he developed his theory of nullification.

Calhoun believed in the "compact" theory of the Union. He maintained that the Constitution was a contract into which the states had entered of their own free will. The states retained their sovereignty, and the federal government was merely their agent for general purposes. If the federal government exceeded its authority and encroached on the powers of the states, the states had a right to resist. Calhoun thought the constitutionality of acts of Congress should be decided by state conventions called for that purpose. If such a convention declared an act of Congress in violation of the Constitution, that act became null and void within the borders of that state. Calhoun insisted that the Constitution did not give Congress the right to levy protective tariffs and that the states had a right to nullify tariff legislation.

On December 19, 1828, the South Carolina legislature published Calhoun's statement (without mentioning his name) as "South Carolina Exposition and Protest," together with resolutions, reproduced below, condemning the tariff. For the time being, South Carolina contented itself with making this protest, hoping that the tariff would be revised after Andrew Jackson became president. But in July 1832, when a new tariff bill was passed by Congress and signed by Jackson, South Carolinians decided to put Calhoun's theory into practice. On November 4, 1832, a special state convention met in Columbia, adopted an ordinance declaring the tariffs of 1828 and 1832 unconstitutional, and announced that no tariff duties would be collected in the state after February 1, 1833. Jackson at once denounced South Carolina's action and asked

Congress to give him authority to use the army and navy, if necessary, to compel South Carolina to obey the law. South Carolina continued defiant. When Congress passed a compromise bill lowering the tariff rate, the "nullies" (as they were called) repealed the nullification ordinance. But they did not disavow the nullification theory.

Calhoun was born in South Carolina in 1782 to an upcountry farmer. After graduating from Yale College, he practiced law briefly. He then married a wealthy Charleston woman and began a political climb that led to Congress, a post in James Monroe's cabinet, and the vice presidency under both John Quincy Adams and Andrew Jackson. He began as a vigorous nationalist, favoring the protective tariff, but moved to states' rights and an antitariff position when it became clear that South Carolina had more to gain from free trade. During the nullification crisis he resigned from the vice presidency in December 1832 for a seat in the Senate. There he became one of the "great triumvirate" (along with Henry Clay and Daniel Webster); an implacable foe of Jackson; and a staunch supporter of South Carolina, the South, and slavery. He died in Washington, D.C., in early 1850.

Questions to Consider. Why was a protective tariff considered so threatening to the Carolinians? Were they fearful of higher prices for imported goods or of reduced markets for their own product, cotton? Why did the "encouragement of domestic industry," originally urged by Alexander Hamilton in 1791, cause such a fierce blowup in 1828 but not before? Was Calhoun trying to speak for all of American agriculture or only for a certain kind? Was it the threat to agriculture or to something else that most disturbed Calhoun? Which of the eight articles of the "Protest" furnishes the best clue to the situation in South Carolina? As to the political issue, why did Calhoun fear what he called "simple consolidated government" as a threat to freedom?

★━━★━━★

South Carolina Exposition and Protest (1828)

JOHN C. CALHOUN

The Senate and House of Representatives of South Carolina, now met, and sitting in General Assembly, through the Hon. William Smith and the Hon. Robert Y. Hayne, the representatives in the Senate of the United States, do, in the name and on behalf of the good people of the said commonwealth,

Jonathan Elliot, ed., *The Debates in the Several State Conventions on the Adoption of the Federal Constitution, &c* (5 v., J. B. Lippincott, Philadelphia, 1836), IV: 580–582.

John C. Calhoun. Calhoun, who served as congressman, vice-president under Andrew Jackson, and then senator from South Carolina, started out as a strong nationalist and then became one of the most vigorous states' righters in the nation. He insisted that sovereignty (supreme power) resided in "the people of the several states" rather than in the people making up the nation as a whole, and that the people of the states had the right to nullify any federal laws they thought threatened their state's welfare. Calhoun developed his doctrine of nullification as a reaction against protective-tariff measures designed to encourage Northern industries but which he thought hurt South Carolina and other Southern states with little or no manufacturing. He was also a states' righter because he wanted to safeguard the institution of slavery from interference by antislavery crusaders in the North. (National Portrait Gallery, Smithsonian Institution, Washington, D.C./Art Resource, NY)

solemnly PROTEST against the system of protecting duties, lately adopted by the federal government, for the following reasons:—

1st. *Because* the good people of this commonwealth believe that the powers of Congress were delegated to it in trust for the accomplishment of certain specified objects which limit and control them, and that every exercise of them for any other purpose, is a violation of the Constitution as unwarrantable as the undisguised assumption of substantive, independent powers not granted or expressly withheld.

2d. *Because* the power to lay duties on imports is, and in its very nature can be, only a means of effecting objects specified by the Constitution; since no free government, and least of all a government of enumerated powers, can of right impose any tax, any more than a penalty, which is not at once justified by public necessity, and clearly within the scope and purview of the social compact; and since the right of confining appropriations of the public money to such legitimate and constitutional objects is as essential to the liberty of the people as their unquestionable privilege to be taxed only by their own consent.

3d. *Because* they believe that the tariff law passed by Congress at its last session, and all other acts of which the principal object is the protection of manufactures, or any other branch of domestic industry, if they be considered as the exercise of a power in Congress to tax the people at its own good will and pleasure, and to apply the money raised to objects not specified in the Constitution, is a violation of these fundamental principles, a breach of a well-defined trust, and a perversion of the high powers vested in the federal government for federal purposes only.

4th. *Because* such acts, considered in the light of a regulation of commerce, are equally liable to objection; since, although the power to regulate commerce may, like all other powers, be exercised so as to protect domestic manufactures, yet it is clearly distinguishable from a power to do so *eo nomine*,[1] both in the nature of the thing and in the common acception of the terms; and because the confounding of them would lead to the most extravagant results, since the encouragement of domestic industry implies an absolute control over all the interests, resources, and pursuits of a people, and is inconsistent with the idea of any other than a simple, consolidated government. . . .

6th. *Because,* whilst the power to protect manufactures is nowhere expressly granted to Congress, nor can be considered as necessary and proper to carry into effect any specified power, it seems to be expressly reserved to the states, by the 10th section of the 1st article of the Constitution.

7th. *Because* even admitting Congress to have a constitutional right to protect manufactures by the imposition of duties, or by regulations of commerce, designed principally for that purpose, yet a tariff of which the operation is

---

1. **eo nomine:** "by that name" (Latin).—*Eds.*

grossly unequal and oppressive, is such an abuse of power as is incompatible with the principles of a free government and the great ends of civil society, justice, and equality of rights and protection.

8th. *Finally*, because South Carolina, from her climate, situation, and peculiar institutions, is, and must ever continue to be, wholly dependent upon agriculture and commerce, not only for her prosperity, but for her very existence as a state; because the valuable products of her soil—the blessings by which Divine Providence seems to have designed to compensate for the great disadvantages under which she suffers in other respects—are among the very few that can be cultivated with any profit by slave labor; and if, by the loss of her foreign commerce, these products should be confined to an inadequate market, the fate of this fertile state would be poverty and utter desolation; her citizens, in despair, would emigrate to more fortunate regions, and the whole frame and constitution of her civil policy be impaired and deranged, if not dissolved entirely.

22

POLITICS AND DEMOCRACY

One of Andrew Jackson's lasting contributions to American history was the popularization of political participation: voter turnout, election to office, party-building. Before Andrew Jackson, political activity remained largely the preserve of a well-to-do, usually educated elite. By 1840, at the end of the presidential administration of Martin Van Buren, Jackson's vice-president, U.S. politics rested on a base of mass adult white male participation unmatched anywhere else in the world. Jackson helped create this new mass-participation system by building a new kind of political party, the "Jacksonian Democrats."

Jackson signaled his approach in his first message to Congress in 1829 when he announced that he would replace long-term office-holders with people of his own choosing. As a New York Democrat asserted, "to the victors belong the spoils," and the Democrats, under Jackson, had carried the 1828 election. Besides contracts and legislative favors, the chief "spoils" available to the president were appointments to federal office, mostly as postal workers and tax collectors in the customs office. Jackson's statement on "rotation in office" provided a disinterested policy rationale for this change, so that voters could decide for themselves whether they agreed. But Democratic activists could meanwhile use Jackson's arguments and rhetoric to enhance their party's popular appeal. Excerpts from this message follow below.

Three years later Jackson issued a ringing message when he vetoed an act to recharter the Second Bank of the United States (BUS). Chartered in 1816 for twenty years, to replace the original Bank of the United States advocated by Treasury Secretary Alexander Hamilton, the mammoth BUS, with headquarters in Philadelphia and branches in twenty-nine other cities, contained private funds as well as government money. It controlled one-fifth of the country's bank notes and one-third of its bank deposits and metal coins. The bank's supporters argued that it was crucial to economic growth because it could make investment loans available anywhere in the country in a way that local banks could not.

But it also had many enemies. Advocates of "cheap money"—state bankers, land speculators, some small business owners—opposed the BUS because it thwarted bank competition and restricted the amount of paper currency in circulation. On the other hand, Eastern working people were suspicious of wages paid in paper money, while Southern planters and Western farmers often looked on anything but gold and silver money as somehow dishonest. And even though its deposits included substantial government funds, the bank's board of directors, which determined the bank's investment policy, was in the hands of private capitalists, especially Nicholas Biddle, Philadelphia's most influential banker.

When President Jackson vetoed the bill to recharter, which had passed overwhelmingly in Congress, he denounced it as dangerous, unpatriotic, unfair, and unconstitutional. He also personalized the fight, telling a supporter, "The Bank is trying to kill me. But I will kill it!" Jackson used his veto power more than any previous president in part because he thought only the president represented the interests of the whole nation as opposed to single states or districts, and he always coupled a veto with a hard-hitting message justifying it. None was more important than this one—excerpts of which are given below—in setting a tone for his administration and promoting the interests of his party.

Andrew Jackson was born in 1767 on the Carolina frontier to poor Scotch-Irish immigrants. But Jackson climbed rapidly to wealth and status through land speculation, law practice, and the purchase of slave laborers. In 1795 he established the Hermitage, a large plantation near Nashville, Tennessee, and headed for Congress the next year. As commander of the Tennessee militia in the War of 1812, Jackson won a victory over the British at the Battle of New Orleans that catapulted him to prominence and led to a Senate seat in 1823 and the presidency in 1828. An ardent nationalist, Jackson quarreled with Senator John C. Calhoun over nullification (once threatening to hang him), with his predecessor, John Quincy Adams, over appointments, and with Nick Biddle over the BUS. These conflicts only added to his popularity and his ability to build a strong Democratic Party using patronage, issues, and personality. Having survived the first attempt to assassinate a president when an unemployed house painter attacked him in 1835, Jackson retired after his second term to the Hermitage, where he died in 1845.

Questions to Consider. In his "Rotation in Office" remarks, Jackson made three main arguments, one having to do with corruption, another with simplicity, a third with democracy. Do you find these arguments persuasive? He did not argue that government should do less or have fewer workers. Why not? Many historians believe that modern economic growth and social stability, as in Europe and the United States, are more likely if a country has dependable civil servants with professional standards and personal integrity. Do you think Jackson's reforms would be more or less likely to produce this result?

In his "Bank Veto Message," why did the president attack monopolies so strongly? How did his criticism of foreign control strengthen his hand? Is it surprising that a vigorous chief executive and opponent of nullification should champion the right of states to tax the BUS? Did his appeal to class differences, as opposed to occupational or sectional ones, signal a new turn in American politics? If so, why might this have occurred in 1832 rather than, say, 1816 or 1824? Who were Jackson's "poor," anyway?

What common themes appear in the two messages? To what extent did they reinforce one another in terms of policy and politics? In neither message did Jackson mention economic growth as an important objective. Why not?

★━━★━━★

Rotation in Office (1829)

ANDREW JACKSON

There are, perhaps, few men who can for any great length of time enjoy office and power without being more or less under the influence of feelings unfavorable to the faithful discharge of their public duties. Their integrity may be proof against improper considerations immediately addressed to themselves, but they are apt to acquire a habit of looking with indifference upon the public interests and of tolerating conduct from which an unpracticed man would revolt. Office is considered as a species of property, and government rather as a means of promoting individual interests than as an instrument created solely for the service of the people. Corruption in some and in others a perversion of correct feelings and principles divert government from its legitimate ends and make it an engine for the support of the few at the expense of the many. The duties of all public officers are, or at least admit of being made, so plain and simple that men of intelligence may readily qualify themselves for their performance; and I can not but believe that more is lost by the long continuance of men in office than is generally to be gained by their experience. I submit, therefore, to your consideration whether the efficiency of the Government would not be promoted and official industry and integrity better secured by a general extension of the law which limits appointments to four years.

James D. Richardson, ed., *A Compilation of the Messages and Papers of the Presidents* (Government Printing Office, Washington, D.C., 1789–1897), II: 448–449.

In a country where offices are created solely for the benefit of the people no one man has any more intrinsic right to official station than another. Offices were not established to give support to particular men at the public expense. No individual wrong is, therefore, done by removal, since neither appointment to nor continuance in office is matter of right. The incumbent became an officer with a view to public benefits, and when these require his removal they are not to be sacrificed to private interests. It is the people, and they alone, who have a right to complain when a bad officer is substituted for a good one. He who is removed has the same means of obtaining a living that are enjoyed by the millions who never held office. The proposed limitation would destroy the idea of property now so generally connected with official station, and although individual distress may be sometimes produced, it would, by promoting that rotation which constitutes a leading principle in the republican creed, give healthful action to the system. . . .

★══★══★

Bank Veto Message (1832)

ANDREW JACKSON

A bank of the United States is in many respects convenient for the Government and useful to the people. Entertaining this opinion, and deeply impressed with the belief that some of the powers and privileges possessed by the existing bank are unauthorized by the Constitution, subversive of the rights of the States, and dangerous to the liberties of the people, I felt it my duty at an early period of my Administration to call the attention of Congress to the practicability of organizing an institution combining all its advantages and obviating these objections. I sincerely regret that in the act before me I can perceive none of these modifications of the bank charter which are necessary, in my opinion, to make it compatable with justice, with sound policy, or with the Constitution of our country.

The present corporate body . . . enjoys an exclusive privilege of banking under the authority of the General Government, a monopoly of its favor and support, and, as a necessary consequence, almost a monopoly of the foreign and domestic exchange. The powers, privileges, and favors bestowed upon it in the original charter, by increasing the value of the stock far above its par value, operated as a gratuity of many millions to the stockholders. . . .

On all hands it is conceded that [the act's] passage will increase at least 20 or 30 per cent more the market price of the stock, subject to the payment of

James D. Richardson, ed., *A Compilation of the Messages and Papers of the Presidents* (Government Printing Office, Washington, D.C., 1897–1907), II: 217–218.

the annuity of $200,000 per year secured by the act, thus adding in a moment one-fourth to its par value. It is not our own citizens only who are to receive the bounty of our Government. More than eight millions of the stock of this bank are held by foreigners. By this act the American Republic proposes virtually to make them a present of some millions of dollars. For these gratuities to foreigners and to some of our own opulent citizens the act secures no equivalent whatever. . . .

Every monopoly and all exclusive privileges are granted at the expense of the public, which ought to receive a fair equivalent. The many millions which this act proposes to bestow on the stockholders of the existing bank must come directly or indirectly out of the earnings of the American people. It is due to them, therefore, if their Government sell monopolies and exclusive privileges, that they should at least exact for them as much as they are worth in open market. . . .

Is there no danger to our liberty and independence in a bank that in its nature has so little to bind it to our country? The president of the bank has told us that most of the State banks exist by its forbearance. Should its influence become concentrated, as it may under the operation of such an act as this, in the hands of a self-elected directory whose interests are identified with those of the foreign stockholders, will there not be cause to tremble for the purity of our elections in peace and for the independence of our country in war? Their power would be great whenever they might choose to exert it; but if this monopoly were regularly renewed every fifteen or twenty years on terms proposed by themselves, they might seldom in peace put forth their strength to influence elections or control the affairs of the nation. But if any private citizen or public functionary should interpose to curtail its powers or prevent a renewal of its privileges, it can not be doubted that he would be made to feel its influence. . . .

If we must have a bank with private stockholders, every consideration of sound policy and every impulse of American feeling admonishes that it should be *purely American.* Its stockholders should be composed exclusively of our own citizens, who at least ought to be friendly to our Government and willing to support it in times of difficulty and danger. . . .

The bank is professedly established as an agent of the executive branch of the Government, and its constitutionality is maintained on that ground. Neither upon the propriety of present action nor upon the provisions of this act was the Executive consulted. It has had no opportunity to say that it neither needs nor wants an agent clothed with such powers and favored by such exemptions. There is nothing in its legitimate functions which makes it necessary or proper. Whatever interest or influence, whether public or private, has given birth to this act, it can not be found either in the wishes or necessities of the executive department, by which present action is deemed premature, and the powers conferred upon its agent not only unnecessary, but dangerous to the Government and country. . . .

It is to be regretted that the rich and powerful too often bend the acts of government to their selfish purposes. Distinctions in society will always exist under every just government. Equality of talents, of education, or of wealth can not be produced by human institutions. In the full enjoyment of the gifts of Heaven and the fruits of superior industry, economy, and virtue, every man is equally entitled to protection by law; but when the laws undertake to add to these natural and just advantages artificial distinctions, to grant titles, gratuities, and exclusive privileges, to make the rich richer and the potent more powerful, and the humble members of society—the farmers, mechanics, and laborers—who have neither the time nor the means of securing like favors to themselves, have a right to complain of the injustice of their Government.

There are no necessary evils in government. Its evils exist only in its abuse. If it would confine itself to equal protection, and, as Heaven does its rains, shower its favors alike on the high and the low, the rich and the poor, it would be an unqualified blessing. In the act before me there seems to be a wide and unnecessary departure from these just principles. . . .

Experience should teach us wisdom. Most of the difficulties our Government now encounters and most of the dangers which impend over our Union have sprung from an abandonment of the legitimate objects of Government by our national legislation, and the adoption of such principles as are embodied in this act. Many of our rich men have not been content with equal protection and equal benefits, but have besought us to make them richer by act of Congress. By attempting to gratify their desires we have in the results of our legislation arrayed section against section, interest against interest, and man against man, in a fearful commotion which threatens to shake the foundations of our Union. It is time to pause in our career to review our principles, and if possible revive that devoted patriotism and spirit of compromise which distinguished the sages of the Revolution and the fathers of our Union.

23

THE TRAIL OF TEARS

American attitudes toward the Native American nations varied widely in the first part of the nineteenth century. Some people urged a policy of assimilation; others proposed the voluntary removal of the Native Americans to lands in the West. But land-hungry Americans in the South and West wanted to push the indigenous peoples off their ancestral lands by force, and a few even favored extermination. When Andrew Jackson, an old "Indian fighter," became president in March 1829, he adopted a policy of forcing the tribes to move to the trans-Mississippi West. The Removal Act of 1830, passed by Congress with his encouragement, proposed that the tribes trade their lands in the United States for new homes in federal territory west of the Mississippi River.

Native Americans everywhere objected to the removal policy, but there was little they could do about it. In Illinois and Florida, they put up forceful resistance, but after several years of bloody warfare they were finally subdued. In Georgia, the Cherokees, a nation in the northwestern part of the state, tried to protect their rights peacefully. Belying the average white's contention that "Indians are savages," the Cherokees had become skilled in agriculture, built fine homes and roads, accepted Christian missionaries, adopted a constitution, and published books in an alphabet invented by Sequoya, a talented hunter who had become a silversmith and a scholar. The Cherokees had treaty commitments from the U.S. government, but neither President Jackson nor the state of Georgia was willing to respect them. In July 1830, when Georgia decided to take over their lands, the Cherokees made a moving appeal to the American people to respect their "national and individual rights" and permit them "to remain on the land of our fathers."

The Cherokees' appeal was in vain. Although some northeastern humanitarians sympathized with the Cherokees, and the Supreme Court in two decisions written by Chief Justice John Marshall ruled in the Cherokees' favor, the state of Georgia asserted its sovereignty over their territory. Jackson sent an army of 7,000 to drive them westward at bayonet point. Over 4,000 of the 15,000 Cherokees who went west along the Trail of Tears in 1838 perished en route. By the time Jackson left office he could boast that his removal policy was rapidly nearing completion.

The "shotgun removal," as it was called, shocked Ralph Waldo Emerson, one of America's greatest writers. "Such a dereliction of all faith and virtue," he cried, "such a denial of justice, and such deafness to screams for mercy were never heard of in time of peace and in the dealing of a nation with its own allies and wards, since the earth was made."

Questions to Consider. In the final section of the appeal, which appears below, note the style in which the Cherokees state their case. Is it coolly argued or does it contain deep-seated feelings? How united were the Cherokees? What rights did they cite? What were their major objections to moving to a new location?

★═══★═══★

Appeal of the Cherokee Nation (1830)

We are aware that some persons suppose it will be for our advantage to remove beyond the Mississippi. We think otherwise. Our people universally think otherwise. Thinking that it would be fatal to their interests, they have almost to a man sent their memorial to Congress, deprecating the necessity of a removal. This question was distinctly before their minds when they signed their memorial. Not an adult person can be found, who has not an opinion on the subject; and if the people were to understand distinctly, that they could be protected against the laws of the neighboring States, there is probably not an adult person in the nation, who would think it best to remove; though possibly a few might emigrate individually. There are doubtless many who would flee to an unknown country, however beset with dangers, privations and sufferings, rather than be sentenced to spend six years in a Georgia prison for advising one of their neighbors not to betray his country. And there are others who could not think of living as outlaws in their native land, exposed to numberless vexations, and excluded from being parties or witnesses in a court of justice. It is incredible that Georgia should ever have enacted the oppressive laws to which reference is here made, unless she had supposed that something extremely terrific in its character was necessary, in order to make the Cherokees willing to remove. We are not willing to remove; and if we could be brought to this extremity, it would be, not by argument; not because our judgment was satisfied; not because our condition will be improved—but only because we cannot endure to be deprived of our national and individual rights, and subjected to a process of intolerable oppression.

We wish to remain on the land of our fathers. We have a perfect and original right to claim this, without interruption or molestation. The treaties with us, and laws of the United States made in pursuance of treaties, guaranty our

E. C. Tracy, *Memoir of the Life of Jeremiah Evarts* (Boston, 1845), 149–158.

The Trail of Tears. In Robert Lindneux's dramatic painting, the Cherokee move toward reservation territory west of the Mississippi River in 1838. Some 4,000 of the 15,000 who began the trip died. But 15,000 was actually only a small portion of the 100,000 Indians driven out of the southeastern United States between 1820 and 1845, and 4,000 was only a small portion of the 25,000 to 30,000 killed in the process. ("Trail of Tears" by Robert Lindneux. Woolaroc Museum, Bartlesville, Oklahoma)

residence, and our privileges, and secure us against intruders. Our only request is, that these treaties may be fulfilled, and these laws executed.

But if we are compelled to leave our country, we see nothing but ruin before us. The country west of the Arkansas territory is unknown to us. From what we can learn of it, we have no prepossessions in its favor. All the inviting parts of it, as we believe, are preoccupied by various Indian nations, to which it has been assigned. They would regard us as intruders, and look upon us with an evil eye. The far greater part of that region is, beyond all controversy, badly supplied with wood and water; and no Indian tribe can live as agriculturists without these articles. All our neighbors, in case of our removal, though crowded into our near vicinity, would speak a language totally different from ours, and practice different customs. The original possessors of that region are now wandering savages, lurking for prey in the neighborhood. They have always been at war, and would be easily tempted to turn their arms against peaceful emigrants. Were the country to which we are urged much better than it is represented to be, and were it free from the objections which we have made to it, still it is not the land of our birth, nor of our affections. It contains neither the scenes of our childhood, nor the graves of our fathers.

24

EMPIRE

When James K. Polk ran for president in 1844, the Democrats campaigned for the reannexation of Texas and the reoccupation of Oregon. Texas, they maintained, had been acquired through the Louisiana Purchase of 1803 and had been unwisely given back. The Oregon country, too, they argued, was part of the United States by virtue of American settlements there in the early nineteenth century; British claims were unjustified. Polk heartily agreed with the Democratic platform on both issues.

Polk compromised with Britain on Oregon, signing a treaty in 1846 that fixed the boundary at the 49th parallel. But his administration went to war with Mexico that same year over Texas and ended by acquiring California and the Southwest for the United States. In fact, Polk had vowed to obtain these territories at any price. When the Mexican government refused to sell them, he maneuvered the United States into war by ordering General Zachary Taylor into a hotly disputed area to provoke a Mexican attack. When that attack came, Polk declared that Mexico "has invaded our territory and shed American blood upon the American soil. . . . War exists by the act of Mexico herself."

Polk's territorial conquests, which mark him as one of the great imperialists of the age, comparable to Disraeli in Britain or the Russian czars, produced a lively debate over the meaning of expansion. Some people, especially New Englanders, thought the Mexican War had been inspired by Southern planters (like Polk himself) greedy for new lands into which to extend slavery. Senator Charles Sumner of Massachusetts called it "a War to Strengthen the 'Slave Power'. . . [and] a War Against the Free States." Others saw both Oregon and the Southwest as tokens in a Northern drive for more farmland and for harbors on the West Coast for the China trade.

The largest group of all saw expansion in terms of what John L. O'Sullivan, the most influential spokesman for westward expansion, called "manifest destiny." According to O'Sullivan, a Democratic editor in New York, the single most important state in national politics, manifest destiny was the "design of Providence"—the right of a teeming, vigorous American nation to take possession of an entire continent and extend the sphere of Anglo-Saxon institutions from sea to sea. By "destiny" O'Sullivan meant that this was foreordained, decreed by fate, bound to happen. By "manifest" he meant that this fate was obvious, that anyone should be able to see it and therefore stand aside and let it happen. That parts of the continent were already occupied by "inferior" Native Americans or held by "imbecile" Mexico was, O'Sullivan insisted, irrelevant. Nature itself would see to it that someday the peoples of the Atlantic and Pacific would "flow together into one."

O'Sullivan's fierce nationalism was perfectly in tune with the mid-nineteenth-century expansionist inclinations of most Americans. From the beginning of settlement, Americans had been lured westward. With Jefferson's acquisition of the Louisiana Territory, they began to harbor visions of a vast American "empire." The War of 1812 partly resulted from land hunger. With the Monroe Doctrine of 1823, Americans declared their special claim to the whole Western Hemisphere.

That claim was made most belligerently in the Mexican War—so belligerently, in fact, that as part of the postwar settlement, the American government offered to pay Mexico $15 million in what Henry David Thoreau and others called "conscience money." But just as its opponents had predicted, the Mexican War divided the victors, triggering an agonizing controversy between North and South over where and whether slavery would be permitted to invade the newly acquired territories.

Born in Ireland in 1813, John L. O'Sullivan immigrated at an early age to New York City, where he became a lawyer, journalist, and ardent Jacksonian. In 1841 O'Sullivan established the *United States Magazine and Democratic Review*, New York's chief Democratic propaganda organ and one of the most jingoistic magazines of the era. O'Sullivan first used the phrase "manifest destiny" in the *Democratic Review* in 1845. Like many Jacksonians, O'Sullivan was tolerant of immigrants and Catholics, but rabidly anti-English and racist. Rewarded with patronage appointments, O'Sullivan at one point joined an expedition to seize Cuba as a slave territory for the United States. He was a Confederate sympathizer during the Civil War. He died in 1895.

Questions to Consider. What specific factors did O'Sullivan cite in arguing that the United States was destined to "overspread the continent"? Why was he so concerned to defend the United States from charges of "spoliation" and "conquest"? How important was sheer population growth to O'Sullivan's argument? Were his numbers accurate? How important were new means of transportation and communication to his vision? Why, given O'Sullivan's strident hostility to England, did he refer constantly to the superiority of "Anglo-Saxon" peoples and institutions and applaud the weight of the "Anglo-Saxon foot"?

■═══■═══■

Annexation (1845)

JOHN L. O'SULLIVAN

Texas is now ours. Already, before these words are written, her Convention has undoubtedly ratified the acceptance, by her Congress, of our proffered invitation into the Union; and made the requisite changes in her already re-publican form of constitution to adopt it to its future federal relations. Her star and her stripe may already be said to have taken their place in the glori-ous blazon of our common nationality; and the sweep of our eagle's wing al-ready includes within its circuit the wide extent of her fair and fertile land. She is no longer to us a mere geographical space—a certain combination of coast, plain, mountain, valley, forest and stream. She is no longer to us a mere country on the map. She comes within the dear and sacred designation of Our Country; no longer a *"pays,"* she is a part of *"la patrie"*; and that which is at once a sentiment and a virtue, Patriotism, already begins to thrill for her too within the national heart. . . .

Why, were other reasoning wanting, in favor of now elevating this ques-tion of the reception of Texas into the Union, out of the lower region of our past party dissensions, up to its proper level of a high and broad nationality, it surely is to be found, found abundantly, in the manner in which other na-tions have undertaken to intrude themselves into it, between us and the proper parties to the case, in a spirit of hostile interference against us, for the avowed object of thwarting our policy and hampering our power, limiting our greatness and checking the fulfilment of our manifest destiny to over-spread the continent allotted by Providence for the free development of our yearly multiplying millions. . . .

It is wholly untrue, and unjust to ourselves, the pretence that the Annexa-tion has been a measure of spoliation, unrightful and unrighteous—of mili-tary conquest under forms of peace and law—of territorial aggrandizement at the expense of justice, and justice due by a double sanctity to the weak. This view of the question is wholly unfounded, and has been before so am-ply refuted in these pages, as well as in a thousand other modes, that we shall not again dwell upon it. The independence of Texas was complete and ab-solute. It was an independence, not only in fact but of right. No obligation of duty towards Mexico tended in the least degree to restrain our right to effect the desired recovery of the fair province once our own—whatever motives of policy might have prompted a more deferential consideration of her feelings and her pride, as involved in the question. If Texas became peopled with an American population, it was by no contrivance of our government, but on

American Progress. This 1872 canvas by John Gast is emblematic of the way Americans thought of the westward experience. At the bottom are prospectors and farmers. At the center are a stagecoach, an ox-drawn covered wagon, and a Pony Express mail rider. At the right, three railroad lines reach from the Mississippi River, in the distance with steamboats, out onto the Great Plains. To the far left, Indians retreat before the onslaught. Miss Liberty, in diaphanous gown, floats over the scene stretching telegraph wire across the continent. This female figure, taken originally from the Marianne figure of the French Revolution, was enormously popular in the nineteenth century, not least because she gave artists a socially acceptable chance to paint—and viewers to observe—the female form in revealing clothes. (Library of Congress)

the express invitation of that of Mexico herself; accompanied with such guaranties of State independence, and the maintenance of a federal system analogous to our own, as constituted a compact fully justifying the strongest measures of redress on the part of those afterwards deceived in this guaranty, and sought to be enslaved under the yoke imposed by its violation. She was released, rightfully and absolutely released, from all Mexican allegiance, or duty of cohesion to the Mexican political body, by the acts and fault of Mexico herself, and Mexico alone. There never was a clearer case. It was not revolution; it was resistance to revolution; and resistance under such circumstances as left independence the necessary resulting state, caused by the abandonment of those with whom her former federal association had existed.

What then can be more preposterous than all this clamor by Mexico and the Mexican interest, against Annexation, as a violation of any rights of hers, any duties of ours? . . .

Nor is there any just foundation of the charge that Annexation is a great pro-slavery measure—calculated to increase and perpetuate that institution. Slavery had nothing to do with it. . . . The country which was the subject of Annexation in this case, from its geographical position and relations, happens to be—or rather the portion of it now actually settled, happens to be—a slave country. But a similar process might have taken place in proximity to a different section of our Union; and indeed there is a great deal of Annexation yet to take place, within the life of the present generation, along the whole line of our northern border. Texas has been absorbed into the Union in the inevitable fulfillment of the general law which is rolling our population westward; the connexion of which with that ratio of growth in population which is destined within a hundred years to swell our numbers to the enormous population of *two hundred and fifty millions* (if not more), is too evident to leave us in doubt of the manifest design of Providence in regard to the occupation of this continent. It was disintegrated from Mexico in the natural course of events, by a process perfectly legitimate on its own part, blameless on ours; and in which all the censures due to wrong, perfidy and folly, rest on Mexico alone. And possessed as it was by a population which was in truth but a colonial detachment from our own, and which was still bound by myriad ties of the very heartstrings to its old relations, domestic and political, their incorporation into the Union was not only inevitable, but the most natural, right and proper thing in the world—and it is only astonishing that there should be any among ourselves to say it nay. . . .

California will, probably, next fall away from the loose adhesion which, in such a country as Mexico, holds a remote province in a slight equivocal kind of dependence on the metropolis. Imbecile and distracted, Mexico never can exert any real governmental authority over such a country. The impotence of the one and the distance of the other, must make the relation one of virtual independence; unless, by stunting the province of all natural growth, and forbidding that immigration which can alone develope its capabilities and fulfill the purposes of its creation, tyranny may retain a military dominion which is no government in the legitimate sense of the term.

In the case of California this is now impossible. The Anglo-Saxon foot is already on its borders. Already the advance guard of the irresistible army of Anglo-Saxon emigration has begun to pour down upon it, armed with the plough and the rifle, and marking its trail with schools and colleges, courts and representative halls, mills and meeting-houses. A population will soon be in actual occupation of California, over which it will be idle for Mexico to dream of dominion. They will necessarily become independent. All this without agency of our government, without responsibility of our people—in the natural flow of events, the spontaneous working of principles, and the adaptation of the tendencies and wants of the human race to the elemental circumstances in the midst of which they find themselves placed. And they will have a right to independence—to self-government—to the possession of the homes conquered from the wilderness by their own labors and dangers, sufferings and sacrifices—a better and a truer right than the artificial title of sovereignty in Mexico a thousand miles distant, inheriting from Spain a title good only against those who have none better. Their right to independence will be the natural right of self-government belonging to any community strong enough to maintain it—distinct in position, origin and character, and free from any mutual obligations of membership of a common political body, binding it to others by the duty of loyalty and compact of public faith. This will be their title to independence; and by this title, there can be no doubt that the population now fast streaming down upon California will both assert and maintain that independence. Whether they will then attach themselves to our Union or not, is not to be predicted with any certainty. Unless the projected rail-road across the continent to the Pacific be carried into effect, perhaps they may not; though even in that case, the day is not distant when the Empires of the Atlantic and Pacific would again flow together into one, as soon as their inland border should approach each other. But that great work, colossal as appears the plan on its first suggestion, cannot remain long unbuilt. Its necessity for this very purpose of binding and holding together in its iron clasp our fast settling Pacific region with that of the Mississippi valley—the natural facility of the route—the ease with which any amount of labor for the construction can be drawn in from the overcrowded populations of Europe, to be paid in the lands made valuable by the progress of the work itself—and its immense utility to the commerce of the world with the whole eastern coast of Asia, alone almost sufficient for the support of such a road—these considerations give assurance that the day cannot be distant which shall witness the conveyance of the representatives from Oregon and California to Washington within less time than a few years ago was devoted to a similar journey by those from Ohio; while the magnetic telegraph will enable the editors of the "San Francisco Union," the "Astoria Evening Post," or the "Nootka Morning News" to set up in type the first half of the President's Inaugural, before the echoes of the latter half shall have died away beneath the lofty porch of the Capitol, as spoken from his lips.

Reform dreams and nightmares. In this drawing, education, worship, and work are the foundations of the good life. The path to evil, by contrast, begins with disobedience to parents and teachers, and then it leads through vanity, fighting, gambling, dueling, and other bad behavior to, finally, the saloon, the prison, and the fires of everlasting punishment. (Library of Congress)

CHAPTER FOUR

The Age of Reform

25

SCHOOLING FOR WOMEN

In March 1776, when the Continental Congress in Philadelphia was beginning to contemplate independence from Britain, Abigail Adams wrote her husband, John, from Braintree, Massachusetts: "I long to hear that you have declared an independency. And, by the way," she added, "in the new code of laws which I suppose it will be necessary for you to make, I desire you would remember the ladies and be more generous and favorable to them than your ancestors. Do not put unlimited power into the hands of the husbands. Remember, all men would be tyrants if they could. If particular care and attention is not paid to the ladies, we are determined to foment a rebellion, and will not hold ourselves bound by any laws in which we have no voice or representation. That your sex are naturally tyrannical is a truth so thoroughly established as to admit of no dispute. . . ." Adams wrote back good-humoredly. "We are obliged to go fairly and softly," he told his wife, "and, in practice, you know we are the subjects. We have only the name of masters, and rather than give this up, which would completely subject us to the despotism of the petticoat, I hope General Washington and all our brave heroes would fight. . . ."

American men had more than "the name of masters." The status of women in Adams's day and for many years afterward was distinctly inferior. Sir William Blackstone, the great eighteenth-century British legal authority, set the standard for the American view. "The husband and wife are one," he proclaimed, "and that one is the husband." Women were regarded as the wards of their husbands, were barred from professions like the law, medicine, and the ministry, and had few opportunities for advanced education.

But the establishment of popular republican government, where citizens governed themselves, began to change attitudes toward education for women. Citizen rule meant that individual voters had to be well informed and self disciplined. Otherwise, they might sail the ship of state onto the rocks. This gave rise to the notion of the "Republican mother," able to instill in her children, boys especially but also girls, the intellectual and moral habits that good citizens would require. And this, people started to argue, meant that women needed to be better educated. Emma Willard's argument to the New York legislature in 1819 for publicly-funded schools for girls (excerpted below) uses this line of reasoning. But she includes other considerations as well. Although New York's legislators rejected Willard's plans as "contrary to God's will," she had more success in Troy, New York, whose citizens contributed enough to found the Troy Female Seminary, which soon had three hundred students and became a model for similar schools.

Emma Willard was born in 1787 in Berlin, Connecticut, where she attended a local private academy. She taught school in Massachusetts and in Middlebury, Vermont, until her marriage to a Middlebury businessman. To supplement the family income and return to education, she opened a female school in Middlebury that offered mathematics, philosophy, and science, subjects not then available to women. Largely self-taught, Willard wrote textbooks in history and geography, introduced teaching techniques that she believed would work well with women, and after founding her seminary in Troy, went to Europe to observe schools there. She retired from active management of the Troy Female Seminary in 1838, but continued to crusade for women's schools and especially teaching jobs for women. She died in Troy in 1870.

Questions to Consider. How prominent in Willard's address was the argument about the need for educated mothers? What other arguments did she use? What did Willard fear was happening to women in the absence of better education? Do any of these concerns surprise you? What sort of people would educated women turn out to be, in Willard's opinion? Would any of her arguments and warnings carry weight today?

★━━★━━★

Address to the New York Legislature (1819)

EMMA WILLARD

Civilized nations have long since been convinced that education, as it respects males, will not, like trade, regulate itself; and hence, they have made it a prime object to provide that sex with everything requisite to facilitate their progress in learning: but female education has been left to the mercy of private adventurers. . . .

Education cannot prosper in any community, unless, from the ordinary motives which actuate the human mind, the best and most cultivated talents

Emma Willard, *An Address to the Public, Particularly to the Members of the Legislature of New-York, Proposing a Plan for Improving Female Education* (Middlebury, 1819).

of that community, can be brought into exercise in that way. Male education flourishes, because, from the guardian care of legislatures, the presidencies and professorships of our colleges are some of the highest objects to which the eye of ambition is directed. Not so with female institutions. Preceptresses of these, are dependent on their pupils for support and are consequently liable to become the victims of their caprice. . . .

Among families, so rich as to be entirely above labour, the daughters are hurried through the routine of boarding school instruction, and at an early period introduced into the gay world. . . . Mark the different treatment, which the sons of these families receive. While their sisters are gliding through the mazes of the midnight dance, they employ the lamp, to treasure up for future use the riches of ancient wisdom; or to gather strength and expansion of mind, in exploring the wonderful paths of philosophy.

. . . When the youth of two sexes has been spent so differently, is it strange, or is nature in fault, if more mature age has brought such a difference of character, that our sex have been considered by the other, as the pampered, wayward babies of society, who must have some rattle put into our hands, to keep us from doing mischief to ourselves or others?

Among women as among the other sex, will be found master spirits, who must have pre-eminence, at whatever price they acquire it. Domestic life cannot hold these, because they prefer to be infamous, rather than obscure. To leave such, without any virtuous road to eminence, is unsafe to community; for not unfrequently, are the secret springs of revolution, set in motion by their intrigues. Such aspiring minds, we will regulate, by education, we will remove obstructions to the course of literature, which has heretofore been their only honorable way to distinction; and we offer them a new object, worthy of their ambition; to govern, and improve the seminaries for their sex. . . .

Where is that wise and heroic country, which has considered, that our rights are sacred, though we cannot defend them? that tho' a weaker, we are an essential part of the body politic, whose corruption or improvement must affect the whole? and which, having thus considered, has sought to give us by education, that rank in the scale of being, to which our importance entitles us? History shows not that country. It shows many, whose legislatures have sought to improve their various vegetable productions, and their breeds of useful brutes; but none, whose public councils have made it an object of their deliberations, to improve the character of their women. . . .

It is the duty of a government, to do all in its power to promote the present and future prosperity of the nation, over which it is placed. This prosperity will depend on the character of its citizens. The characters of these will be formed by their mothers; and it is through the mothers, that the government can control the characters of its future citizens, to form them such as will ensure their country's prosperity. If this is the case, then it is the duty of our present legislators to begin now, to form the characters of the next generation, by controlling that of the females, who are to be their mothers, while it is yet with them a season of improvement.

. . . It is not a masculine education which is here recommended . . . a female institution might possess the respectability, permanency, and uniformity of operation of those appropriated to males, and yet differ from them, so as to be adapted to that difference of character and duties, to which the softer sex should be formed. . . .

It is highly important, that females should be conversant with those studies, which will lead them to understand the operations of the human mind. The chief use to which the philosophy of the mind can be applied, is to regulate education by its rule. . . . Natural philosophy has not often been taught to our sex. Yet why should we be kept in ignorance of the great machinery of nature, and left to the vulgar notion, that nothing is curious but what deviates from her common course? If mothers were acquainted with science, they would communicate very many of its principles to their children in early youth. . . .

Conclusion

1. Females, by having their understandings cultivated, their reasoning powers developed and strengthened, may be expected to act more from the dictates of reason, and less from those of fashion and caprice.

2. With minds thus strengthened they would be taught systems of morality, enforced by the sanctions of religion; and they might be expected to acquire juster and more enlarged views of their duty, and stronger and higher motives to its performance.

3. This plan of education, offers all that can be done to preserve female youth from a contempt of useful labour. The pupils would become accustomed to it, in conjunction with the high objects of literature, and the elegant pursuits of the fine arts; and it is to be hoped that both from habit and association, they might in future life, regard it as respectable. . . . If housewifery could be raised to a regular art, and taught upon philosophical principles, it would become a higher and more interesting occupation; and ladies of fortune, like wealthy agriculturalists, might find, that to regulate their business, was an agreeable employment.

4. The pupils might be expected to acquire a taste for moral and intellectual pleasures, which would buoy them above a passion for show and parade. . . .

5. By being enlightened in moral philosophy, and in that, which teaches the operations of the mind, females would be enabled to perceive the nature and extent, of that influence, which they possess over their children. . . .

26

THE EVANGELICAL IMPULSE

American Protestantism grew dramatically in the first half of the nineteenth century. Leading the way were the Baptist and Methodist churches, which grew fivefold, and the Presbyterians, which grew threefold. But every Protestant denomination increased its numbers, including some—Unitarian Universalists, Disciples of Christ, Seventh-Day Adventists, and others—that had not existed before 1800. This exploding growth was partly a simple function of westward expansion, which opened vast fields for recruiting, but the churches grew in Eastern towns and cities as well. Most now preached a doctrine of free will that left salvation in the hands not of God, as with Calvinism, but of the individual, making it easier to move people to "come to Jesus." They accompanied this new doctrine with highly emotional revivalist preaching, and founded whole strings of seminaries and colleges to train the future evangelists of their particular denomination.

The churches became engines of reform as well as of conversion, gathering themselves into an "empire of benevolence" that distributed millions of free Bibles and religious pamphlets, founded Sunday schools and orphanages, sent missionaries to the frontier and abroad, and waged a startlingly successful campaign to shut down businesses and government functions, including mail delivery, on Sunday. Pacifism became a part of some creeds, anti-Catholicism of others. Eventually Northern ministers would intensify the rising sectionalism of the country and split their own denominations along regional lines by taking up the greatest mid-century reform of them all: the struggle to abolish slavery.

Always and everywhere, they labored to convert the godless— hard-living seamen, hardened prisoners, prostitutes and procurers—and lift them from the ways of sin. Of the sins afflicting the nation, none seemed more deadly, at least in the early decades of the new century, than the heavy drinking of alcohol. The problem was certainly real. Grain farmers were distilling corn into whiskey so cheap that it became more popular than rum, the old colonial favorite; German immigrants made beer so plentiful that it overwhelmed cider. By the 1830s

Americans consumed an average of five gallons of alcohol per capita per year, putting the United States alongside Scotland, Ireland, Sweden, and Russia as heavy-drinking cultures. The consequences for family life, job performance, and piety seemed obvious and ominous.

The evangelists attacked with gusto. They preached temperance, or moderation, then moved on to total abstinence. They worked in the churches. They also worked through organizations such as the American Temperance Society, which had thousands of local chapters; the Washingtonian Society of recovered alcoholics; and the Cold-Water Army—children who urged adults not to drink. They urged self-discipline but also laws to limit or stop the manufacture and sale of alcohol. The temperance movement was nationwide, South as well as North; and sometimes ecumenical, as Catholic temperance advocates joined with their evangelical counterparts when German and Irish immigration rose in the 1840s. And it was partially successful. Many "took the pledge" not to drink, and went "on the [water] wagon." Some legislatures restricted alcohol. By mid-century, per capita consumption was down, in some places substantially, and it never returned to its early Herculean levels.

Lyman Beecher, a pioneer temperance evangelist, was born in Connecticut in 1775. The son and grandson of blacksmiths, Beecher attended Yale, was ordained a Presbyterian minister, and assumed pulpits in New York, Connecticut, and Boston before heading to Cincinnati in 1832 to become president of the new Lane Theological Seminary. By then he had a formidable reputation as a fiery preacher and reformer who conducted "continuous revivals" in which he assailed intemperance, secularism, and Catholicism. His sermons on intemperance, one of which is excerpted below, were widely read, even in Europe; his intemperate anti-Catholicism helped foment a mob attack on a Boston convent. At Lane Seminary, Beecher's abolitionist sympathies came under criticism, and he resigned in 1850. His thirteen children, among them novelist Harriet, educational reformer Catharine, and antislavery activists Edward and Henry, kept the reform torch aloft. Numerous and influential, the Beechers were a virtual race apart: "Sinners, saints, and Beechers." Some said Lyman fathered more brains than any other man in America. He died at his son's home in Brooklyn in 1863.

Questions to Consider. Why did Beecher think that "young men" were a key group in the temperance fight? What attitude did he urge churches to take toward drinkers? What role should businesses and consumers play? To whom did he address his direst warnings? Do you find them moving today? If not, why not? How important to this struggle does Christian conversion seem to have been for Beecher and his fellow evangelists?

■══■══■

The Remedy for Intemperance (1828)

LYMAN BEECHER

Let us now take an inventory of the things which can be done to resist the progress of intemperance. . . .

The young men of our land may set glorious examples of voluntary abstinence from ardent spirits, and, by associations for that purpose, may array a phalanx of opposition against the encroachments of the destroyer; while men of high official standing and influence may cheer us by sending down the good example of their firmness and independence in the abolition of long-established, but corrupting habits. . . .

All denominations of Christians in the nation may with great ease be united in the effort to exclude the use and the commerce in ardent spirits. They alike feel and deplore the evil, and, united, have it in their power to put a stop to it. This union may be accomplished through the medium of a national society. There is no object for which a national society is more imperiously demanded, or for which it can be reared under happier auspices. God grant that three years may not pass away before the entire land shall be marshaled, and the evils of intemperance be seen like a dark cloud passing off, and leaving behind a cloudless day!

The Churches of our Lord Jesus Christ of every name can do much to aid in this reformation. They are organized to shine as lights in the world, and to avoid the very appearance of evil. A vigilant discipline is doubtless demanded in the cases of members who are of a lax and doubtful morality in respect to intemperance. It is not enough to cut off those who are past reformation, and to keep those who, by close watching, can be preserved in the use of their feet and tongue. Men who are mighty to consume strong drink are unfit members of that kingdom which consisteth not in "meat and drink," but in "righteousness and peace." The time, we trust, is not distant, when the use of ardent spirits will be proscribed by a vote of all the Churches in our land, and when the commerce in that article shall, equally with the slave-trade, be regarded as inconsistent with a creditable profession of Christianity.

The Friends,[1] in excluding ardent spirits from the list of lawful articles of commerce, have done themselves immortal honor; and in the temperance of their families, and their thrift in business, have set an example which is worthy the admiration and imitation of all the Churches in our land. . . .

Much may be accomplished to discountenance the commerce in ardent spirits by a silent, judicious distribution of patronage in trade.

---

1. The Society of Friends, or Quakers.—*Eds.*

W. H. Daniels, *The Temperance Reform* (Cincinnati, Chicago, and St. Louis, 1878), 79–90.

GRAND, NATIONAL, TEMPERANCE BANNER.
Dedicated to every Son & Daughter of Temperance, throughout the Union.

A Grand National Temperance Banner. The temperance movement tried everything to make people give up alcohol—sermons, lectures, personal testimonials, parades and marches, songs, leaflets, newspapers, posters, and banners. One of the most popular prints of the day reproduced a banner of a young man rejecting liquor and the evils associated with it—cards, dice, and a voluptuous woman. Instead, he chooses the glass of water offered by a virtuously dressed woman, presumably more wifely and domestic. The woman with the liquor wears a clinging gown that reveals her breasts and thighs, wears her hair unpinned and flowing over her shoulders, and hooks her alluring hand through the man's arm. The man's strength of character is self-evident. It takes a strong individual to resist such charms. (Library of Congress)

Let that portion of the community who would exile from society the traffic in ardent spirits bestow their custom upon those who will agree to abandon it, and a regard to interest will soon produce a competition in well-doing. The temperate population of a city or town are the best customers, and have it in their power to render the commerce in ardent spirits disadvantageous to those who engage in it. . . .

. . . Could my voice be extended through the land to all orders and descriptions of men, I would "cry aloud and spare not." To the watchmen upon Zion's walls, appointed to announce the approach of danger, and to say unto the wicked man, "Thou shalt surely die," I would say, Can we hold our peace, or withhold the influence of our example in such an emergency as this, and be guiltless of blood? Are we not called upon to set examples of entire abstinence? How otherwise shall we be able to preach against intemperance, and reprove, rebuke, and exhort? Talk not of "habit," and of "prudent use," and a little for the "stomach's sake." This is the way in which men become drunkards. Our security and our influence demand immediate and entire abstinence. If nature would receive a shock by such a reformation, it proves that it has already been too long delayed, and can safely be deferred no longer.

To the Churches of our Lord Jesus Christ—whom he hath purchased with his blood, that he might redeem them from all iniquity, and purify them to himself a peculiar people—I would say, Beloved in the Lord, the world hath need of your purified example; for who will make a stand against the encroachments of intemperance if professors of religion will not? Will you not, then, abstain from the use of it entirely, and exile it from your families? Will you not watch over one another with keener vigilance, and lift an earlier note of admonition, and draw tighter the bands of brotherly discipline, and with a more determined fidelity cut off those whom admonition cannot reclaim? Separate, brethren, between the precious and the vile, the living and the dead, and burn incense between them, that the plague may be stayed. . . .

The friends of the Lord and his Christ, with laudable enterprise, are rearing temples to Jehovah, and extending his word and ordinances through the land; while the irreligious influence of this single crime balances, or nearly balances, the entire account.

And now, ye venerable and honorable men, raised to seats of legislation in a nation which is the freest, and is destined to become the greatest, and may become the happiest upon earth, can you, will you behold unmoved the march of the mighty evil? Shall it mine in darkness, and lift fearlessly its giant form in daylight, and deliberately dig the grave of our liberties, and entomb the last hope of enslaved nations, and nothing be done by the national government to stop the destroyer? With the concurrent aid of an enlightened public sentiment, you possess the power of a most efficacious legislation; and, by your example and influence, you of all men possess the best opportunities of forming a correct and irresistible public sentiment on the side of temperance. Much power to you is given to check and extirpate this evil, and to roll down to distant ages, broader and deeper and purer, the streams of national prosperity. Save us by your wisdom and firmness, save us by your own example, and, "as in duty bound, we will ever pray." . . .

To the affectionate husband I would say, Behold the wife of thy bosom, young and beautiful as the morning; and yet her day may be overcast with clouds, and all thy early hopes be blasted. Upon her the fell destroyer may lay his hand, and plant in that healthful frame the seeds of disease, and transmit to successive generations the inheritance of crime and woe. Will you not watch over her with ever-wakeful affection, and keep far from your abode the occasions of temptation and ruin? Call around you the circle of your healthful and beautiful children. Will you bring contagion into such a circle as this? Shall those sparkling eyes become inflamed, those rosy cheeks purpled and bloated, that sweet breath be tainted, those ruby lips blistered, and that vital tone of unceasing cheerfulness be turned into tremor and melancholy? Shall those joints so compact be unstrung, that dawning intellect be clouded, those affectionate sensibilities benumbed, and those capacities for holiness and heaven be filled with sin and "fitted for destruction?" O, thou father, was it for this that the Son of God shed his blood for thy precious offspring; that, abandoned, and even tempted, by thee, they should destroy themselves and pierce thy heart with many sorrows? Wouldst thou let the wolf into thy sheep-fold among the tender lambs? wouldst thou send thy flock to graze about a den of lions?

Close, then, thy doors against a more ferocious destroyer, and withhold the footsteps of thy immortal progeny from places of resort more dangerous than the lions' den. Should a serpent of vast dimensions surprise in the field one of your little group, and wreath about his body its cold, elastic folds—tightening with every yielding breath its deadly grip—how would his cries pierce your soul, and his strained eyeballs and convulsive agonies and imploring hands add wings to your feet, and supernatural strength to your arms! But in this case you could approach with hope to his rescue. The keen edge of steel might sunder the elastic fold and rescue the victim, who, the moment he is released, breathes freely and is well again. But the serpent Intemperance twines about the body of your child a deadlier grip, and extorts a keener cry of distress, and mocks your effort to relieve him by a fiber which no steel can sunder.

And now, I would say, Resolve upon reformation by entire abstinence while the argument is clear, and the impression of it is fresh, and your judgment is convinced, and your conscience is awake, be persuaded, not almost, but altogether. The present moment may be the one which decides your destiny forever. As you decide now upon abstinence or continued indulgence, so may your character be through time and through eternity. Resolve, also, instantly to exclude ardent spirits from your family, and put out of sight the memorials of past folly and danger. And if for medical purposes you retain ardent spirits in your house, let it be among other drugs, and labeled, "Touch not, taste not, handle not."

27

OF HUMAN BONDAGE

After the rapid spread of the Cotton Kingdom had made slavery so profitable, persuading significant numbers of slaveholders to free their slaves seemed hopeless. It became virtually impossible when Southern states passed laws that outlawed public debates on the issue of slavery and made manumission (voluntarily freeing one's slaves) illegal.

Furthermore, persuading Northerners to support nonviolent abolitionism was almost as difficult as persuading Southerners. The cause appeared hopelessly impractical. In addition, most white Northerners considered blacks inferior and did not want them around, free or otherwise. Recognizing this difficulty, the American Colonization Society had tried—unsuccessfully—to encourage gradual manumission by raising money to send freed slaves to Africa. The problem remained when William Lloyd Garrison of Boston founded the militant American Anti-Slavery Society in 1833. His chief goals were to persuade Northerners on two points: that immediate abolition was feasible; and that slaves, once free, would make acceptable citizens and neighbors.

Women played a major role in nineteenth-century reform movements, including the antislavery struggle. They helped sensitize the Protestant churches to the evils of slavery and organized petition drives urging Congress to abolish the slave trade. At a time when the male-dominant mainstream culture of the United States was intolerant of women who commented on political issues, they wrote and sometimes spoke out against slavery. One of their great early successes was Lydia Maria Child's *An Appeal in Favor of That Class of Americans Called Africans,* which appeared in 1833. Child's book (excerpted below) blended anecdote, logic, and historical scholarship and was written in a clear, compelling style. It helped convert thousands of wavering Northerners to the cause of immediate abolitionism and significantly strengthened the role of the Garrisonians in the unfolding antislavery crusade.

Born in 1802 into a family of Massachusetts Unitarians, Lydia Maria Child was, at age thirty-one, already the best-known woman writer in America when *An Appeal* appeared. She had several novels and domestic "how-to" works to her credit and had founded the country's first children's magazine, the *Juvenile Miscellany,* in 1826. Though she was influential with reformers, Child's *Appeal* badly damaged her popularity. Sales of her books fell sharply, and the *Juvenile Miscellany* foundered in 1834. From 1840 to 1849 she and her husband edited the *National Anti-Slavery Standard* in New York City. In 1852 they moved to a Massachusetts farm, where Lydia wrote extensively on religion, women's rights, capital punishment, slavery, and, following the Civil War, the plight of the freedmen. She died in Wayland, Massachusetts, in 1880.

Questions to Consider. It was an article of faith for most Americans in the early nineteenth century that women were different from men— that they saw the world differently and expressed themselves differently. Does Lydia Maria Child's *Appeal* seem "feminine" to you? Did she raise points or use arguments that a man might not have? Many Americans of the time thought abolitionists were humorless and self-righteous. Does Child seem to have been humorless? What was her primary method of persuasion? Why did she discuss the slave trade so extensively? What did she mean when she said that efforts to regulate slavery were like efforts to regulate murder?

★━━★━━★

That Class of Americans Called Africans (1833)

LYDIA MARIA CHILD

A judicious and benevolent friend lately told me the story of one of her relatives, who married a slave-owner, and removed to his plantation. The lady in question was considered very amiable, and had a serene, affectionate expression of countenance. After several years' residence among her slaves, she visited New England. "Her history was written in her face," said my friend; "its expression had changed into that of a fiend. She brought but few slaves with her; and those few were of course compelled to perform additional labor. One faithful negro-woman nursed the twins of her mistress, and did all the washing, ironing, and scouring. If, after a sleepless night with the restless babes, (driven from the bosom of their own mother,) she performed her toilsome avocations with diminished activity, her mistress, with her own lady-like hands, applied the cowskin, and the neighborhood resounded with the cries of her victim. The instrument of punishment was actually kept hanging

Lydia Maria Child, *An Appeal in Favor of That Class of Americans Called Africans* (New York, 1833), 28–37, 141–146.

A slave auction. Nothing appalled foreign visitors more than the sight of slave sales, especially in the capital of the republic, Washington, D.C. This picture from the *London News* shows what British travelers made of the institution of the slave auction. The auctioneer calls out the bid on the slave family on the block; male slaves await their turn at either foot of the block. So normal was the scene that many of the men in the room pay no attention; to notice might even open them to accusations of sympathy, anathema in the Old South. Only the buyers in front of the block, concerned (like their forebears in 1619) to buy the most labor for the lowest price, seem to notice. (Library of Congress)

in the entry, to the no small disgust of her New-England visiters. For my part," continued my friend, "I did not try to be polite to her; for I was not hypocrite enough to conceal my indignation."

The following occurred near Natchez, and was told to me by a highly intelligent man, who, being a diplomatist and a courtier, was very likely to make the best of national evils: A planter had occasion to send a female slave some distance on an errand. She did not return so soon as he expected, and he grew angry. At last he gave orders that she should be severely whipped when she came back. When the poor creature arrived, she pleaded for mercy, saying she had been so very ill, that she was obliged to rest in the fields; but she was ordered to receive another dozen lashes, for having had the impudence to speak. She died at the whipping-post; nor did she perish alone— a new-born baby died with her. The gentleman who told me this fact, witnessed the poor creature's funeral. It is true, the master was universally blamed and shunned for the cruel deed; but the laws were powerless.

I shall be told that such examples as these are of rare occurrence; and I have no doubt that instances of excessive severity are far from being common. I believe that a large proportion of masters are as kind to their slaves as they can be, consistently with keeping them in bondage; but it must be allowed that this, to make the best of it, is very stinted kindness. And let it never be forgotten that the negro's fate depends entirely on the character of his master; and it is a mere matter of chance whether he fall into merciful or unmerciful hands; his happiness, nay, his very life, depends on chance. . . .

But it is urged that it is the interest of planters to treat their slaves well. This argument no doubt has some force; and it is the poor negro's only security. But it is likewise the interest of men to treat their cattle kindly; yet we see that passion and short-sighted avarice do overcome the strongest motives of interest. Cattle are beat unmercifully, sometimes unto death; they are ruined by being over-worked; weakened by want of sufficient food; and so forth. Besides, it is sometimes directly *for* the interest of the planter to work his slaves beyond their strength. When there is a sudden rise in the prices of sugar, a certain amount of labor in a given time is of more consequence to the owner of a plantation than the price of several slaves; he can well *afford* to waste a few lives. This is no idle hypothesis—such calculations are gravely and openly made by planters. Hence, it is the slave's prayer that sugars may be cheap. When the negro is old, or feeble from incurable disease, is it his master's *interest* to feed him well, and clothe him comfortably? Certainly not: it then becomes desirable to get rid of the human brute as soon as convenient. It is a common remark, that it is not quite safe, in most cases, for even parents to be entirely dependant on the generosity of their children; and if human nature be such, what has the slave to expect, when he becomes a mere bill of expense? . . .

Among other apologies for slavery, it has been asserted that the Bible does not forbid it. Neither does it forbid the counterfeiting of a bank-bill. It is the *spirit* of the Holy Word, not its particular *expressions,* which must be a rule for our conduct. How can slavery be reconciled with the maxim, "Do unto others, as ye would that others should do unto you"? Does not the command, "Thou shalt not *steal,*" prohibit *kidnapping?* And how does whipping men to death agree with the injunction, "Thou shalt do no *murder*"? Are we not told "to loose the bands of wickedness, to undo the heavy burdens, to let the oppressed go free, and to break every yoke"? It was a Jewish law that he who stole a man, or sold him, or he in whose hands the stolen man was found, should suffer death; and he in whose house a fugitive slave sought an asylum was forbidden to give him up to his master. Modern slavery is so unlike Hebrew servitude, and its regulations are so diametrically opposed to the rules of the Gospel, which came to bring deliverance to the captive, that it is idle to dwell upon this point. . . .

I shall perhaps be asked why I have said so much about the slave-*trade,* since it was long ago abolished in this country. There are several good reasons for it. In the first place, it is a part of the system; for if there were no slaves, there could be no slave-trade; and while there are slaves, the slave-trade *will* continue. In the next place, the trade is still briskly carried on in Africa, and slaves are smuggled into these States through the Spanish colonies. In the third place, a very extensive internal slave-trade is carried on in this country. The breeding of negro-cattle for the foreign markets, (of Louisiana, Georgia, Alabama, Arkansas, and Missouri,) is a very lucrative branch of business. Whole coffles of them, chained and manacled, are driven through our Capital on their way to auction. Foreigners, particularly those who come here with enthusiastic ideas of American freedom, are amazed and disgusted at the sight. A troop of slaves once passed through Washington on the fourth of July, while drums were beating, and standards flying. One of the captive negroes raised his hand, loaded with irons, and waving it toward the starry flag, sung with a smile of bitter irony, "Hail Columbia! *happy* land!" . . .

A free man of color is in constant danger of being seized and carried off by these slave-dealers. Mr. Cooper, a Representative in Congress from Delaware, told Dr. Torrey, of Philadelphia, that he was often afraid to send his servants out in the evening, lest they should be encountered by kidnappers. Wherever these notorious slave-jockeys appear in our Southern States, the free people of color hide themselves, as they are obliged to do on the coast of Africa. . . .

Finally, I have described some of the horrors of the slave-trade, because when our constitution was formed, the government pledged itself not to abolish this traffic until 1808. We began our career of freedom by granting a twenty years' lease of iniquity—twenty years of allowed invasion of other men's rights—twenty years of bloodshed, violence, and fraud! And this will be told in our annals—this will be heard of to the end of time!

While the slave-trade was allowed, the South could use it to advance their views in various ways. In their representation to Congress, five slaves counted the same as three freemen; of course, every fresh cargo was not only an increase of property, but an increase of *political power.* Ample time was allowed to lay in a stock of slaves to supply the new slave states and territories that might grow up; and when this was effected, the prohibition of foreign commerce in human flesh, operated as a complete *tariff,* to protect the domestic supply.

Every man who buys a slave promotes this traffic, by raising the value of the article; every man who owns a slave, indirectly countenances it; every man who allows that slavery is a lamentable *necessity,* contributes his share to support it; and he who votes for admitting a slave-holding State into the Union, fearfully augments the amount of this crime. . . .

The abolitionists think it a duty to maintain at all times, and in all places, that slavery *ought* to be abolished, and that it *can* be abolished. When error is so often repeated it becomes very important to repeat the truth; especially as good men are apt to be quiet, and selfish men are prone to be active. They propose no *plan*—they leave that to the wisdom of Legislatures. But they never swerve from the *principle* that slavery is both wicked and unnecessary.—

Their object is to turn the public voice against this evil, by a plain exposition of facts.

The Anti-Slavery Society is loudly accused of being seditious, fanatical, and likely to promote insurrections. It seems to be supposed, that they wish to send fire and sword into the South, and encourage the slaves to hunt down their masters. Slave-owners wish to have it viewed in this light, because they know the subject will not bear discussion; and men here, who give the tone to public opinion, have loudly repeated the charge—some from good motives, and some from bad. I once had a very strong prejudice against anti-slavery—(I am ashamed to think *how* strong—for mere prejudice should never be stubborn,) but a candid examination has convinced me, that I was in an error. I made the common mistake of taking things for granted, without stopping to investigate.

Ridicule and reproach has been abundantly heaped upon the laborers in this righteous cause. Power, wealth, talent, pride, and sophistry, are all in arms against them; but God and truth is on their side. The cause of anti-slavery is rapidly gaining ground. Wise heads as well as warm hearts, are joining in its support. In a few years I believe the opinion of New-England will be unanimous in its favor. Maine, which enjoys the enviable distinction of never having had a slave upon her soil, has formed an Anti-Slavery Society composed of her best and most distinguished men. Those who are determined to be on the popular side, should be cautious how they move just now: It is a trying time for such characters, when public opinion is on the verge of a great change.

Men who *think* upon the subject, are fast coming to the conclusion that slavery can never be much ameliorated, while it is allowed to exist. What Mr. Fox said of the *trade* is true of the *system*—"you may as well try to *regulate* murder."

28

THE STRUGGLES OF LABOR

American manufacturing changed dramatically after the War of 1812. Before the war, skilled artisans created custom goods from start to finish in their own homes and shops. After the war, as a result of wider demand and improvements in technology, a "factory system" emerged in the Northeast, beginning with the giant New England textile mills, driven by water power, and spreading rapidly to steam-powered shoe factories and machine shops. Human labor in thrall to mechanization became the foundation of the factory system; large mills and impersonal corporations became its chief features. Consumers benefited from more affordable mass-produced goods. Once-independent artisans slowly but surely fell to the status of wage workers—"hands."

One result was economic inequality on an unprecedented scale for a nonslave system. By the 1850s, the top 10 percent of the Northern population owned perhaps 60 percent of the section's wealth. The labor force, increasingly proletarian (wage-earning), saw its condition deteriorate. It was not uncommon for an adult male factory worker to earn a dollar for a fourteen-hour day; women and children sometimes received less. By the 1840s the nation was debating this maldistribution of wealth and income, now painfully noticeable, almost as intensely as it debated slavery, and it was taken to be a threat to democracy as well as the general welfare.

Among the most outspoken participants in that debate were proponents of labor unions. The earliest unions consisted of skilled artisans in a particular craft—carpentry, for example, or barrel making or printing. In the 1820s and 1830s craft unions began to grow and consolidate, first in their respective cities, then nationwide as multicraft workers' alliances. One of the most important of these early unions was the General Trades' Union of New York, which formed the core of the National Trades' Union of the 1830s.

Below are excerpts from a speech by Ely Moore, a New York printer, labor organizer, and Democratic activist, to the first National Trades' Union convention in 1834. Using class conflict rhetoric that foreshadowed Karl Marx's *Communist Manifesto,* Moore argued that working men were becoming vassals to their employers, and that the unequal distribution of wealth subverted the "natural rights of man" and was hostile to the "spirit and genius" of democracy. Moore's speech, fairly typical of the era, was ultimately fairly moderate in substance. But it still raised the hackles of conservatives, who were as unnerved by his criticism of "undue accumulation" as they were by his cry for workers to unite against the "aristocracy."

The biggest craft unions were in the Northern seaboard cities, especially Philadelphia, New York, and Boston, where an enormous construction boom had spurred employment and therefore union efforts in the building trades. The carpenters of Boston mounted a successful strike as early as the 1820s and remained active in the next decade, which witnessed much labor organizing. But by the mid-1840s construction had slumped and there were thousands of unorganized immigrant workers willing to take nearly any wage just to live. This hit "journeymen" craftsmen—ordinary wage earners as opposed to contractors, or "masters"—particularly hard. The second selection, "Resolutions of the Journeymen Carpenters of Boston," gives a taste of the arguments used by labor in this early formative era. It conveys, among other things, the importance of non-wage issues and the pressures that stemmed from the assumption that men had to be the main, if not the sole, breadwinners for their family.

Ely Moore was born in New Jersey in 1798, attended public schools, and moved to New York, where he became a printer, land speculator, and politician. He was the first president of the New York General Trades' Union in 1833, edited the *National Trades' Union*, a labor journal, and was head of the National Trades' Union until 1836. That year Moore, a popular orator, was elected to Congress as a Democrat and served until 1839. Thereafter, he held various political patronage positions (posts he received for supporting successful Democratic candidates) in New York City and Kansas, where he moved in 1855. He died in Lecompton, Kansas, in 1861.

Questions to Consider. What were the different forces that, in Moore's view, had produced the drift toward "vassalage" and "supremacy"? Why did he think this drift was dangerous? Why did he propose labor unions as a remedy instead of government action? What remedies besides legislation and unionization might he have urged? Why did he spend so much time defending the idea of labor unions? Do you find Moore's arguments about the dangers of inequality and the legitimacy of labor unions persuasive? Would you say that they are less relevant today than in the nineteenth century, or more?

■═══■═══■

Address to the General Trades' Union (1833)

ELY MOORE

Wherever man exists, under whatever form of government, or whatever be the structure or organization of society, . . . selfishness will appear, operating either for evil or for good. To curb it sufficiently by legislative enactments is impossible. Much can be done, however, towards restraining it within proper limits by unity of purpose and concert of action on the part of the *producing* classes. To contribute toward the achievement of this great end is one of the objects of the "General Trades' Union." Wealth, we all know, constitutes the aristocracy of this country. Happily no distinctions are known among us save what wealth and worth confer. . . . The greatest danger, therefore, which threatens the stability of our Government and the liberty of the people is an undue accumulation and distribution of wealth. And I do conceive that real danger is to be apprehended from this source, notwithstanding that tendency to distribution which naturally grows out of the character of our statutes of conveyance, of inheritance, and descent of property; but by securing to the producing classes a fair, certain, and equitable compensation for their toil and skill, we insure a more just and equal distribution of wealth than can ever be effected by statutory law.

. . . We ask . . . what better means can be devised for promoting a more equal distribution of wealth than for the producing classes to *claim,* and by virtue of union and concert, *secure their claims* to their respective portions? And why should not those who have the toil have the enjoyment also? Or why should the sweat that flows from the brow of the laborer be converted into a source of revenue for the support of the crafty or indolent?

It has been averred, with great truth, that all governments become cruel and aristocratical in their character and bearing in proportion as one part of the community is elevated and the other depressed, and that misery and degradation to the many is the inevitable result of such a state of society. And we regard it to be equally true that, in proportion as the line of distinction between the employer and employed is *widened,* the condition of the latter inevitably verges toward a state of vassalage, while that of the former as certainly approximates toward supremacy; and that whatever system is calculated to make the many dependent upon or subject to the few not only tends to the subversion of the natural rights of man, but is hostile to the best interests of the community, as well as to the spirit and genius of our Government. Fully persuaded that the foregoing positions are incontrovertible, we,

Ely Moore, *Address Before the General Trades' Union of New York City* (New York, 1833), 7–14, 19–20.

in order to guard against the encroachments of aristocracy, to preserve our natural and political rights, to elevate our moral and intellectual condition, to promote our pecuniary interests, to narrow the line of distinction between the journeyman and employer, to establish the honor and safety of our respective vocations upon a more secure and permanent basis, and to alleviate the distresses of those suffering from want of employment have deemed it expedient to form ourselves into a "General Trades' Union."

It may be asked, how these desirable objects are to be achieved by a general union of trades? How the encroachments of aristocracy, for example, are to be arrested by our plan? We answer, by enabling the producer to enjoy the full benefit of his productions, and thus diffuse the streams of wealth more generally and, consequently, more equally throughout all the ramifications of society. . . .

There are, doubtless, many individuals who are resolved, right or wrong, to misrepresent our principles, impeach our measures, and impugn our motives. Be it so. They can harm us not. . . . We have the consolation of knowing that all good men, all who love their country, and rejoice in the improvement of the condition of their fellow men, will acknowledge the policy of our views and the purity of our motives. . . . And why, let me ask, should the character of our Union be obnoxious to censure? Wherefore is it wrong in principle? Which of its avowed objects reprehensible? What feature of it opposed to the public good? I defy the ingenuity of man to point to a single measure which it recognizes that is wrong in itself or in its tendency. What, is it wrong for men to unite for the purpose of resisting the encroachments of aristocracy? Wrong to restrict the principle of selfishness to its proper and legitimate bounds and objects? Wrong to oppose monopoly and mercenary ambition? Wrong to consult the interests and seek the welfare of the producing classes? Wrong to attempt the elevation of our moral and intellectual standing? Wrong to establish the honor and safety of our respective vocations upon a more secure and permanent basis? I ask—in the name of heaven I ask—can it be wrong for men to attempt the melioration of their condition and the preservation of their natural and political rights?

I am aware that the charge of "illegal combination" is raised against us. The cry is as senseless as 'tis stale and unprofitable. Why, I would inquire, have not journeymen the same right to ask their own price for their own property or services that employers have? or that merchants, physicians, and lawyers have? Is that equal justice which makes it an offense for journeymen to combine for the purpose of maintaining their present prices or raising their wages, while employers may combine with impunity for the purpose of lowering them? I admit that such is the common law. All will agree, however, that it is neither wise, just, nor politic, and that it is directly opposed to the spirit and genius of our free institutions and ought therefore, to be abrogated. . . .

Again, it is alleged that it is setting a dangerous precedent for journeymen to combine for the purpose of coercing a compliance with their terms. It may, indeed, be dangerous to aristocracy, dangerous to monopoly, dangerous to oppression, but not to the general good or the public tranquillity. Internal danger to a state is not to be apprehended from a general effort on the part of the people to improve and exalt their condition, but from an alliance of the crafty, designing, and intriguing few. What! tell us, in this enlightened age, that the welfare of the people will be endangered by a voluntary act of the people themselves? That the people will wantonly seek their own destruction? That the safety of the state will be plotted against by three-fourths of the members comprising the state! O how worthless, how poor and pitiful, are all such arguments and objections! . . .

My object in inviting you to a consideration of this subject at the present time is to impress upon your minds the importance of the situation which you, in reality, ought to occupy in society. This you seem to have lost sight of in a very great degree; and, from some cause or other, have relinquished your claims to that consideration to which, as mechanics and as men, you are entitled. You have, most unfortunately for yourselves and for the respectability of your vocations, become apparently unconscious of your own worth, and been led to regard your callings as humble and inferior, and your stations as too subordinate in life. And why? why is it so? Why should the producer consider himself inferior to the consumer? Or why should the mechanic, who builds a house, consider himself less important than the owner or occupant? It is strange, indeed, and to me perfectly unaccountable that the artificer, who prepares the accommodations, the comforts, and embellishments of life, should consider himself of less consequence than those to whose pleasure and convenience he ministers. . . .

<hr>

Resolutions of the Journeymen Carpenters of Boston (1845)

Notice to house carpenters and housewrights in the country. An advertisement having appeared in the papers of this city, giving information that there is at this time a great demand for workmen in this branch of mechanical business in this city, it is considered a duty to state for the benefit of our brethren of the trade that we are not aware of any considerable demand for labor in this business, as there is, at this time, a very considerable number of journeymen carpenters who are out of employ, and the probable inducement which led to the communication referred to arises from a disposition manifested on the part of the builders in this city to make their own terms as to the price of

J. R. Commons et al., eds., *A Documentary History of American Industrial Society* (Cleveland, 1910), VI: 76.

labor and the number of hours of labor which shall hereafter constitute a day's work. It being a well-known fact that the most unreasonable requirements have been hitherto extracted with regard to the terms of labor of journeymen mechanics in this city; and it is further well known that in the cities of New York, Philadelphia, Baltimore, and most of the other cities a much more liberal and equitable course of policy has been adopted by the master-builders, on this subject, giving to their journeymen that fair and liberal support to which they are unquestionably entitled. It is an undoubted fact that, in the present system, it is impossible for a journeyman housewright and house carpenter to maintain a family at the present time with the wages which are now usually given to the journeymen house carpenters in this city.

29

PUBLIC OR PRIVATE

The era from the 1830s until the Civil War produced intense reform movements, especially in the Northeast. "In the history of the world," exclaimed Ralph Waldo Emerson, "the doctrine of Reform had never such a scope as at the present hour." Some reformers were religious; they took seriously Christianity's emphasis on spiritual equality and Jesus's concern for the lowly and humble. Some drew inspiration from the Declaration of Independence, with its insistence on natural rights, and were eager to make its social and political ideas a reality. Many believed that human nature was perfectible and that with better social arrangements men and women would be able to live more fully and freely than they ever had before. Hence the struggle for temperance, women's rights, humane prisons and asylums, better working conditions, and a host of communitarian schemes such as Mormonism.

Reformers also focused on education. Believing that the foundation of democracy was an educated citizenry, they were shocked by the disparity between that ideal and the sorry state of schooling. In most mid-Atlantic states paupers were educated at public expense; in the South, public schools were almost nonexistent; in the West, the sparse population was simply unable to establish adequate schools. Even in New England, where an educational tradition stretched back to the Puritan insistence that as many people as possible should read the Bible, school systems were largely dysfunctional.

The signs were everywhere. Essayist Bronson Alcott taught eighty students in one tiny room. Buildings were usually frigid and joyless, on sites selected with less regard to comfort "than if the children were animals." Anything would do, especially if it was "so useless for everything else as to be given to the district." Teachers were unavailable and untrained. Supplies were minimal. Common (public) school "revivalists" therefore went to work to persuade towns and villages to build more and better schools; to fill them with comfortable desks, blackboards, books, maps, blocks, and writing materials; to establish standards and train professional (mostly female) teachers; and to make elementary education compulsory.

No one was more devoted to the cause than Horace Mann. A Boston lawyer and politician from Franklin, Massachusetts, Mann had suffered through a miserable childhood and a wretched education. In 1837 he stunned his friends by quitting, at age forty-one, both the law and the presidency of the Massachusetts senate to become secretary of the state's fledgling board of education. There, with little formal power save persuasion, Mann worked a revolution in the state's school system. Largely as a result of his efforts, Massachusetts became a model for common schools across the North.

But there were powerful opposing forces. Prosperous families, in particular, liked to send their children to private schools. One of Mann's greatest challenges was therefore to convince parents to send their children to public schools, as his 1838 *Report on the Common Schools* (excerpted below) makes clear. The report also reflected Mann's view that the common school experience would promote the opportunity, social unity, and compassion that would make students good future citizens: "If we do not prepare children to become good citizens—if we do not . . . enrich their minds with knowledge, imbue their hearts with the love of truth and duty . . . then our republic must go down to destruction."

Mann's devotion to educational reform never faltered. After serving twelve years as secretary of the Massachusetts board of education, he served a term in the U.S. House of Representatives, where he supported efforts to halt the expansion of slavery. In 1853 Mann became the first president of Antioch College in Ohio, where he died in 1859.

Questions to Consider. According to Horace Mann, what was the main purpose of the common school system? To what extent did Mann's enthusiasm for public schools reflect his view of human nature? Why did some people value private education more than public? What did Mann think would be the social consequences of this preference? What did Mann seem to value most, opportunity for individuals or well-being for the society? Do you find his arguments persuasive? Some say they are especially relevant today. Do you agree?

◼━◼━◼

Report on the Common Schools (1838)

HORACE MANN

The object of the common school system of Massachusetts was to give to every child in the Commonwealth a free, straight, solid path-way, by which he could walk directly up from the ignorance of an infant to a knowledge of the primary duties of a man; and could acquire a power and an invincible will to discharge them. Have our children such a way? Are they walking in it? Why do so many, who enter it, falter therein? Are there not many, who miss it altogether? What can be done to reclaim them? What can be done to rescue faculties, powers, divine endowments, graciously designed for individual and social good, from being perverted to individual and social calamity? These are the questions of deep and intense interest, which I have proposed to myself, and upon which I have sought for information and counsel. . . .

An . . . [important] topic . . . is the apathy of the people themselves towards our common schools. The wide usefulness of which this institution is capable is shorn away on both sides, by two causes diametrically opposite. On one side there is a portion of the community who do not attach sufficient value to the system to do the things necessary to its healthful and energetic working. They may say excellent things about it, they may have a conviction of its general utility; but they do not understand, that the wisest conversation not embodied in action, that convictions too gentle and quiet to coerce performance, are little better than worthless. The prosperity of the system always requires some labor. It requires a conciliatory disposition, and oftentimes a little sacrifice of personal preferences. . . .

Through remissness or ignorance on the part of parent and teacher, the minds of children may never be awakened to a consciousness of having, within themselves, blessed treasures of innate and noble faculties, far richer than any outward possessions can be; they may never be supplied with any foretaste of the enduring satisfactions of knowledge; and hence, they may attend school for the allotted period, merely as so many male and female automata, between four and sixteen years of age. As the progenitor of the human race, after being perfectly fashioned in every limb and organ and feature, might have lain till this time, a motionless body in the midst of the beautiful garden of Eden, had not the Creator breathed into him a living soul; so children, without some favoring influences to woo out and cheer their faculties, may remain mere inanimate forms, while surrounded by the paradise of knowledge. It is generally believed, that there is an increasing class of people

Horace Mann, *First Annual Report of the Board of Education* (Boston, 1838), 47–58.

New England schoolroom, 1857. Horace Mann's reform efforts succeeded to an astonishing degree in the towns and villages of the Northern states. By modern standards, however, even the new and newly refurbished schools were sometimes stark and gloomy, as this photograph of a girls' class suggests. Even when teachers were better trained and paid, they relied on strict discipline and drill to educate their students. (The Metropolitian Museum of Art, Gift of I. N. Phelps Stokes, Edward S. Hawes, Alice Mary Hawes, Marion Augusta Hawes, 1937)

amongst us, who are losing sight of the necessity of securing ample opportunities for the education of their children. And thus, on one side, the institution of common schools is losing its natural support, if it be not incurring actual opposition.

Opposite to this class, who tolerate, from apathy, a depression in the common schools, there is another class who affix so high a value upon the culture of their children, and understand so well the necessity of a skillful preparation of means for its bestowment, that they turn away from the common schools, in their depressed state, and seek, elsewhere, the helps of a more enlarged and thorough education. Thus the standard, in descending to a point corresponding with the views and wants of one portion of society, falls below the demands and the regards of another. Out of different feelings grow different plans; and while one remains fully content with the common school, the other builds up the private school or the academy.

The education fund is thus divided into two parts. Neither of the halves does a quarter of the good which might be accomplished by a union of the whole. One party pays an adequate price, but has a poor school; the other has a good school, but at more than four-fold cost. Were their funds and their interest combined, the poorer school might be as good as the best; and the dearest almost as low as the cheapest. This last mentioned class embraces a considerable portion, perhaps a majority of the wealthy persons in the state; but it also includes another portion, numerically much greater, who, whether rich or poor, have a true perception of the sources of their children's individual and domestic well-being, and who consider the common necessaries of their life, their food and fuel and clothes, and all their bodily comforts as superfluities, compared with the paramount necessity of a proper mental and moral culture of their offspring.

The maintenance of free schools rests wholly upon the social principle. It is emphatically a case where men, individually powerless, are collectively strong. The population of Massachusetts, being more than *eighty* to the square mile, gives it the power of maintaining common schools. Take the whole range of the western and south-western states, and their population, probably, does not exceed a dozen or fifteen to the square mile. Hence, except in favorable localities, common schools are impossible; as the population upon a territory of convenient size for a district, is too small to sustain a school. Here, nothing is easier. But by dividing our funds, we cast away our natural advantages. We voluntarily reduce ourselves to the feebleness of a state, having but half our density of population.

It is generally supposed, that this severance of interests, and consequent diminution of power, have increased much of late, and are now increasing in an accelerated ratio. This is probable, for it is a self-aggravating evil. Its origin and progress are simple and uniform. Some few persons . . . finding the advantages of the common school inadequate to their wants, unite to establish a private one. They transfer their children from the former to the latter. The heart goes with the treasure. The common school ceases to be visited by those whose children are in the private. Such parents . . . have now no personal motive to vote for or advocate any increase of the town's annual appropriation for schools; to say nothing of the temptation to discourage such increase in indirect ways, or even to vote directly against it. If, by this means, some of the best scholars happen to be taken from the common school, the standard of that school is lowered. The lower classes in a school have no abstract standard of excellence, and seldom aim at higher attainments than such as they daily witness. All children, like all men, rise easily to the common level. There, the mass stop; strong minds only ascend higher. But raise the standard, and, by a spontaneous movement, the mass will rise again and reach it. Hence the removal of the most forward scholars from a school is not a small misfortune. . . .

The refusal of a town to maintain the free town school drives a portion of its inhabitants to establish the private school or academy. When established, these institutions tend strongly to diminish the annual appropriations of the town; they draw their ablest recruits from the common schools; and, by being able to offer higher compensation, they have a pre-emptive right to the best qualified teachers; while, simultaneously, the district schools are reduced in length, deteriorated in quality, and, to some extent, bereft of talents competent for instruction. . . .

. . . The patrons of the private school plead the moral necessity of sustaining it, because, they say, some of the children in the public school are so addicted to profanity or obscenity, so prone to trickishness or to vulgar and mischievous habits, as to render a removal of their own children from such contaminating influences an obligatory precaution. But would such objectors bestow that guardian care, that parental watchfulness upon the common schools, which an institution, so wide and deep-reaching in its influences, demands of all intelligent men, might not these repellent causes be mainly abolished? Reforms ought to be originated and carried forward by the intelligent portion of society; by those who can see most links in the chain of causes and effects; and that intelligence is false to its high trusts, which stands aloof from the labor of enlightening the ignorant and ameliorating the condition of the unfortunate. And what a vision must rise before the minds of all men, endued with the least glimmer of foresight, in the reflection, that, after a few swift years, those children, whose welfare they now discard, and whose associations they deprecate, will constitute more than *five sixths* of the whole body of that community, of which their own children will be only a feeble minority, vulnerable at every point, and utterly incapable of finding a hiding-place for any earthly treasure, where the witness, the juror and the voter cannot reach and annihilate it!

The theory of our laws and institutions undoubtedly is, *first*, that in every district of every town in the Commonwealth, there should be a free district school, sufficiently safe, and sufficiently good, for all the children within its territory, where they may be well instructed in the rudiments of knowledge, formed to propriety of demeanor, and imbued with the principles of duty: and, *secondly*, in regard to every town, having such an increased population as implies the possession of sufficient wealth, that there should be a school of an advanced character, offering an equal welcome to each one of the same children, whom a peculiar destination, or an impelling spirit of genius, shall send to its open doors,—especially to the children of the poor. . . .

After the state shall have secured to all its children, that basis of knowledge and morality, which is indispensable to its own security; after it shall have supplied them with the instruments of that individual prosperity, whose aggregate will constitute its own social prosperity; then they may be emancipated from its tutelage, each one to go withersoever his well-instructed mind shall determine.

30

INDIVIDUALISM

The "transcendentalists" were a loose group of New England thinkers, writers, and reformers who came to prominence in the 1830s and 1840s. Transcendentalists shared a faith in the spiritual qualities of nature, in the special mission of young people to throw off the "dead hand" of the past, and in the primacy of the free individual over the stifling community. Opposed to slavery, concerned with women's rights and intellectual freedom, they founded journals, organized "utopian" communities, contributed to reform movements. But their bent was individualistic. They were therefore different from reformers such as Horace Mann or Ely Moore, who preached progress through collective action on behalf of institutions that would bring people together instead of drive them apart—public schools, for example, or labor unions. Transcendentalists, by contrast, wanted to "transcend"—rise above, escape from—institutional or social constraints.

Notable transcendentalists included Henry David Thoreau, who lived alone in a cabin at Walden Pond; Bronson Alcott, the father of novelist Louisa May Alcott; and Margaret Fuller, editor and early feminist. But the movement's leading figure was Ralph Waldo Emerson. Indeed, if Jefferson was the prophet of American democracy and Jackson its hero, Ralph Waldo Emerson might have been its high priest. Emerson, a Harvard graduate who abandoned his Unitarian ministry to become "a lay preacher to the world," reflected all the chief points of the transcendentalist credo. In the woods was "perpetual youth" and the true source of "reason and faith." Man should shrug off the "dry bones of the past," walk with his "own feet," work with his "own hands," speak with his "own mind." Audiences recognized immediately that Emerson was preaching a kind of individual "liberation," a message perfectly in tune with the self-conscious democracy of the young republic and its youthful, pushy middle class. Excerpted below is "Self-Reliance," Emerson's single most popular essay. The essay was enormously influential in its day—it helped make Emerson a star and energized countless thousands—and it has been strikingly, powerfully appealing, especially to young people, ever since.

Born in Boston in 1803 to a long line of New England clergymen, Ralph Waldo Emerson graduated from Harvard, taught for a few years, became a Unitarian minister, then gradually, in part through his reading of English and German philosophers, grew skeptical and gave up his Boston pulpit. In 1834 he moved to Concord, Massachusetts, where he published *Nature* (1834), "The American Scholar" (1837), "The Divinity School Address" (1838), and other important works over the next twenty-five years. He also became one of the country's most sought-after lecturers, acclaimed in both the United States and England. Never an avid personal participant in social reform movements, he spent his final years quietly in Concord, where he died in 1882.

Questions to Consider. Why did Emerson argue that a true man must be a nonconformist? What specific social groups threatened the nonconformist? Which of these groups posed the greatest threat? What sort of listener would be most likely to respond to the statement, "All history resolves itself very easily into the biography of a few stout and earnest persons"? Why did Emerson say that reliance on property showed a lack of self-reliance? What sort of property should people be most ashamed to have? Were Emerson's views of politics and social reform healthy or unhealthy? Emerson was a memorable phrase maker. Can you find phrases in this essay that are familiar?

★━━★━━★

Self-Reliance (1841)

RALPH WALDO EMERSON

Trust thyself: every heart vibrates to that iron string. Accept the place the divine Providence has found for you; the society of your contemporaries, the connexion of events. Great men have always done so and confided themselves childlike to the genius of their age, betraying their perception that the absolutely trustworthy was seated at their heart, working through their hands, predominating in all their being. And we are now men, and must accept in the highest mind the same transcendent destiny; and not minors and invalids in a protected corner, not cowards fleeing before a revolution, but guides, redeemers, and benefactors, obeying the Almighty effort, and advancing on Chaos and the Dark. . . .

The nonchalance of boys who are sure of a dinner, and would disdain as much as a lord to do or say aught to conciliate one, is the healthy attitude of

Ralph Waldo Emerson, *Essays and English Traits* (New York, 1909), 47–64.

human nature. A boy is in the parlour what the pit is in the playhouse; independent, irresponsible, looking out from his corner on such people and facts as pass by, he tries and sentences them on their merits, in the swift summary way of boys, as good, bad, interesting, silly, eloquent, troublesome. He cumbers himself never about consequences, about interests: he gives an independent, genuine verdict. You must court him: he does not court you. But the man is, as it were, clapped into jail by his consciousness. As soon as he has once acted or spoken with eclat, he is a committed person, watched by the sympathy or the hatred of hundreds whose affections must now enter into his account. There is no Lethe for this. Ah, that he could pass again into his neutrality! Who can thus avoid all pledges, and having observed, observe again from the same unaffected, unbiassed, unbribable, unaffrighted innocence, must always be formidable. He would utter opinions on all passing affairs, which being seen to be not private but necessary, would sink like darts into the ear of men, and put them in fear.

These are the voices which we hear in solitude, but they grow faint and inaudible as we enter into the world. Society everywhere is in conspiracy against the manhood of every one of its members. Society is a joint-stock company in which the members agree for the better securing of his bread to each shareholder, to surrender the liberty and culture of the eater. The virtue in most request is conformity. Self-reliance is its aversion. It loves not realities and creators, but names and customs.

Whoso would be a man must be a nonconformist. He who would gather immortal palms must not be hindered by the name of goodness, but must explore if it be goodness. Nothing is at last sacred but the integrity of your own mind. Absolve you to yourself, and you shall have the suffrage of the world. I remember an answer which when quite young I was prompted to make to a valued adviser who was wont to importune me with the dear old doctrines of the church. On my saying, What have I to do with the sacredness of traditions, if I live wholly from within? my friend suggested—"But these impulses may be from below, not from above." I replied, "They do not seem to me to be such; but if I am the Devil's child, I will live then from the Devil." No law can be sacred to me but that of my nature. Good and bad are but names very readily transferable to that or this; the only right is what is after my constitution, the only wrong what is against it. A man is to carry himself in the presence of all opposition as if every thing were titular and ephemeral but he. I am ashamed to think how easily we capitulate to badges and names, to large societies and dead institutions. Every decent and well-spoken individual affects and sways me more than is right. I ought to go upright and vital. . . .

What I must do, is all that concerns me, not what the people think. This rule, equally arduous in actual and in intellectual life, may serve for the whole distinction between greatness and meanness. It is the harder, because you will always find those who think they know what is your duty better than you know it. It is easy in the world to live after the world's opinion; it is easy in solitude to live after our own; but the great man is he who in the midst of the crowd keeps with perfect sweetness the independence of solitude. . . .

But why should you keep your head over your shoulder? Why drag about this corpse of your memory, lest you contradict somewhat you have stated in this or that public place? Suppose you should contradict yourself; what then? It seems to be a rule of wisdom never to rely on your memory alone, scarcely even in acts of pure memory, but to bring the past for judgment into the thousand-eyed present, and live ever in a new day. In your metaphysics you have denied personality to the Deity: yet when the devout motions of the soul come, yield to them heart and life, though they should clothe God with shape and color. Leave your theory as Joseph his coat in the hand of the harlot, and flee.

A foolish consistency is the hobgoblin of little minds, adored by little statesmen and philosophers and divines. With consistency a great soul has simply nothing to do. He may as well concern himself with his shadow on the wall. Speak what you think now in hard words, and to-morrow speak what to-morrow thinks in hard words again, though it contradict every thing you said to-day.—'Ah, so you shall be sure to be misunderstood.'—Is it so bad then to be misunderstood? Pythagoras was misunderstood, and Socrates, and Jesus, and Luther, and Copernicus, and Galileo, and Newton, and every pure and wise spirit that ever took flesh. To be great is to be misunderstood. . . .

I hope in these days we have heard the last of conformity and consistency. Let the words be gazetted and ridiculous henceforward. Instead of the gong for dinner, let us hear a whistle from the Spartan fife. Let us never bow and apologize more. A great man is coming to eat at my house. I do not wish to please him: I wish that he should wish to please me. I will stand here for humanity, and though I would make it kind, I would make it true. Let us affront and reprimand the smooth mediocrity and squalid contentment of the times, and hurl in the face of custom, and trade, and office, the fact which is the upshot of all history, that there is a great responsible Thinker and Actor working wherever a man works; that a true man belongs to no other time or place, but is the centre of things. Where he is, there is nature. He measures you, and all men, and all events. Ordinarily every body in society reminds us of somewhat else or of some other person. Character, reality, reminds you of nothing else; it takes place of the whole creation. The man must be so much that he must make all circumstances indifferent. Every true man is a cause, a country, and an age; requires infinite spaces and numbers and time fully to accomplish his design;—and posterity seem to follow his steps as a train of clients. A man Caesar is born, and for ages after, we have a Roman Empire. Christ is born, and millions of minds so grow and cleave to his genius, that he is confounded with virtue and the possible of man. An institution is the lengthened shadow of one man; as, Monachism, of the Hermit Antony; the Reformation, of Luther; Quakerism, of Fox; Methodism, of Wesley; Abolition,

of Clarkson. Scipio, Milton called "the height of Rome"; and all history resolves itself very easily into the biography of a few stout and earnest persons.

Let a man then know his worth, and keep things under his feet. Let him
not peep or steal, or skulk up and down with the air of a charity-boy, a bas-
tard, or an interloper, in the world which exists for him. But the man in the
street finding no worth in himself which corresponds to the force which built
a tower or sculptured a marble god, feels poor when he looks on these. To
him a palace, a statue, or a costly book have an alien and forbidding air,
much like a gay equipage, and seem to say like that, "Who are you, sir?" Yet
they all are his, suitors for his notice, petitioners to his faculties that they will
come out and take possession. The picture waits for my verdict: it is not to
command me, but I am to settle its claims to praise. That popular fable of the
sot who was picked up dead drunk in the street, carried to the duke's house,
washed and dressed and laid in the duke's bed, and, on his waking, treated
with all obsequious ceremony like the duke, and assured that he had been insane, owes its popularity to the fact, that it symbolizes so well the state of
man, who is in the world a sort of sot, but now and then wakes up, exercises
his reason, and finds himself a true prince. . . .

The relations of the soul to the divine spirit are so pure that it is profane to
seek to interpose helps. It must be that when God speaketh, he should communicate not one thing, but all things; should fill the world with his voice;
should scatter forth light, nature, time, souls, from the centre of the present
thought; and new date and new create the whole. Whenever a mind is simple, and receives a divine wisdom, old things pass away,—means, teachers,
texts, temples fall; it lives now and absorbs past and future into the present
hour. All things are made sacred by relation to it,—one as much as another.
All things are dissolved to their centre by their cause, and in the universal
miracle petty and particular miracles disappear. If, therefore, a man claims to
know and speak of God, and carries you backward to the phraseology of
some old mouldered nation in another country, in another world, believe
him not. Is the acorn better than the oak which is its fulness and completion?
Is the parent better than the child into whom he has cast his ripened being?
Whence then this worship of the past? The centuries are conspirators against
the sanity and authority of the soul. Time and space are but physiological col-
ors which the eye makes, but the soul is light; where it is, is day; where it was,
is night; and history is an impertinence and an injury, if it be anything more
than a cheerful apologue or parable of my being and becoming.

Man is timid and apologetic; he is no longer upright; he dares not say 'I
think,' 'I am,' but quotes some saint or sage. He is ashamed before the blade
of grass or the blowing rose. These roses under my window make no reference to former roses or to better ones; they are for what they are; they exist
with God to-day. There is no time to them. There is simply the rose; it is perfect in every moment of its existence. Before a leaf-bud has burst, its whole
life acts; in the full-blown flower, there is no more; in the leafless root, there
is no less. Its nature is satisfied, and it satisfies nature, in all moments alike.

But man postpones or remembers; he does not live in the present, but with reverted eye laments the past, or, heedless of the riches that surround him, stands on tiptoe to foresee the future. He cannot be happy and strong until he too lives with nature in the present. . . .

. . . The reliance on Property, including the reliance on governments which protect it, is the want of self-reliance. Men have looked away from themselves and at things so long, that they have come to esteem the religious, learned, and civil institutions, as guards of property, and they deprecate assaults on these, because they feel them to be assaults on property. They measure their esteem of each other, by what each has, and not by what each is. But a cultivated man becomes ashamed of his property, out of new respect for his nature. Especially he hates what he has, if he see that it is accidental,—came to him by inheritance, or gift, or crime; then he feels that it is not having; it does not belong to him, has no root in him, and merely lies there, because no revolution or no robber takes it away. But that which a man is, does always by necessity acquire, and what the man acquires is living property, which does not wait the beck of rulers, or mobs, or revolutions, or fire, or storm, or bankruptcies, but perpetually renews itself wherever the man breathes. "Thy lot or portion of life," said the Caliph Ali, "is seeking after thee; therefore be at rest from seeking after it." Our dependence on these foreign goods leads us to our slavish respect for numbers. The political parties meet in numerous conventions; the greater the concourse, and with each new uproar of announcement, The delegation from Essex! The Democrats from New Hampshire! The Whigs of Maine! the young patriot feels himself stronger than before by a new thousand of eyes and arms. In like manner the reformers summon conventions, and vote and resolve in multitude. Not so, O friends! will the God deign to enter and inhabit you, but by a method precisely the reverse. It is only as a man puts off all foreign support, and stands alone, that I see him to be strong and to prevail.

31

Balm for the Afflicted

Dorothea L. Dix, a Boston schoolteacher, was interested in most ante-bellum reforms but especially in the treatment of the mentally ill. One Sunday, in March 1841, she went to the House of Correction in East Cambridge to hold a Sunday school class for the women inmates. She was horrified by the filth, neglect, and misery she discovered among the insane who were kept in the jail.

Dix's experience in East Cambridge turned her into an earnest reformer. She persuaded local authorities to improve conditions in the jail. She also began touring Massachusetts—visiting jails, almshouses, and houses of correction—to gather information about the treatment of the mentally ill. Having gathered a shocking collection of facts, she drew up a tract entitled *Memorial to the Legislature of Massachusetts,* which called for drastic reforms, and had it presented to the Massachusetts legislature in January 1843. The memorial raised a storm; Dix was called a sensationalist, a troublemaker, and a liar. But leading humanitarians supported her and, in the end, the lawmakers appropriated money for enlarging and improving the state hospital for the insane in Worcester.

Dorothea L. Dix, born in Hampden, Maine, in 1802, and brought up by her grandmother in Boston, had never intended to be a reformer. Shy and sickly as a young woman, she taught in a girls' school, wrote children's stories and books on religious subjects, and led a retired life. But she was a friend and disciple of the great Unitarian preacher William Ellery Channing, who believed human nature could be bettered, and she also knew reformers like Samuel Gridley Howe, who ran a school for the blind and agitated for prison reform. There was something natural, then, about her turn to activism after her Sunday morning in East Cambridge in 1841. After the Massachusetts legislature responded affirmatively to her 1843 petition, she was in the field of reform for good. She continued her crusade for better asylums until the end of her life. She went from one state to another, following the procedure she had used in Massachusetts: gathering facts, drawing up petitions, winning public opinion over to the need for reform, and persuading states to do something about it. "I have travelled over more than ten thousand miles in the last three years," she wrote in 1845. "Have visited eighteen state penitentiaries, three hundred county jails and houses of correction, more than five hundred almshouses and other institutions, besides hospitals and houses of refuge."

One of Dix's proudest accomplishments, an act of Congress setting aside federal land in support of asylums, came to naught when President Franklin Pierce, a Democrat, vetoed the measure. Even so, she was responsible for the founding or enlarging of thirty-two mental hospitals in the United States and abroad. Her success owed much, no doubt, to the public's desire to control social deviants. But her own motivations were profoundly humanitarian, a trait that showed itself again when she served as superintendent of nurses for the Union in the Civil War. By the time she died in 1887, in a New Jersey hospital founded by her efforts, she was regarded as one of the most distinguished women in the nation.

Questions to Consider. Notice the method that Dix employed in her *Memorial* to rouse the interest of the Massachusetts legislators and persuade them to take action—that is, reporting in horrendous detail the conditions she had uncovered. Do you think the technique is convincing? Are there any similarities between Dix's method and those of investigative reporters today? For what reasons were the mentally ill badly treated? Why did Dix think the mentally ill should be separated from criminals? To what motives in the legislators did she appeal in her call for action? What did she reveal about her own motivations and outlook?

★▬★▬★

Memorial on Asylums (1843)

DOROTHEA DIX

Gentlemen,—I respectfully ask to present this Memorial, believing that the cause, which actuates to and sanctions so unusual a movement, presents no equivocal claim to public consideration and sympathy. . . .

About two years since leisure afforded opportunity and duty prompted me to visit several prisons and almshouses in the vicinity of this metropolis, I found, near Boston, in the jails and asylums for the poor, a numerous class brought into unsuitable connection with criminals and the general mass of paupers. I refer to idiots and insane persons, dwelling in circumstances not

D. L. Dix, *Memorial to the Legislature of Massachusetts* (Munroe and Francis, Boston, 1843), 3–32.

Dorothea Lynde Dix. Dix invariably dressed in proper Victorian attire, with her lustrous hair in a tight prim bun. The more she traveled and testified on behalf of asylums—daring behavior for an antebellum woman—the more decorous she dressed. During the Civil War, she thought Union army nurses, too, should look proper, in order to ward off soldierly advances and preserve the good reputation of the nursing corps. (Boston Athenaeum)

only adverse to their own physical and moral improvement, but productive of extreme disadvantages to all other persons brought into association with them. I applied myself diligently to trace the causes of these evils, and sought to supply remedies. As one obstacle was surmounted, fresh difficulties appeared. Every new investigation has given depth to the conviction that it is only by decided, prompt, and vigorous legislation the evils to which I refer, and which I shall proceed more fully to illustrate, can be remedied. I shall be obliged to speak with great plainness, and to reveal many things revolting to the taste, and from which my woman's nature shrinks with peculiar sensitiveness. But truth is the highest consideration. *I tell what I have seen*—painful and shocking as the details often are—that from them you may feel more deeply the imperative obligation which lies upon you to prevent the possibility of a repetition or continuance of such outrages upon humanity. . . .

I come to present the strong claims of suffering humanity. I come to place before the Legislature of Massachusetts the condition of the miserable, the desolate, the outcast. I come as the advocate of helpless, forgotten, insane, and idiotic men and women; of beings sunk to a condition from which the most unconcerned would start with real horror; of beings wretched in our prisons, and more wretched in our almshouses. . . .

I must confine myself to few examples, but am ready to furnish other and more complete details, if required.

If my pictures are displeasing, coarse, and severe, my subjects, it must be recollected, offer no tranquil, refined, or composing features. The condition of human beings, reduced to the extremest states of degradation and misery cannot be exhibited in softened language, or adorn a polished page.

I proceed, gentlemen, briefly to call your attention to the *present state of* insane persons confined within this Commonwealth, *in cages, closets, cellars stalls, pens! Chained, naked, beaten with rods,* and *lashed* into obedience. . . .

It is the Commonwealth, not its integral parts, that is accountable for most of the abuses which have lately and do still exist. I repeat it, it is defective legislation which perpetuates and multiplies these abuses. In illustration of my subject, I offer the following extracts from my Note-book and Journal:—

Springfield. In the jail, one lunatic woman, furiously mad, a State pauper, improperly situated, both in regard to the prisoners, the keepers, and herself. It is a case of extreme self-forgetfulness and oblivion to all the decencies of life, to describe which would be to repeat only the grossest scenes. She is much worse since leaving [the asylum of] Worcester. In the almshouse of the same town is a woman apparently only needing judicious care, and some well-chosen employment, to make it unnecessary to confine her in solitude, in a dreary unfurnished room. Her appeals for employment and companionship are most touching, but the mistress replied "she had no time to attend to her." . . .

Lincoln. A woman in a cage. *Medford.* One idiotic subject chained, and in one in a close stall for seventeen years. *Pepperell.* One often doubly chained, hand and foot; another violent; several peaceable now. *Brookfield.* One man caged, comfortable. *Granville.* One often closely confined; now losing the use of his limbs from want of exercise. *Charlemont.* One man caged. *Savoy.* One man caged. *Lenox.* Two in the jail, against whose unfit condition there the jailer protests.

Dedham. The insane disadvantageously placed in the jail. In the almshouse, two females in stalls, situated in the main building; lie in wooden bunks filled with straw; always shut up. One of these subjects is supposed curable. The overseers of the poor have declined giving her a trial at the hospital, as I was informed, on account of expense.

Besides the above, I have seen many who, part of the year, are chained or caged. The use of cages all but universal. Hardly a town but can refer to some not distant period of using them; chains are less common; negligences frequent; wilful abuse less frequent than sufferings proceeding from ignorance, or want of consideration. I encountered during the last three months many poor creatures wandering reckless and unprotected through the country. . . . But I cannot particularize. In traversing the State, I have found hundreds of insane persons in every variety of circumstance and condition, many whose situation could not and need not be improved; a less number, but that very large, whose lives are the saddest pictures of human suffering and degradation.

I give a few illustrations; but description fades before reality.

Danvers. November. Visited the almshouse. A large building, much out of repair. Understand a new one is in contemplation. Here are from fifty-six to sixty inmates, one idiotic, three insane; one of the latter in close confinement at all times.

Long before reaching the house, wild shouts, snatches of rude songs, imprecations and obscene language, fell upon the ear, proceeding from the occupant of a low building, rather remote from the principal building to which my course was directed. Found the mistress, and was conducted to the place which was called "the home" of the *forlorn* maniac, a young woman, exhibiting a condition of neglect and misery blotting out the faintest idea of comfort, and outraging every sentiment of decency. She had been, I learnt, "a respectable person, industrious and worthy. Disappointments and trials shook her mind, and, finally, laid prostrate reason and self-control. She became a maniac for life. She had been at Worcester Hospital for a considerable time, and had been returned as incurable." The mistress told me she understood that, "while there, she was comfortable and decent." Alas, what a change was here exhibited! She had passed from one degree of violence to another, in swift progress. There she stood, clinging to or beating upon the bars of her caged apartment, the contracted size of which afforded space only for increasing accumulations of filth, a *foul* spectacle. There she stood with naked arms and dishevelled hair, the unwashed frame invested with fragments of unclean garments, the air so extremely offensive, though ventilation was afforded on all sides save one, that it was not possible to remain beyond a few moments without retreating for recovery to the outward air. Irritation of body, produced by utter filth and exposure, incited her to the horrid process of tearing off her skin by inches. Her face, neck, and person were thus disfigured to hideousness. To my exclamation of horror, the mistress replied: "Oh, we can't help it. Half the skin is off sometimes. We can do nothing with her; and it makes no difference what she eats, for she consumes her own filth as readily as the food which is brought her."

Men of Massachusetts, I beg, I implore, I demand pity and protection for these of my suffering, outraged sex. Fathers, husbands, brothers, I would supplicate you for this boon; but what do I say? I dishonor you, divest you at once of Christianity and humanity, does this appeal imply distrust. If it comes burdened with a doubt of your righteousness in this legislation, then blot it out; while I declare confidence in your honor, not less than your humanity. Here you will put away the cold, calculating spirit of selfishness and self-seeking; lay off the armor of local strife and political opposition; here and now, for once, forgetful of the earthly and perishable, come up to these halls and consecrate them with one heart and one mind to works of righteousness and just judgment. . . .

Injustice is also done to the *convicts;* it is certainly very wrong that they should be doomed day after day and night to listen to the ravings of madmen and madwomen. This is a kind of punishment that is not recognized by our statutes, and is what the criminal ought not to be called upon to undergo. The confinement of the criminal and of the insane in the same building is subversive of that good order and discipline which should be observed in every well-regulated prison. I do most sincerely hope that more permanent provision will be made for the pauper insane by the State, either to restore Worcester Insane Asylum to what it was originally designed to be or else make some just appropriation for the benefit of this very unfortunate class of our "fellow-beings."

Gentlemen, I commit to you this sacred cause. Your action upon this subject will affect the present and future condition of hundreds and of thousands. In this legislation, as in all things, may you exercise that "wisdom which is the breath of the power of God."

32

WOMEN'S RIGHTS

In the first part of the nineteenth century, women in increasing numbers began asking for equality before the law and asserting their right to be educated, enter the professions, and participate in public affairs along with men. Some women became active in reform, participating in the temperance movement, the fight against slavery, and the crusade for world peace. But even as reformers they were required to take a subordinate position. When a woman tried to speak at a temperance convention in New York she was shouted down. One man yelled, "Shame on the woman, shame on the woman!" And when several women attended the World Anti-Slavery Convention in London in 1840, men refused to seat them as delegates and made them sit in a curtained enclosure out of the public view. Two delegates—Lucretia Mott and Elizabeth Cady Stanton—began talking of holding a convention to battle for their own rights.

In July 1848 the first organized meeting for women's rights ever held met in Seneca Falls, New York, attended by two hundred delegates, including thirty-two men. Stanton drew up the Declaration of Sentiments, using the Declaration of Independence as a model. She also drafted a series of resolutions that were adopted by the convention. Only one of her demands ran into trouble: the right to vote. Woman suffrage still seemed so outlandish that it took the eloquence of Frederick Douglass, a black abolitionist and journalist, to persuade the delegates to adopt it by a small majority. Many people were shocked by the Seneca Falls convention. They denounced the "Reign of Petticoats" and warned against the "Insurrection among Women." But many distinguished Americans—including Ralph Waldo Emerson, John Greenleaf Whittier, and William Lloyd Garrison—supported the movement.

Elizabeth Cady Stanton, who drafted the Seneca Falls Declaration, was born in Johnstown, New York, in 1815. She attended Emma Willard's seminary in Troy, and while studying law with her father, became aware of the injustices suffered by women from American legal practices. When she married the abolitionist lawyer Henry B. Stanton in 1840, she insisted that the word *obey* be omitted from the ceremony. At an antislavery convention that she attended with her husband the same year, she got to know Lucretia Mott, and the two of them began working together for women's rights. Following the Seneca Falls Conference, Stanton joined Mott (and later Susan B. Anthony) in sponsoring conventions, writing articles, delivering lectures, and appearing before legislative bodies on behalf of the cause. Despite Stanton's grace and charm, she was considered a dangerous radical for espousing woman suffrage and easier divorce laws for women. During the Civil War she helped organize the Women's Loyal National League and urged emancipation. After the war she resumed her work for woman suffrage, became president of the National Woman Suffrage Association, lectured on family life, wrote for *Revolution,* a women's rights weekly, and contributed to the three-volume *History of Woman Suffrage,* published in the 1880s. One of the most distinguished feminist leaders in the country, she died in New York City in 1902.

Questions to Consider. Many years passed before the women's rights movement in America began achieving some of its objectives. But the Seneca Falls convention marks the formal beginning of the organized movement to advance women's position, so it merits careful study. Do you think there were any advantages in using the Declaration of Independence as a model for the Declaration of Sentiments? Does the Seneca Falls Declaration emphasize legal, economic, or political rights? Were any rights overlooked? Some of those who signed the declaration withdrew their names when the suffrage resolution met with ridicule. Why do you suppose this happened? How radical do the Seneca Falls demands seem today? Which demands have been met by legislation since 1848?

The Seneca Falls Declaration of 1848

ELIZABETH CADY STANTON

When, in the course of human events, it becomes necessary for one portion of the family of man to assume among the people of the earth a position different from that which they have hitherto occupied, but one to which the laws of nature and of nature's God entitle them, a decent respect to the opinions of

Susan B. Anthony, Elizabeth Cady Stanton, and Matilda Joslyn Gage, eds., *History of Woman Suffrage* (3 v., Susan B. Anthony, Elizabeth Cady Stanton, and Matilda Joslyn Gage, Rochester, N.Y., 1889), I: 75–80.

Elizabeth Cady Stanton with two of her children about the time of the Seneca Falls Convention of 1848. (Elizabeth Cady Stanton Trust)

mankind requires that they should declare the causes that impel them to such a course.

We hold these truths to be self-evident: that all men and women are created equal; that they are endowed by their Creator with certain inalienable rights; that among these are life, liberty, and the pursuit of happiness; that to secure these rights governments are instituted, deriving their just powers from the consent of the governed. . . . But when a long train of abuses and usurpations, pursuing invariably the same object evinces a design to reduce them under absolute despotism, it is their duty to throw off such government, and to provide new guards for their future security. Such has been the patient sufferance of the women under this government, and such is now the necessity which constrains them to demand the equal station to which they are entitled.

The history of mankind is a history of repeated injuries and usurpations on the part of man toward woman, having in direct object the establishment of an absolute tyranny over her. To prove this, let facts be submitted to a candid world.

He has never permitted her to exercise her inalienable right to the elective franchise.

He has compelled her to submit to laws, in the formation of which she had no voice.

He has withheld from her rights which are given to the most ignorant and degraded men—both natives and foreigners.

Having deprived her of this first right of a citizen, the elective franchise, thereby leaving her without representation in the halls of legislation, he has opposed her on all sides.

He has made her, if married, in the eye of the law, civilly dead.

He has taken from her all right in property, even to the wages she earns.

He has made her, morally, an irresponsible being, as she can commit many crimes with impunity, provided they be done in the presence of her husband. In the covenant of marriage, she is compelled to promise obedience to her husband, he becoming, to all intents and purposes, her master—the law giving him power to deprive her of her liberty, and to administer chastisement.

He has so framed the laws of divorce, as to what shall be the proper causes, and in case of separation, to whom the guardianship of the children shall be given, as to be wholly regardless of the happiness of women—the law, in all cases, going upon a false supposition of the supremacy of man, and giving all power into his hands.

After depriving her of all rights as a married woman, if single, and the owner of property, he has taxed her to support a government which recognizes her only when her property can be made profitable to it.

He has monopolized nearly all the profitable employments, and from those she is permitted to follow, she receives but a scanty remuneration. He closes against her all the avenues to wealth and distinction which he considers most honorable to himself. As a teacher of theology, medicine, or law, she is not known.

He has denied her the facilities for obtaining a thorough education, all colleges being closed against her.

He allows her in Church, as well as State, but a subordinate position, claiming Apostolic authority for her exclusion from the ministry, and, with some exceptions, from any public participation in the affairs of the Church.

He has created a false public sentiment by giving to the world a different code of morals for men and women, by which moral delinquencies which exclude women from society, are not only tolerated, but deemed of little account in man.

He has usurped the prerogative of Jehovah himself, claiming it as his right to assign for her a sphere of action, when that belongs to her conscience and to her God.

He has endeavored, in every way that he could, to destroy her confidence in her own powers, to lessen her self-respect, and to make her willing to lead a dependent and abject life.

Now, in view of this entire disfranchisement of one-half the people of this country, their social and religious degradation—in view of the unjust laws above mentioned, and because women do not feel themselves aggrieved, oppressed, and fraudulently deprived of their most sacred rights, we insist that they have immediate admission to all the rights and privileges which belong to them as citizens of the United States.

In entering upon the great work before us, we anticipate no small amount of misconception, misrepresentation, and ridicule; but we shall use every instrumentality within our power to effect our object. We shall employ agents, circulate tracts, petition the State and National legislatures, and endeavor to enlist the pulpit and the press in our behalf. We hope this Convention will be followed by a series of Conventions embracing every part of the country.

Resolutions

WHEREAS, The great precept of nature is conceded to be, that "man shall pursue his own true and substantial happiness." Blackstone in his Commentaries remarks, that this law of Nature being coequal with mankind, and dictated by God himself, is of course superior in obligation to any other. It is binding over all the globe, in all countries and at all times; no human laws are of any validity if contrary to this, . . . therefore,

Resolved, That such laws as conflict, in any way, with the true and substantial happiness of woman, are contrary to the great precept of nature and of no validity, for this is "superior in obligation to any other."

Resolved, That all laws which prevent woman from occupying such a station in society as her conscience shall dictate, or which place her in a position inferior to that of man, are contrary to the great precept of nature, and therefore of no force or authority.

Resolved, That woman is man's equal—was intended to be so by the Creator, and the highest good of the race demands that she should be recognized as such.

Resolved, That the women of this country ought to be enlightened in regard to the laws under which they live, that they may no longer publish their degradation by declaring themselves satisfied with their present position, nor their ignorance, by asserting that they have all the rights they want.

Resolved, That inasmuch as man, while claiming for himself intellectual superiority, does accord to woman moral superiority, it is pre-eminently his duty to encourage her to speak and teach, as she has an opportunity, in all religious assemblies.

Resolved, That the same amount of virtue, delicacy, and refinement of behavior that is required of woman in the social state, should also be required of man, and the same transgressions should be visited with equal severity on both man and woman.

Resolved, That the objection of indelicacy and impropriety, which is so often brought against woman when she addresses a public audience, comes with a very ill-grace from those who encourage, by their attendance, her appearance on the stage, in the concert, or in feats of the circus.

Resolved, That woman has too long rested satisfied in the circumscribed limits which corrupt customs and a perverted application of the Scriptures have marked out for her, and that it is time she should move in the enlarged sphere which her great Creator has assigned her.

Resolved, That it is the duty of the women of this country to secure to themselves their sacred right to the elective franchise.

Resolved, That the equality of human rights results necessarily from the fact of the identity of the race in capabilities and responsibilities.

Resolved, therefore, That, being invested by the Creator with the same capabilities, and the same consciousness of responsibility for their exercise, it is demonstrably the right and duty of woman, equally with man, to promote every righteous cause by every righteous means; and especially in regard to the great subjects of morals and religion, it is self-evidently her right to participate with her brother in teaching them, both in private and in public, by writing and by speaking, by any instrumentalities proper to be used, and in any assemblies proper to be held; and this being a self-evident truth growing out of the divinely implanted principles of human nature, any custom or authority adverse to it, whether modern or wearing the hoary sanction of antiquity, is to be regarded as a self-evident falsehood, and at war with mankind.

33

THE ANTISLAVERY IMPULSE

At a time when the male-dominant mainstream culture of the United States was intolerant of women who commented on political issues, many women wrote and spoke out against slavery. No woman was more important in this struggle than Harriet Beecher Stowe, whose novel *Uncle Tom's Cabin* made the nation feel "what an accursed thing slavery is." Some readers believed the novel moved the nation closer to civil war—a view apparently shared by Abraham Lincoln, who remarked on meeting Stowe, "So this is the little lady who made this big war."

Uncle Tom's Cabin may not have "caused" the Civil War. But by 1852, when the book was published, the nation was enveloped in an atmosphere of sectional suspicion and hatred. The Compromise of 1850, an effort to cobble North and South together, was unraveling because Northerners resisted the Fugitive Slave Law. In 1854 bitter fighting between proslavery and antislavery forces broke out in "Bleeding Kansas." In 1856 Preston Brooks, a representative from South Carolina, brutally beat Charles Sumner, an antislavery senator from Massachusetts, as he sat at his desk in the Senate chamber. For Northerners, the episode was a symbol of Southern bestiality. For Southerners, Brooks was a hero.

As these events inflamed sectional feelings, *Uncle Tom's Cabin* engaged readers to an extraordinary degree. It was so sensational and moving a tale about life under slavery that it became a testament of Northern abolitionists and compelled readers who had never given slavery much thought to feel responsible for its horrors. In the South, which instantly denounced the novel, it was actually dangerous to possess a copy. Sales were so great that Stowe's Boston publisher could not find enough paper to meet the demand. Thousands of Americans attended stage versions. No other novel in history has matched the influence of *Uncle Tom's Cabin*, which brought the author international acclaim and made her a much sought-after lecturer.

In the excerpt below, Stowe shows us two of the most famous figures in all of American literature: "Uncle" Tom, whose Kentucky master has sold him "down the river" to New Orleans for financial reasons;

and Simon Legree, owner of a cotton plantation in the frontier regions of interior Louisiana, who has just bought Tom. In characters and scenes such as these, Stowe could depict plantation slavery in the raw, enabling her to explore, among other things, the nature of slave labor, slave living conditions, slave culture, plantation discipline and control, and the significance of religion to both masters and slaves.

Harriet Beecher Stowe was born in Connecticut in 1811. The daughter of Lyman Beecher, a famous Calvinist minister, she went to Cincinnati in 1832 with her father, who became president of Lane Theological Seminary. She married a Lane professor in 1836, started to write magazine stories, and after moving to Maine in 1850, where her husband taught and preached, began work on a novel, *Uncle Tom's Cabin.* The novel was based on what she learned of the South while living in Ohio, just across the river from the slave plantations of Kentucky, and from her brother who had worked in New Orleans. She continued to write for the next twenty years, producing a steady stream of novels, stories, and articles about slavery and life in old New England. She died in Hartford in 1896.

Questions to Consider. What is Simon Legree's purpose in treating Tom the way he does at the beginning of the excerpt? How does Legree view the economics of slaveholding? What are the multiple purposes, in the novel, of slave singing? How does Legree use his two black labor bosses, Sambo and Quimbo, to control both the plantation and each other? Why does Stowe include the section on picking cotton? What effect does the final scene have on you? Other slaves in the novel escape northward to freedom. Why doesn't Tom?

★━━★━━★

Uncle Tom's Cabin (1852)

HARRIET BEECHER STOWE

On the lower part of a small, mean boat, on the Red River, Tom sat,—chains on his wrists, chains on his feet, and a weight heavier than chains lay on his heart. All had faded from his sky,—moon and star; all had passed by him, as the trees and banks were now passing, to return no more. . . .

Mr. Simon Legree, Tom's master, had purchased slaves at one place and another, in New Orleans, to the number of eight, and driven them, handcuffed, in couples of two and two, down to the good steamer Pirate, which lay at the levee, ready for a trip up the Red River.

Harriet Beecher Stowe, *Uncle Tom's Cabin* (New York, 1852), 360–383.

Having got them fairly on board, and the boat being off, he came round, with that air of efficiency which ever characterized him, to take a review of them. Stopping opposite to Tom, who had been attired for sale in his best broadcloth suit, with well-starched linen and shining boots, he briefly expressed himself as follows:—

"Stand up."

Tom stood up.

"Take off that stock!" and, as Tom, encumbered by his fetters, proceeded to do it, he assisted him, by pulling it, with no gentle hand, from his neck, and putting it in his pocket.

Legree now turned to Tom's trunk, which, previous to this, he had been ransacking, and, taking from it a pair of old pantaloons and a dilapidated coat, which Tom had been wont to put on about his stable-work, he said, liberating Tom's hands from the handcuffs, and pointing to a recess in among the boxes,—

"You go there, and put these on."

Tom obeyed, and in a few moments returned.

"Take off your boots," said Mr. Legree.

Tom did so.

"There," said the former, throwing him a pair of coarse, stout shoes, such as were common among the slaves, "put these on."

In Tom's hurried exchange, he had not forgotten to transfer his cherished Bible to his pocket. It was well he did so; for Mr. Legree, having refitted Tom's handcuffs, proceeded deliberately to investigate the contents of his pockets. He drew out a silk handkerchief, and put it into his own pocket. Several little trifles, which Tom had treasured, chiefiy because they had amused Eva, he looked upon with a contemptuous grunt, and tossed them over his shoulder into the river.

Tom's Methodist hymn-book, which, in his hurry, he had forgotten, he now held up and turned over.

"Humph! pious, to be sure. So, what 's yer name,—you belong to the church, eh?"

"Yes, Mas'r," said Tom, firmly.

"Well, I 'll soon have *that* out of you. I have none o' yer bawling, praying, singing niggers on my place; so remember. Now, mind yourself," he said, with a stamp and a fierce glance of his gray eye, directed at Tom, "*I'm* your church now! You understand,—you 've got to be as I say."

Something within the silent black man answered *No!* and, as if repeated by an invisible voice, came the words of an old prophetic scroll, as Eva had often read them to him,—"Fear not! for I have redeemed thee. I have called thee by my name. Thou art MINE!"

But Simon Legree heard no voice. That voice is one he never shall hear. He only glared for a moment on the downcast face of Tom, and walked off. He took Tom's trunk, which contained a very neat and abundant wardrobe, to the forecastle, where it was soon surrounded by various hands of the boat.

With much laughing, at the expense of niggers who tried to be gentlemen, the articles very readily were sold to one and another, and the empty trunk finally put up at auction. It was a good joke, they all thought, especially to see how Tom looked after his things, as they were going this way and that; and then the auction of the trunk, that was funnier than all, and occasioned abundant witticisms.

This little affair being over, Simon sauntered up again to his property.

"Now, Tom, I've relieved you of any extra baggage, you see. Take mighty good care of them clothes. It'll be long enough 'fore you get more. I go in for making niggers careful; one suit has to do for one year, on my place." . . .

"Now," said he, doubling his great, heavy fist into something resembling a blacksmith's hammer, "d' ye see this fist? Heft it!" he said, bringing it down on Tom's hand. "Look at these yer bones! Well, I tell ye this yer fist has got as hard as iron *knocking down niggers.* I never see the nigger, yet, I could n't bring down with one crack," said he, bringing his fist down so near to the face of Tom that he winked and drew back. "I don't keep none o' yer cussed overseers; I does my own overseeing; and I tell you things *is* seen to. You's every one on ye got to toe the mark, I tell ye; quick,—straight,—the moment I speak. That's the way to keep in with me. Ye won't find no soft spot in me, nowhere. So, now, mind yerselves; for I don't show no mercy!"

The women involuntarily drew in their breath, and the whole gang sat with downcast, dejected faces. Meanwhile, Simon turned on his heel, and marched up to the bar of the boat for a dram.

"That's the way I begin with my niggers," he said, to a gentlemanly man, who had stood by him during his speech. "It's my system to begin strong,—just let 'em know what to expect." . . .

"You have a fine lot there."

"Real," said Simon. "There's that Tom, they told me he was suthin uncommon. I paid a little high for him, 'tendin' him for a driver and a managing chap; only get the notions out that he's larnt by being treated as niggers never ought to be, he'll do prime! The yellow woman I got took in in. I rayther think she's sickly, but I shall put her through for what she's worth; she may last a year or two. I don't go for savin' niggers. Use up, and buy more, 's my way,—makes you less trouble, and I'm quite sure it comes cheaper in the end;" and Simon sipped his glass.

"And how long do they generally last?" said the stranger.

"Well, donno; 'cordin' as their constitution is. Stout fellers last six or seven years; trashy ones gets worked up in two or three. I used to, when I fust begun, have considerable trouble fussin' with 'em, and trying to make 'em hold out,—doctorin' on 'em up when they's sick, and givin' on 'em clothes and blankets, and what not, tryin' to keep 'em all sort o' decent and comfortable. Law, 't was n't no sort o' use; I lost money on 'em, and 't was heaps o' trouble. Now, you see, I just put 'em straight through, sick or well. When one nigger's dead, I buy another; and I find it comes cheaper and easier, every way." . . .

The boat moved on,—freighted with its weight of sorrow,—up the red, muddy, turbid current, through the abrupt, tortuous windings of the Red River; and sad eyes gazed wearily on the steep red-clay banks, as they glided by in dreary sameness. At last the boat stopped at a small town, and Legree, with his party, disembarked.

. . . [Now on the road,] the whole company were seeking Legree's plantation, which lay a good distance off. . . .

Simon [astride his big horse] rode on, . . . apparently well pleased, occasionally pulling away at a flask of spirit, which he kept in his pocket.

"I say, *you!*" he said, as he turned back and caught a glance at the dispirited faces behind him. "Strike up a song, boys,—come!"

The men looked at each other, and the *"come"* was repeated, with a smart crack of the whip which the driver carried in his hands. Tom began a Methodist hymn,—

> "Jerusalem, my happy home,
>   Name ever dear to me!
> When shall my sorrows have an end,
> Thy joys when shall"—

"Shut up, you black cuss!" roared Legree; "did ye think I wanted any o' yer infernal old Methodism? I say, tune up, now, something real rowdy,— quick!"

One of the other men struck up one of those unmeaning songs, common among the slaves.

> "Mas'r see'd me cotch a coon,
>   High boys, high!
> He laughed to split,—d' ye see the moon,
>   Ho! ho! ho! boys, ho!
> Ho! yo! hi—e! oh!"

The singer appeared to make up the song to his own pleasure, generally hitting on rhyme, without much attempt at reason; and all the party took up the chorus, at intervals,—

> "Ho! ho! ho! boys, ho!
> High—e—oh! high—e—oh!"

It was sung very boisterously, and with a forced attempt at merriment; but no wail of despair, no words of impassioned prayer, could have had such a depth of woe in them as the wild notes of the chorus. As if the poor, dumb heart, threatened,—prisoned,—took refuge in that inarticulate sanctuary of music, and found there a language in which to breathe its prayer to God! There was a prayer in it, which Simon could not hear. He only heard the boys singing noisily, and well pleased; he was making them "keep up their spirits." . . .

"Ye see what ye 'd get!" said Legree, caressing the dogs with grim satisfaction, and turning to Tom and his companions. "Ye see what ye 'd get, if ye
try to run off. These yer dogs has been raised to track niggers; and they 'd jest
as soon chaw one on ye up as to eat their supper. So, mind yerself! How now,
Sambo!" he said, to a ragged fellow, without any brim to his hat, who was of-
ficious in his attentions. "How have things been going?"

"Fust-rate, Mas'r."

"Quimbo," said Legree to another, who was making zealous demonstra-
tions to attract his attention, "ye minded what I telled ye?"

"Guess I did, did n't I?"

These two colored men were the two principal hands on the plantation.
Legree had trained them in savageness and brutality as systematically as he
had his bull-dogs; and, by long practice in hardness and cruelty, brought
their whole nature to about the same range of capacities. It is a common remark, and one that is thought to militate strongly against the character of the
race, that the Negro overseer is always more tyrannical and cruel than the
white one. This is simply saying that the Negro mind has been more crushed
and debased than the white. It is no more true of this race than of every oppressed race, the world over. The slave is always a tyrant, if he can get a
chance to be one.

Legree, like some potentates we read of in history, governed his plantation
by a sort of resolution of forces. Sambo and Quimbo cordially hated each
other; the plantation hands, one and all, cordially hated them; and by play-
ing off one against another, he was pretty sure, through one or the other of
the three parties, to get informed of whatever was on foot in the place.

Nobody can live entirely without social intercourse; and Legree encouraged his two black satellites to a kind of coarse familiarity with him,—a familiarity, however, at any moment liable to get one or the other of them into
trouble; for, on the slightest provocation, one of them always stood ready, at
a nod, to be a minister of his vengeance on the other. . . .

It was late in the evening when the weary occupants of the shanties came
flocking home,—men and women, in soiled and tattered garments, surly and
uncomfortable, and in no mood to look pleasantly on new-comers. The small
village was alive with no inviting sounds; hoarse, gutteral voices contending
at the handmills where their morsel of hard corn was yet to be ground into
meal, to fit it for the cake that was to constitute their only supper. From the
earliest dawn of the day, they had been in the fields, pressed to work under
the driving lash of the overseers; for it was now in the very heat and hurry of
the season, and no means was left untried to press every one up to the top of
their capabilities. "True," says the negligent lounger; "picking cotton is n't
hard work," Is n't it? And it is n't much inconvenience, either, to have one
drop of water fall on your head; yet the worst torture of the inquisition is produced by drop after drop, drop after drop, falling moment after moment,
with monotonous succession, on the same spot; and work, in itself not hard,
becomes so, by being pressed, hour after hour, with unvarying, unrelenting

sameness, with not even the consciousness of free-will to take from its te-
diousness. Tom looked in vain among the gang, as they poured along, for
companionable faces. He saw only sullen, scowling, imbruted men, and feeble, discouraged women, or women that were not women,—the strong push-
ing away the weak,—the gross, unrestricted animal selfishness of human
beings, of whom nothing good was expected and desired; and who, treated
in every way like brutes, had sunk as nearly to their level as it was possible
for human beings to do. To a late hour in the night the sound of the grinding
was protracted; for the mills were few in number compared with the
grinders, and the weary and feeble ones were driven back by the strong, and
came on last in their turn. . . .

Slowly the weary, dispirited creatures wound their way into the room,
and, with crouching reluctance, presented their baskets to be weighed.

Legree noted on a slate, on the side of which was pasted a list of names,
the amount.

Tom's basket was weighed and approved; and he looked, with an anxious
glance, for the success of the woman he had befriended.

Tottering with weakness, she came forward, and delivered her basket. It
was of full weight, as Legree well perceived; but, affecting anger, he said,—

"What, you lazy beast! short again! stand aside, you 'll catch it, pretty soon!"

The woman gave a groan of utter despair, and sat down on a board. . . .

"And now," said Legree, "come here, you Tom. You see, I told ye I did n't
buy ye jest for the common work; I mean to promote ye, and make a driver
of ye; and to-night ye may jest as well begin to get yer hand in. Now, ye jest
take this yer gal and flog her; ye 've seen enough on 't to know how."

"I beg Mas'r's pardon," said Tom; "hopes Mas'r won't set me at that. It 's
what I an't used to,—never did,—and can't do, no way possible."

"Ye 'll larn a pretty smart chance of things ye never did know, before I 've
done with ye!" said Legree, taking up a cowhide, and striking Tom a heavy
blow across the cheek, and following up the infliction by a shower of blows.

"There!" he said, as he stopped to rest; "now will ye tell me ye can't do it?"

"Yes, Mas'r," said Tom, putting up his hand, to wipe the blood that trick-
led down his face. "I 'm willin' to work night and day, and work while there
's life and breath in me; but this yer thing I can't feel it right to do; and, Mas'r,
I *never* shall do it,—*never!*"

Tom had a remarkably smooth, soft voice, and a habitually respectful
manner, that had given Legree an idea that he would be cowardly, and easily
subdued. When he spoke these last words, a thrill of amazement went
through every one; the poor woman clasped her hands, and said, "O Lord!"
and every one involuntarily looked at each other, and drew in their breath, as
if to prepare for the storm that was about to burst.

Legree looked stupefied and confounded; but at last burst forth,—

"What! ye blasted black beast! tell *me* ye don't think it *right* to do what I tell
ye! What have any of you cussed cattle to do with thinking what 's right? I 'll
put a stop to it! Why, what do ye think ye are? May be ye think ye 're a gen-

tleman, master Tom, to be a telling your master what 's right, and what an't! So you pretend it 's wrong to flog the gal!"

"I think so, Mas'r," said Tom; "the poor crittur 's sick and feeble; 't would be downright cruel, and it 's what I never will do, nor begin to. Mas'r, if you mean to kill me, kill me; but, as to my raising my hand agin any one here, I never shall,—I 'll die first!"

Tom spoke in a mild voice, but with a decision that could not be mistaken. Legree shook with anger; his greenish eyes glared fiercely, and his very whiskers seemed to curl with passion; but, like some ferocious beast, that plays with its victim before he devours it, he kept back his strong impulse to proceed to immediate violence, and broke out into bitter raillery.

"Well, here 's a pious dog, at last, let down among us sinners!—a saint, a gentleman, and no less, to talk to us sinners about our sins! Powerful holy crittur, he must be! Here, you rascal, you make believe to be so pious,—did n't you never hear, out of yer Bible, 'Servants, obey yer masters'? An't I yer master? Did n't I pay down twelve hundred dollars, cash, for all there is inside yer old cussed black shell? An't yer mine, now, body and soul?" he said, giving Tom a violent kick with his heavy boot; "tell me!"

In the very depth of physical suffering, bowed by brutal oppression, this question shot a gleam of joy and triumph through Tom's soul. He suddenly stretched himself up, and, looking earnestly to heaven, while the tears and blood that flowed down his face mingled, he exclaimed,—

"No! no! no! my soul an't yours, Mas'r! You have n't bought it,—ye can't buy it! It 's been bought and paid for, by one that is able to keep it;—no matter, no matter, you can't harm me!"

"I can't!" said Legree, with a sneer; "we 'll see,—we 'll see! Here, Sambo, Quimbo, give this dog such a breakin' in as he won't get over, this month!"

34

PATRIOTISM AND SLAVERY

No reform movement was more sophisticated than the antislavery crusade in spreading its message, and it soon became clear to abolitionists that Southerners, both white and black, would be particularly effective messengers. After all, they knew the slave system firsthand, and had crossed the line to oppose it. This kind of firsthand testimony was difficult to refute.

The Grimké sisters, Sarah and Angelina, are good examples. Born into a wealthy South Carolina slaveholding family, they grew to abhor the slave system and eventually moved to Philadelphia, where they became Quakers, wrote pamphlets, organized private meetings, and eventually spoke publicly to large mixed crowds about their own experiences with slavery. When conservatives denounced them on the grounds that women should not speak in public, they became activists on behalf of women's rights as well. Similarly, James G. Birney was an Alabama slaveholder who freed his own slaves, moved to Ohio to write and speak against slavery, and in 1840 was nominated for president by the Liberty Party, the country's first antislavery political organization.

Even more important to the cause were former slaves. Several thousand slaves escaped from the South in the decades before the Civil War, living and working in the free states or Canada, despite the constant threat of being captured and returned to their owners under the provisions of the U.S. Constitution and the Fugitive Slave Law. Dozens published the story of their lives in bondage and how they escaped. Together the stories formed a "fugitive slave narrative" literature that became crucial to both the abolitionist cause and historians struggling to understand the institution of slavery.

The Narrative of the Life of Frederick Douglass (1845), one of the great classics of the fugitive literature, provided vivid details about plantation life and culture and recounted how the Maryland-born Douglass escaped in 1838 at age twenty-one and became an agent and lecturer for the American Anti-Slavery Society. After lecturing in Great Britain to earn money to try to buy his freedom and thus avoid the chronic threat of being recaptured by slave catchers, Douglass moved to Rochester, New York, a center of antislavery sentiment, where he published a weekly paper and continued to lecture.

The "Fourth of July" speech excerpted below (actually delivered on July 5) was one of Douglass's finest efforts, but all of his public appearances attracted great attention. An admirer recalled immense audiences that "laughed and wept by turns, completely carried away by the wondrous gifts of his pathos and humor." Another remembered his "flashing eye" and the "depth and sonorousness" of his voice. He was "such an ideal of an orator as the listeners never forgot." Douglass published an updated version of his autobiography in 1855 (and newer ones in 1885 and 1892). When the Civil War broke out he helped raise two African American regiments for the Union. He served as marshal of the District of Columbia and consul general to Haiti before his death in Washington in 1895.

Questions to Consider. Douglass, unlike most abolitionists, did not appeal to religious sentiment in this address. What was his chief appeal? What were his ultimate goals in making the speech? Why did he sound ironic, even sarcastic? Was he trying to make his listeners ashamed? Would the speech have been more effective if it had not sounded so angry? Do you find Douglass's response to this criticism valid and persuasive? Why did he say that the Declaration of Independence was "the ring-bolt" to the chain of national destiny and praise the Revolutionary generation for overcoming "prudence" and "timidity"? Were his bitter criticisms of the United States in 1852 fair? What did he expect people to do?

★━━★━━★

Slavery and the Fourth of July (1852)

FREDERICK DOUGLASS

This . . . is the Fourth of July. It is the birthday of your National Independence, and of your political freedom. This, to you, is what the Passover was to the emancipated people of God. It carries your minds back to the day, and to the act of your great deliverance; and to the signs, and to the wonders, associated with that act, and that day. This celebration also marks the beginning of another year of your national life; and reminds you that the Republic

Frederick Douglass, *What to a Slave is the Fourth of July?* (Rochester, N.Y., 1852).

of America is now 76 years old. I am glad, fellow-citizens, that your nation is so young. Seventy-six years, though a good old age for a man, is but a mere speck in the life of a nation. Three score years and ten is the allotted time for individual men; but nations number their years by thousands. According to this fact, you are, even now, only in the beginning of your national career, still lingering in the period of childhood. I repeat, I am glad this is so. There is hope in the thought, and hope is much needed, under the dark clouds which lower above the horizon. The eye of the reformer is met with angry flashes, portending disastrous times; but his heart may well beat lighter at the thought that America is young, and that she is still in the impressible stage of her existence. . . .

Your fathers, who had not adopted the fashionable idea of this day, of the infallibility of government, and the absolute character of its acts, presumed to differ from the home government in respect to the wisdom and the justice of some of those burdens and restraints. They went so far in their excitement as to pronounce the measures of government unjust, unreasonable, and oppressive, and altogether such as ought not to be quietly submitted to. I scarcely need say, fellow-citizens, that my opinion of those measures fully accords with that of your fathers. . . .

Feeling themselves harshly and unjustly treated by the home goverment, your fathers, like men of honesty, and men of spirit, earnestly sought redress. They petitioned and remonstrated; they did so in a decorous, respectful, and loyal manner. Their conduct was wholly unexceptionable. This, however, did not answer the purpose. They saw themselves treated with sovereign indifference, coldness and scorn. Yet they persevered. They were not the men to look back. . . .

Oppression makes a wise man mad. Your fathers were wise men, and if they did not go mad, they became restive under this treatment. They felt themselves the victims of grievous wrongs, wholly incurable in their colonial capacity. With brave men there is always a remedy for oppression. Just here, the idea of a total separation of the colonies from the crown was born! It was a startling idea, much more so, than we, at this distance of time, regard it. The timid and the prudent (as has been intimated) of that day, were, of course, shocked and alarmed by it. . . .

The Declaration of Independence is the ring-bolt to the chain of your nation's destiny; so indeed, I regard it. The principles contained in that instrument are saving principles. Stand by those principles, be true to them on all occasions, in all places, against all foes, and at whatever cost.

From the round top of your ship of state, dark and threatening clouds may be seen. Heavy billows, like mountains in the distance, disclose to the leeward huge forms of flinty rocks! That bolt drawn, that chain broken, and all is lost. Cling to this day—cling to it, and to its principles, with the grasp of a storm-tossed mariner to a spar at midnight. . . .

Fellow-citizens, I am not wanting in respect for the fathers of this republic.

The signers of the Declaration of Independence were brave men. They were great men too—great enough to give fame to a great age. . . .

My business, if I have any here to-day, is with the present. The accepted time with God and his cause is the ever-living now. We have to do with the past only as we can make it useful to the present and to the future.

. . . Now is the time, the important time. Your fathers have lived, died, and have done their work, and have done much of it well. You live and must die, and you must do your work. You have no right to enjoy a child's share in the labor of your fathers, unless your children are to be blest by your labors. You have no right to wear out and waste the hard-earned fame of your fathers to cover your indolence. . . .

Fellow-citizens, pardon me, allow me to ask, why am I called upon to speak here to-day? What have I, or those I represent, to do with your national independence? Are the great principles of political freedom and of natural justice, embodied in that Declaration of Independence, extended to us?

. . . I am not included within the pale of this glorious anniversary! Your high independence only reveals the immeasurable distance between us. The blessings in which you, this day, rejoice, are not enjoyed in common. The rich inheritance of justice, liberty, prosperity and independence, bequeathed by your fathers, is shared by you, not by me. The sunlight that brought life and healing to you, has brought stripes and death to me. This Fourth of July is *yours*, not *mine*. *You* may rejoice, *I* must mourn. To drag a man in fetters into the grand illuminated temple of liberty, and call upon him to join you in joyous anthems, were inhuman mockery and sacrilegious irony. Do you mean, citizens, to mock me, by asking me to speak to-day? . . .

Fellow-citizens; above your national, tumultuous joy, I hear the mournful wail of millions! Whose chains, heavy and grievous yesterday, are, to-day, rendered more intolerable by the jubilant shouts that reach them. If I do forget, if I do not faithfully remember those bleeding children of sorrow this day, "may my right hand forget her cunning, and may my tongue cleave to the roof of my mouth!" To forget them, to pass lightly over their wrongs, and to chime in with the popular theme, would be treason most scandalous and shocking, and would make me a reproach before God and the world.

My subject, then fellow-citizens, is AMERICAN SLAVERY. I shall see, this day, and its popular characteristics, from the slave's point of view. Standing, there, identified with the American bondman, making his wrongs mine, I do not hesitate to declare, with all my soul, that the character and conduct of this nation never looked blacker to me than on this Fourth of July! Whether we turn to the declarations of the past, or to the professions of the present, the conduct of the nation seems equally hideous and revolting. America is false to the past, false to the present, and solemnly binds herself to be false to the future. Standing with God and the crushed and bleeding slave on this occasion, I will, in the name of humanity which is outraged, in the name of liberty which is fettered, in the name of the constitution and the Bible, which are disregarded and trampled upon, dare to call in question and to denounce, with all the emphasis I can command, everything that serves to perpetuate slavery—the great sin and shame of America! . . .

. . . Must I undertake to prove that the slave is a man? That point is conceded already. Nobody doubts it. The slaveholders themselves acknowledge it in the enactment of laws for their government. They acknowledge it when they punish disobedience on the part of the slave. There are seventy-two crimes in the State of Virginia, which, if committed by a black man, (no matter how ignorant he be), subject him to the punishment of death; while only two of the same crimes will subject a white man to the like punishment. What is this but the acknowledgement that the slave is a moral, intellectual and responsible being? The manhood of the slave is conceded. It is admitted in the fact that Southern statute books are covered with enactments forbidding, under severe fines and penalties, the teaching of the slave to read or to write. When you can point to any such laws, in reference to the beasts of the field, then I may consent to argue the manhood of the slave. When the dogs in your streets, when the fowls of the air, when the cattle on your hills, when the fish of the sea, and the reptiles that crawl, shall be unable to distinguish the slave from a brute, then will I argue with you that the slave is a man! . . .

Would you have me argue that man is entitled to liberty? That he is the rightful owner of his own body? You have already declared it. Must I argue the wrongfulness of slavery?. . . To do so, would be to make myself ridiculous, and to offer an insult to your understanding. There is not a man beneath the canopy of heaven, that does not know that slavery is wrong for *him.*

What, am I to argue that it is wrong to make men brutes, to rob them of their liberty, to work them without wages, to keep them ignorant of their relations to their fellow-men, to beat them with sticks, to flay their flesh with the lash, to load their limbs with irons, to hunt them with dogs, to sell them at auction, to sunder their families, to knock out their teeth, to burn their flesh, to starve them into obedience and submission to their masters? Must I argue that a system thus marked with blood, and stained with pollution, is wrong? No! I will not. I have better employments for my time and strength, than such arguments would imply.

What, then, remains to be argued? Is it that slavery is not divine; that God did not establish it; that our doctors of divinity are mistaken? There is blasphemy in the thought. That which is inhuman, cannot be divine. Who can reason on such a proposition? They that can, may; I cannot. The time for such argument is past. . . .

What, to the American slave, is your Fourth of July? I answer: a day that reveals to him, more than all other days in the year, the gross injustice and cruelty to which he is the constant victim. To him, your celebration is a sham; your boasted liberty, an unholy license; your national greatness, swelling vanity; your sounds of rejoicing are empty and heartless; your denunciations of tyrants, brass-fronted impudence; your shouts of liberty and equality, hollow mockery; your prayers and hymns, your sermons and thanksgivings, with all your religious parade, and solemnity, are, to him, mere bombast, fraud, deception, impiety, and hypocrisy—a thin veil to cover up crimes which would disgrace a nation of savages. There is not a nation on the earth guilty of practices, more shocking and bloody, than are the people of these United States, at this very hour.

Union soldiers at Missionary Ridge, East Tennessee. The Civil War saw the large-scale introduction of modern means of combat, from railroads to observation balloons to ironclad naval vessels to heavy long-distance mortars, even to submarines and barbed wire. But no weapons were more deadly than the rifled musket and cannon, both of which spun shots with deadly accuracy over long distances, making frontal assaults all but suicidal and producing hundreds of thousands of dead and wounded. This 1863 battle, which turned a seeming Rebel victory into a triumph for the United States, took place just before General Sherman introduced "scorched earth" tactics in Georgia and Carolina and the armies of Generals Grant and Lee became expert at trenching in Virginia. Either approach, though ominous for the future, was preferable to the bloodletting of mass assaults against rifled muskets and cannon. (Minnesota Historical Society)

CHAPTER FIVE

Coming Apart

35

RACE, SLAVERY, AND THE CONSTITUTION

The spread of slavery during the early nineteenth century divided the nation and so fanned the flames of sectionalism that the United States was able to remain united only by careful political compromise between North and South. The Missouri Compromise of 1820 admitted Maine, a free state, and Missouri, a slave state, to the Union about the same time, thus preserving the balance between the two sections; it also barred slavery from all territories north of a line (36°30′N) drawn westward from Missouri's southern border. The Compromise of 1850 admitted California as a free state but organized New Mexico and Utah on the principle of popular sovereignty, with slavery left to the inhabitants' decision.

In 1854 Congress violated the Missouri Compromise line. By the Kansas-Nebraska Act of that year, sponsored by Illinois Senator Stephen A. Douglas, who wanted settlers to decide whether or not to have slavery, territory north of 36°30′N was opened to slavery on a "local option" basis. The result was a bloody conflict in Kansas between free-soil settlers opposed to slavery there and those favoring slavery. In 1857, moreover, Chief Justice Roger B. Taney's opinion in the *Dred Scott* case placed the Supreme Court squarely behind the institution of slavery. (A Missouri slave, Dred Scott, had sued his master for freedom, basing his case on the fact that they had lived for a time in free territory.) Speaking for the majority of the justices, Taney announced that blacks could not be American citizens and that Congress could not prohibit slavery even in territories under its direct jurisdiction. The *Dred Scott* decision made all previous compromises over slavery unconstitutional. It also exacerbated sectional tensions. Proslavery Southerners were anxious to extend slavery into new areas; antislavery Northerners were just as determined to do all they could to prevent the further expansion of human bondage despite the Court's ruling. Even Northerners who were not abolitionists opposed Taney's decision. They did not like the idea of Southerners bringing their slaves into the federal territories.

Roger Taney was born in 1777 in Maryland, where he practiced law for a time and then entered politics. An early supporter of Andrew Jackson, he became attorney general in 1831 and helped draft Jackson's message to Congress in 1832 vetoing the recharter bill for the Bank of the United States. In 1836 Jackson made Taney chief justice of the Supreme Court. Taney's major opinion before *Dred Scott* was an antimonopoly decision in the *Charles River Bridge* case in 1837. After the *Dred Scott* decision, Taney's prestige declined rapidly, and it all but disappeared after the Republican victory in 1860. He died in Washington four years later.

Scott himself became free because his master died, and the widow married an abolitionist who arranged for Scott's freedom. Scott became a hotel porter in St. Louis and died there of tuberculosis a year after the Supreme Court decision.

Questions to Consider. The *Dred Scott* decision purports to cite historical facts as well as to advance opinions about those facts. How accurate is Taney's statement that American blacks had never possessed any of the rights and privileges the U.S. Constitution confers on citizens? Why did he make a careful distinction between the rights of citizenship that a state may confer and the rights conferred by the federal Constitution? Note that Taney insisted that Dred Scott, not being a citizen, was "not entitled to sue in the courts." If he believed this, why did he agree to rule on the case at all? Was he correct in saying that when the nation was founded "no one thought of disputing" the idea that "the negro might justly and lawfully be reduced to slavery"? Do you think his reference to the constitutional provision permitting the slave trade until 1808 strengthened his arguments? Note that in order to find the Missouri Compromise unconstitutional, Taney maintained that the clause in the Constitution giving Congress power to regulate the federal territories applied only to territories belonging to the United States at the time the Constitution was adopted. Do you think he made a convincing case for this assertion? Would Taney's insistence that Congress cannot prohibit slavery in the federal territories logically apply to whites as well as blacks?

★═══★═══★

Dred Scott v. *Sanford* (1857)

ROGER B. TANEY

The question is simply this: Can a negro, whose ancestors were imported into this country, and sold as slaves, become a member of the political community formed and brought into existence by the Constitution of the United

19 *Howard* 393 (1857).

States, and as such become entitled to all the rights, and privileges, and immunities, guaranteed by that instrument to the citizen? One of which rights is the privilege of suing in a court of the United States in the cases specified in the Constitution. . . .

The words "people of the United States" and "citizens" are synonymous terms, and mean the same thing. They both describe the political body who, according to our republican institutions, form the sovereignty, and who hold the power and conduct the government through their representatives. They are what we familiarly call the "sovereign people," and every citizen is one of this people, and a constituent member of this sovereignty. The question before us is, whether the class of persons described in the plea in abatement compose a portion of this people, and are constituent members of this sovereignty? We think they are not, and that they are not included, and were not intended to be included, under the word "citizens" in the Constitution, and can, therefore, claim none of the rights and privileges which that instrument provides for and secures to citizens of the United States. On the contrary, they were at that time considered as a subordinate and inferior class of beings, who had been subjugated by the dominant race, and whether emancipated or not, yet remained subject to their authority, and had no rights or privileges but such as those who held the power and the government might choose to grant them. . . .

The question then arises, whether the provisions of the Constitution, in relation to the personal rights and privileges to which the citizen of a State should be entitled, embraced the negro African race, at that time in this country, or who might afterwards be imported, who had then or should afterwards be made free in any State; and to put it in the power of a single State to make him a citizen of the United States, and endue him with the full rights of citizenship in every other State without their consent. Does the Constitution of the United States act upon him whenever he shall be made free under the laws of a State, and raised there to the rank of a citizen, and immediately clothe him with all the privileges of a citizen in every other State, and in its own courts?

The court think the affirmative of these propositions cannot be maintained. And if it cannot, the plaintiff in error could not be a citizen of the State of Missouri, within the meaning of the Constitution of the United States, and, consequently, was not entitled to sue in its courts. . . .

It is difficult at this day to realize the state of public opinion in relation to that unfortunate race, which prevailed in the civilized and enlightened portions of the world at the time of the Declaration of Independence, and when the Constitution of the United States was framed and adopted. . . .

They had for more than a century before been regarded as beings of an inferior order; and altogether unfit to associate with the white race, either in social or political relations; and so far inferior that they had no rights which the white man was bound to respect; and that the negro might justly and lawfully be reduced to slavery for his benefit. . . . This opinion was at that time fixed and universal in the civilized portion of the white race. It was regarded as an axiom in morals as well as in politics, which no one thought of disputing, or supposed to be open to dispute; and men in every grade and position in society daily and habitually acted upon it in their private pursuits, as well as in matters of public concern, without doubting for a moment the correctness of this opinion. . . .

But there are two clauses in the Constitution which point directly and specifically to the negro race as a separate class of persons, and show clearly that they were not regarded as a portion of the people or citizens of the Government then formed.

One of these clauses reserves to each of the thirteen States the right to import slaves until the year 1808, if he thinks it proper. And the importation which it thus sanctions was unquestionably of persons of the race of which we are speaking, as the traffic in slaves in the United States had always been confined to them. And by the other provision the States pledge themselves to each other to maintain the right of property of the master, by delivering up to him any slave who may have escaped from his service, and be found within their respective territories. . . . And these two provisions show, conclusively, that neither the description of persons therein referred to, nor their descendants, were embraced in any of the other provisions of the Constitution; for certainly these two clauses were not intended to confer on them or their posterity the blessings of liberty, or any of the personal rights so carefully provided for the citizen. . . .

Indeed, when we look to the condition of this race in the several States at the time, it is impossible to believe that these rights and privileges were intended to be extended to them. . . .

The Act of Congress, upon which the plaintiff relies, declares that slavery and involuntary servitude, except as a punishment for crime, shall be forever prohibited in all that part of the territory ceded by France, under the name of Louisiana, which lies north of thirty-six degrees thirty minutes north latitude, and not included within the limits of Missouri. And the difficulty which meets us at the threshold of this part of the inquiry is, whether Congress was authorized to pass this law under any of the powers granted to it by the Constitution; for if the authority is not given by that instrument, it is the duty of this court to declare it void and inoperative, and incapable of conferring freedom upon any one who is held as a slave under the laws of any one of the States.

The counsel for the plaintiff has laid much stress upon that article in the Constitution which confers on Congress the power "to dispose of and make all needful rules and regulations respecting the territory or other property belonging to the United States," but, in the judgment of the court, that provision has no bearing on the present controversy, and the power there given, whatever it may be, is confined, and was intended to be confined, to the territory which at that time belonged to, or was claimed by, the United States, and was within their boundaries as settled by the treaty with Great Britain, and can have no influence upon a territory afterwards acquired from a foreign Government. It was a special provision for a known and particular territory, and to meet a present emergency, and nothing more. . . .

If this clause is construed to extend to territory acquired by the present Government from a foreign nation, outside of the limits of any charter from the British Government to a colony, it would be difficult to say, why it was deemed necessary to give the Government the power to sell any vacant lands belonging to the sovereignty which might be found within it; and if this was necessary, why the grant of this power should precede the power to legislate over it and establish a Government there; and still more difficult to say, why it was deemed necessary so specially and particularly to grant the power to make needful rules and regulations in relation to any personal or movable property it might acquire there. For the words, *other property* necessarily, by every known rule of interpretation, must mean property of a different description from territory or land. And the difficulty would perhaps be insurmountable in endeavoring to account for the last member of the sentence, which provides that "nothing in this Constitution shall be so construed as to prejudice any claims of the United States or any particular State," or to say how any particular State could have claims in or to a territory ceded by a foreign Government, or to account for associating this provision with the preceding provisions of the clause, with which it would appear to have no connection. . . .

The rights of private property have been guarded. . . . Thus the rights of property are united with the rights of person, and placed on the same ground by the fifth amendment to the Constitution. . . . An Act of Congress which deprives a person of the United States of his liberty or property merely because he came himself or brought his property into a particular Territory of the United States, and who had committed no offense against the laws, could hardly be dignified with the name of due process of law. . . .

It seems, however, to be supposed, that there is a difference between property in a slave and other property, and that different rules may be applied to it in expounding the Constitution of the United States. And the laws and usages of nations, and the writings of eminent jurists upon the relation of master and slave and their mutual rights and duties, and the powers which governments may exercise over it, have been dwelt upon in the argument.

But . . . if the Constitution recognizes the right of property of the master in a slave, and makes no distinction between that description of property and other property owned by a citizen, no tribunal, acting under the authority of the United States, whether it be legislative, executive, or judicial, has a right to draw such a distinction, or deny to it the benefit of the provisions and guarantees which have been provided for the protection of private property against the encroachments of the Government.

Now . . . the right of property in a slave is distinctly and expressly affirmed in the Constitution. The right to traffic in it, like an ordinary article of merchandise and property, was guaranteed to the citizens of the United

States, in every State that might desire it, for twenty years. And the Government in express terms is pledged to protect it in all future time, if the slave escapes from his owner. . . . And no word can be found in the Constitution which gives Congress a greater power over slave property, or which entitles property of that kind to less protection than property of any other description. The only power conferred is the power coupled with the duty of guarding and protecting the owner in his rights.

Upon these considerations, it is the opinion of the court that the Act of Congress which prohibited a citizen from holding and owning property of this kind in the territory of the United States north of the line therein mentioned, is not warranted by the Constitution, and is therefore void; and that neither Dred Scott himself, nor any of his family, were made free by being carried into this territory; even if they had been carried there by the owner, with the intention of becoming a permanent resident.

36

LIBERTY AND UNION

The great vehicle for antislavery politics was the Republican Party. Founded in Ripon, Wisconsin, in 1854, the new party rapidly absorbed members of earlier, smaller antislavery organizations by pledging itself to oppose the further extension of slavery in the United States. In the election of 1856, the Republicans showed amazing strength: their candidate, John C. Frémont, won 1,339,932 popular and 114 electoral votes to Democratic candidate James Buchanan's 1,832,955 popular and 174 electoral votes. During the next four years the party broadened its appeal to attract industrialists and workers as well as farmers, professional people, and religious leaders who were opposed to slavery. It also developed able party leaders and made impressive gains at the state and congressional levels.

The Republican Party's 1860 platform not only upheld the Union and reiterated its stand against the extension of slavery but also contained a number of economic planks that would appeal to industrialists in the Northeast and farmers in the West. It favored a protective tariff, the building of a transcontinental railroad, and a homestead act giving free land to settlers. Adopted in Chicago in May 1860, the platform conformed closely to the views of such moderates as William H. Seward and Horace Greeley of New York, Benjamin F. Wade and Salmon P. Chase of Ohio, and its standard-bearer, Abraham Lincoln of Illinois. Only when leading abolitionists threatened to walk out of the convention did Republican leaders incorporate a reaffirmation of the Declaration of Independence into their platform. But though the Republicans took a moderate position in their platform, the victory of Lincoln in the 1860 election triggered secession and civil war.

Questions to Consider. To what did the Republican platform refer when it announced that events of the past four years had established the necessity of organizing a new party? Do you agree with the statement that the principles of the Declaration of Independence are "essential to the preservation of our Republican institutions"? Do you agree with the assertion that "threats of Disunion" are equivalent to "an avowal of contemplated treason"? In denouncing "the lawless invasion by armed force of the soil of any State or Territory," what did the platform makers have in mind? What did the platform say about Kansas and the *Dred Scott* decision? What dominated the platform, the slavery issue or economic issues? On balance, to whom was the platform supposed to appeal?

★═══★═══★

The Republican Party Platform of 1860

Resolved, That we, the delegated representatives of the Republican electors of the United States, in Convention assembled, in discharge of the duty we owe to our constituents and our country, unite in the following declarations:

1. That the history of the nation, during the last four years, has fully established the propriety and necessity of the organization and perpetuation of the Republican party, and that the causes which called it into existence are permanent in their nature, and now, more than ever before, demand its peaceful and constitutional triumph.

2. That the maintenance of the principles promulgated in the Declaration of Independence and embodied in the Federal Constitution, "That all men are created equal; that they are endowed by their Creator with certain inalienable rights; that among these are life, liberty and the pursuit of happiness; that, to secure these rights, governments are instituted among men, deriving their just powers from the consent of the governed," is essential to the preservation of our Republican institutions, and that the Federal Constitution, the Rights of the States, and the Union of the States, must and shall be preserved.

3. That to the Union of the States this nation owes its unprecedented increase in population, its surprising development of material resources, its rapid augmentation of wealth, its happiness at home and its honor abroad; and we hold in abhorrence all schemes for Disunion, come from whatever source they may; And we congratulate the country that no Republican member of Congress has uttered or countenanced the threats of Disunion so often made by Democratic members, without rebuke and with applause from their political associates; and we denounce those threats of Disunion, in case of a popular overthrow of their ascendancy, as denying the vital principles of a free government, and as an avowal of contemplated treason, which it is the imperative duty of an indignant People sternly to rebuke and forever silence.

Francis Curtis, *The Republican Party* (2 v., G. P. Putnam's Sons, New York, 1904), I: 355–358.

4. That the maintenance inviolate of the rights of the States, and especially the right of each State to order and control its own domestic institutions according to its own judgment exclusively, is essential to that balance of powers on which the perfection and endurance of our political fabric depends; and we denounce the lawless invasion by armed forces of the soil of any State or Territory, no matter under what pretext, as among the gravest of crimes.

5. That the present Democratic Administration has far exceeded our worst apprehensions, in its measureless subserviency to the exactions of a sectional interest, as especially evinced in its desperate exertions to force the infamous Lecompton constitution[1] upon the protesting people of Kansas; in construing the personal relation between master and servant to involve an unqualified property in persons; in its attempted enforcement, everywhere, on land and sea, through the intervention of Congress and of the Federal Courts of the extreme pretensions of a purely local interest; and in its general and unvarying abuse of the power intrusted to it by a confiding people. . . .

7. That the new dogma that the Constitution, of its own force, carries Slavery into any or all of the Territories of the United States, is a dangerous political heresy, at variance with the explicit provisions of that instrument itself, with contemporaneous exposition, and with legislative and judicial precedent; is revolutionary in its tendency, and subversive of the peace and harmony of the country.

8. That the normal condition of all the territory of the United States is that of freedom; That as our Republican fathers, when they had abolished slavery in all our national territory, ordained that "no person should be deprived of life, liberty, or property, without due process of law," it becomes our duty, by legislation, whenever such legislation is necessary, to maintain this provision of the Constitution against all attempts to violate it; and we deny the authority of Congress, of a territorial legislature, or of any individuals, to give legal existence to Slavery in any Territory of the United States.

9. That we brand the recent re-opening of the African slave-trade, under the cover of our national flag, aided by perversions of judicial power, as a crime against humanity and a burning shame to our country and age; and we call upon Congress to take prompt and efficient measures for the total and final suppression of that execrable traffic.

10. That in the recent vetoes, by their Federal Governors, of the acts of the Legislatures of Kansas and Nebraska, prohibiting Slavery in those territories, we find a practical illustration of the boasted Democratic principle of Non-Intervention and Popular Sovereignty embodied in the Kansas-Nebraska bill, and a demonstration of the deception and fraud involved therein.

---

1. **Lecompton constitution:** A proslavery constitution adopted by a proslavery legislature in 1857 and not submitted to a popular vote.—*Eds.*

11. That Kansas should, of right, be immediately admitted as a State under the Constitution recently formed and adopted by her people, and accepted by the House of Representatives.

12. That, while providing revenue for the support of the General Government by duties upon imports, sound policy requires such an adjustment of these imposts as to encourage the development of the industrial interests of the whole country; and we commend that policy of national exchanges which secures to the working men liberal wages, to agriculture remunerating prices, to mechanics and manufacturers an adequate reward for their skill, labor and enterprise, and to the nation commercial prosperity and independence.

13. That we protest against any sale or alienation to others of the Public Lands held by actual settlers, and against any view of the Homestead policy which regards the settlers as paupers or supplicants for public bounty; and we demand the passage by Congress of the complete and satisfactory Homestead measure which has already passed the House.

14. That the Republican Party is opposed to any change in our Naturalization Laws or any State legislation by which the rights of our citizenship hitherto accorded to immigrants from foreign lands shall be abridged or impaired; and in favor of giving a full and efficient protection to the rights of all classes of citizens, whether native or naturalized, both at home and abroad.

15. That appropriations by Congress for River and Harbor improvements of a National character, required for the accommodation and security of an existing commerce, are authorized by the Constitution, and justified by the obligations of Government to protect the lives and property of its citizens.

16. That a Railroad to the Pacific Ocean is imperatively demanded by the interests of the whole country; that the Federal Government ought to render immediate and efficient aid in its construction; and that, as preliminary thereto, a daily Overland Mail should be promptly established.

37

FLIGHT FROM UNION

The election of 1860 centered on slavery and the Union. The Republicans ran Abraham Lincoln for president on a platform opposing the further extension of slavery. The Democrats split over the issue. The Northern Democrats ran Illinois Senator Stephen A. Douglas on a platform calling for "popular sovereignty," that is, the right of people in the federal territories to decide for themselves whether they wanted slavery. The Southern Democrats ran Kentucky's John C. Breckenridge on a frankly proslavery platform demanding federal protection of slavery in the territories. A fourth party, the Constitutional Union party, which ran John Bell of Tennessee, tried to play down the slavery issue by emphasizing the preservation of the Union. This division of Lincoln's opponents made his victory an almost foregone conclusion. Though Lincoln did not win the majority of popular votes cast in the election, he won more popular votes than any of his three opponents and he also took the majority of electoral votes. But he received not one electoral vote in the South.

Even before Lincoln's election, Mississippi had contemplated withdrawing from the Union if the Republicans won. When Lincoln did win, Governor John J. Pettus issued a proclamation denouncing the "Black Republicans," held a conference with the state's congressional delegation, including Jefferson Davis, and recommended a state convention to take action on secession. Late in November 1860, the Mississippi legislature met in Jackson, received the governor's recommendation, and passed a bill providing for elections the following month for a convention to meet on January 7 "to consider the then existing relations between the government of the United States and the government and people of the State of Mississippi." It also passed a series of resolutions outlining the reasons for adopting secession as "the proper remedy" for the state's grievances.

On December 20, South Carolina seceded from the Union. Shortly afterward ten other states followed its lead: Mississippi, Florida, Alabama, Georgia, Louisiana, Texas, Virginia, Arkansas, Tennessee, and North Carolina. In February 1861, delegates from the seceding states met in Montgomery, Alabama, to adopt a constitution for the Confederate States of America. They chose Mississippi's Jefferson Davis as president. On April 12, the Civil War began.

Questions to Consider. The Mississippi resolutions contained a succinct summary of the outlook of Southern secessionists. To what extent did they depend on John C. Calhoun's "compact" theory of the Union? Were the resolutions correct in stating that the Northern states had "assumed a revolutionary position" toward the Southern states? Was the charge that the Northern states had violated the Constitution in their behavior toward the South valid? Was it accurate to say that Northerners sought an abolitionist amendment to the Constitution? To what "incendiary publications" do the resolutions refer? What "hostile invasion of a Southern State" did the drafters of the resolutions have in mind? Do you see any similarities between the arguments advanced here and those appearing in the Declaration of Independence?

★════★════★

Mississippi Resolutions on Secession (1860)

Whereas, The Constitutional Union was formed by the several States in their separate sovereign capacity for the purpose of mutual advantage and protection;

That the several States are distinct sovereignties, whose supremacy is limited so far only as the same has been delegated by voluntary compact to a Federal Government, and when it fails to accomplish the ends for which it was established, the parties to the compact have the right to resume, each State for itself, such delegated powers;

That the institution of slavery existed prior to the formation of the Federal Constitution, and is recognized by its letter, and all efforts to impair its value or lessen its duration by Congress, or any of the free States, is a violation of the compact of Union and is destructive of the ends for which it was ordained, but in defiance of the principles of the Union thus established, the people of the Northern States have assumed a revolutionary position towards the Southern States;

That they have set at defiance that provision of the Constitution which was intended to secure domestic tranquillity among the States and promote their general welfare, namely: "No person held to service or labor in one State, under the laws thereof, escaping into another, shall, in consequence of any law

John K. Bettersworth, ed., *Mississippi in the Confederacy* (Louisiana State University Press, Baton Rouge, 1961), 22–24. Reprinted by permission of Louisiana State University Press.

Private Tresvant ("Tris") Childers, Confederate States of America, displaying his rebel spirit for the camera. Childers was born on an Alabama plantation in 1835, enlisted in an artillery regiment in 1862, and fought in Florida, Tennessee, and Alabama before surrendering on May 4, 1865. Some years after the war he moved to Arkansas to farm, although he was unable to purchase his modest holdings outright until 1910. (Private Collection)

or regulation therein, be discharged from such service or labor, but shall be delivered up on claim of the party to whom such service or labor may be due;"

That they have by voluntary associations, individual agencies and State legislation interfered with slavery as it prevails in the slave-holding States;

That they have enticed our slaves from us, and by State intervention obstructed and prevented their rendition under the fugitive slave law;

That they continue their system of agitation obviously for the purpose of encouraging other slaves to escape from service, to weaken the institution in the slave-holding States by rendering the holding of such property insecure, and as a consequence its ultimate abolition certain;

That they claim the right and demand its execution by Congress to exclude slavery from the Territories, but claim the right of protection for every species of property owned by themselves;

That they declare in every manner in which public opinion is expressed their unalterable determination to exclude from admittance into the Union any new State that tolerates slavery in its Constitution, and thereby force Congress to a condemnation of that species of property;

That they thus seek by an increase of abolition States "to acquire two-thirds of both houses" for the purpose of preparing an amendment to the Constitution of the United States, abolishing slavery in the States, and so continue the agitation that the proposed amendment shall be ratified by the Legislatures of three-fourths of the States;

That they have in violation of the comity of all civilized nations, and in violation of the comity established by the Constitution of the United States, insulted and outraged our citizens when travelling among them for pleasure, health or business, by taking their servants and liberating the same, under the forms of State laws, and subjecting their owners to degrading and ignominious punishment;

That to encourage the stealing of our property they have put at defiance that provision of the Constitution which declares that fugitives from justice (escaping) into another State, on demand of the Executive authority of that State from which he fled, shall be delivered up;

That they have sought to create domestic discord in the Southern States by incendiary publications;

That they encouraged a hostile invasion of a Southern State to excite insurrection, murder and rapine;

That they have deprived Southern citizens of their property and continue an unfriendly agitation of their domestic institutions, claiming for themselves perfect immunity from external interference with their domestic policy. . . .

That they have elected a majority of Electors for President and Vice-President on the ground that there exists an irreconcilable conflict between the two sections of the Confederacy in reference to their respective systems of labor and in pursuance of their hostility to us and our institutions, thus declaring to the civilized world that the powers of this Government are to be used for the dishonor and overthrow of the Southern Section of this great Confederacy. Therefore,

Be it resolved by the Legislature of the State of Mississippi, That in the opinion of those who now constitute the said Legislature, the secession of each aggrieved State is the proper remedy for these injuries.

38

Union Inviolate

Fifteen states had significant slave populations when Abraham Lincoln was elected president of the United States on November 6, 1860. One of these, South Carolina, seceded from the Union in late December; others appeared ready to follow early in the new year. To forestall this mass exit, various last-minute compromise proposals emerged in Congress, including the so-called Crittenden Plan. This plan called for two constitutional amendments, the first guaranteeing slavery forever in the states where it already existed, and the second dividing the territories between slavery and freedom. President-elect Lincoln had no objection to the first proposed amendment, but he was unalterably opposed to the second, which would have nullified the free-soil plank of the Republican Party. A territorial division, Lincoln wrote, would only encourage planter expansionism and thus "put us again on the highroad to a slave empire," and on this point "I am inflexible."

Taking this as their cue, five more states—Georgia, Florida, Alabama, Mississippi, and Louisiana—seceded in January 1861. Texas followed on February 1. Seven states were therefore already gone, at least by their own declaration, as Lincoln prepared to deliver his inaugural address on March 4. The stakes were enormously high. Eight slave states, all in the strategically significant upper South, still remained in the Union. Should war begin, their allegiance would be invaluable and the inaugural address could help achieve that. Moreover, in the event of war, the North would have to unite behind the goals of the new president and his party. The address could articulate those unifying goals.

Lincoln believed his first inaugural address could be the most important speech of his life. Like most American politicians, he was a lawyer by trade, and the numerous legalistic formulations of the speech perhaps reflect this background. But the crisis Lincoln faced was fundamentally a constitutional—that is, a legalistic—crisis: Could a nation permit secessionist activity and remain a nation? What compromise with basic principles was possible before constitutional rights were destroyed? Because these were questions partly of constitutional law, Lincoln addressed them partly in legal language. But, as always in his great speeches, he also relied on common sense, common sentiments of patriotism, and, particularly in his conclusion, common familiarity with the cadences of the single most popular work in nineteenth-century America—the King James Bible.

Born to a frontier farming family in Kentucky in 1809, Abraham Lincoln grew up in Indiana and Illinois. As a young man he worked as a farmer, rail-splitter, boatsman, and storekeeper before turning to law and politics. He was enormously successful as a lawyer and served several years in the Illinois legislature and one term in the House of Representatives. Largely a self-educated man, Lincoln read and reread such books as the Bible, Aesop's fables, the works of Shakespeare, and the poems of Robert Burns. He also developed great skill as a writer. In 1858, his debates with Stephen Douglas over slavery brought him national prominence and helped him win the Republican nomination for president in 1860. Although he made restoration of the Union his primary objective during the Civil War, in time he also made it clear that, eventually, it must be a Union without slavery. On April 14, 1865, while attending a performance at Ford's Theatre in Washington, he was shot by actor John Wilkes Booth, a Confederate sympathizer. Lincoln died the next morning.

Questions to Consider. In what ways did Lincoln try to reassure Southerners about his intentions? Could he have said more without compromising his principles? What *was* his basic operating principle in this crisis? What did Lincoln see as the "only substantial dispute" between North and South, and why did he think secession would only make this dispute worse? Was he right in thinking that "deliberate" would be better than "hurried"? To what impulse was Lincoln trying to appeal when he referred to "the better angels of our nature"?

★━━★━━★

First Inaugural Address (1861)

ABRAHAM LINCOLN

I consider that in view of the Constitution and the laws, the Union is unbroken, and to the extent of my ability I shall take care, as the Constitution itself expressly enjoins me, that the laws of the Union be faithfully executed in all the States. Doing this I deem to be only a simple duty on my part, and I shall perform it so far as practicable unless my rightful masters, the American people,

James D. Richardson, ed., *A Compilation of the Messages and Papers of the Presidents* (Government Printing Office, Washington, D.C., 1897–1907), VI: 6–12.

The bombardment of Fort Sumter, May 4, 1861. The people of Charleston watched the bombing of Fort Sumter from the rooftops of their homes. (Library of Congress)

shall withhold the requisite means or in some authoritative manner direct the contrary. I trust this will not be regarded as a menace, but only as the declared purpose of the Union that it *will* constitutionally defend and maintain itself.

In doing this there needs to be no bloodshed or violence, and there shall be none unless it be forced upon the national authority. The power confided to me will be used to hold, occupy, and possess the property and places belonging to the Government and to collect the duties and imposts; but beyond what may be necessary for these objects, there will be no invasion, no using of force against or among the people anywhere. . . .

Plainly the central idea of secession is the essence of anarchy. A majority held in restraint by constitutional checks and limitations, and always changing easily with deliberate changes of popular opinions and sentiments, is the only true sovereign of a free people. Whoever rejects it does of necessity fly to anarchy or to despotism. Unanimity is impossible. The rule of a minority, as a permanent arrangement, is wholly inadmissible; so that, rejecting the majority principle, anarchy or despotism in some form is all that is left. . . .

One section of our country believes slavery is *right* and ought to be extended, while the other believes it is *wrong* and ought not to be extended. This is the only substantial dispute. The fugitive-slave clause of the Constitution and the law for the suppression of the foreign slave trade are each as well enforced, perhaps, as any law can ever be in a community where the moral sense of the people imperfectly supports the law itself. The great body of the people abide by the dry legal obligation in both cases, and a few break over in each. This, I think, can not be perfectly cured, and it would be worse in both cases *after* the separation of the sections than before. The foreign slave trade, now imperfectly suppressed, would be ultimately revived without restriction in one section, while fugitive slaves, now only partially surrendered, would not be surrendered at all by the other.

Physically speaking, we can not separate. We can not remove our respective sections from each other nor build an impassable wall between them. A husband and wife may be divorced and go out of the presence and beyond the reach of each other, but the different parts of our country can not do this. They can not but remain face to face, and intercourse, either amicable or hostile, must continue between them. Is it possible, then, to make that intercourse more advantageous or more satisfactory *after* separation than *before?* Can aliens make treaties easier than friends can make laws? Can treaties be more faithfully enforced between aliens than laws can among friends? Suppose you go to war, you can not fight always; and when, after much loss on both sides and no gain on either, you cease fighting, the identical old questions, as to terms of intercourse, are again upon you. . . .

My countrymen, one and all, think calmly and *well* upon this whole subject. Nothing valuable can be lost by taking time. If there be an object to *hurry* any of you in hot haste to a step which you would never take *deliberately*, that object will be frustrated by taking time; but no good object can be frustrated by it. Such of you as are now dissatisfied still have the old Constitution unimpaired, and, on the sensitive point, the laws of your own framing under it; while the new Administration will have no immediate power, if it would, to change either. If it were admitted that you who are dissatisfied hold the right side in the dispute, there still is no single good reason for precipitate action. Intelligence, patriotism, Christianity, and a firm reliance on Him who has never yet forsaken this favored land are still competent to adjust in the best way all our present difficulty.

In *your* hands, my dissatisfied fellow-countrymen, and not in *mine,* is the momentous issue of civil war. The Government will not assail *you*. You can have no conflict without being yourselves the aggressors. *You* have no oath registered in heaven to destroy the Government, while *I* shall have the most solemn one to "preserve, protect, and defend it."

I am loath to close. We are not enemies, but friends. We must not be enemies. Though passion may have strained it must not break our bonds of affection. The mystic chords of memory, stretching from every battlefield and patriot grave to every living heart and hearthstone all over this broad land, will yet swell the chorus of the Union, when again touched, as surely they will be, by the better angels of our nature.

39

Anthems of War

Singing played an important role in the Civil War in a way that is hard for people surrounded by radios, disks, and concerts to understand. Songs helped soldiers set a cadence for marching. Soldiers sang in camp to ward off homesickness and for something to do besides drink or fight. On the home front people gathered around parlor pianos to sing topical songs about the war from sheet music. They sang about the soldiering life in "Marching Through Georgia" and "Tenting on the Old Camp Ground," about the battlefield in "Comrades, I Am Dying!" and "The Dying Volunteer," and about domestic scenes in "When This Cruel War Is Over" and "When Johnny Comes Marching Home," one of the enduring favorites.

Everyone, in the field or at home, sang the great patriotic songs of the age, "Battle Cry of Freedom" and "Battle Hymn of the Republic" in the United States, for example, and "Maryland My Maryland," "The Bonnie Blue Flag," and "Dixie" in the Confederacy. Songs like these built fervor, defined the cause, created collective solidarity, and sustained morale. They may in fact have been indispensable to the conflict. Even in the Confederacy, with comparatively few publishers, instruments, or distribution outlets, sheet music outsold books, pamphlets, and magazines by five to one. The songs of the two sections were in many respects similar: simple, sentimental, belligerent. Set frequently to older tunes—folk ballads, hymns, popular songs, European melodies—the words frequently changed as the circumstances of the war changed or the popular mood changed. Songs written for one side sometimes ended up on the other side with new, sometimes sarcastic or comic, words.

Amidst the sameness and sentimentality, however, there were significant ideological differences, which may be seen in the following two popular examples, one Southern, the other Northern. The author of "Maryland My Maryland" was James Ryder Randall, a Maryland native who was teaching in Louisiana when word arrived that war had broken out and that Baltimore residents had attacked a Massachusetts regiment, with casualties on both sides. Randall, seeking to rally

Southern morale and spur Maryland to join the rebellion, wrote his poem for a New Orleans newspaper. A pro-Confederate printer set it to the music of "Tannenbaum, O Tannenbaum" and published it in sheet music form with the Maryland coat of arms on the cover. As it turned out, Maryland remained in the Union despite the rebel sentiments of Baltimore. But the song was immensely popular anyway and became a favorite Confederate marching song.

"Battle Hymn of the Republic," one of the greatest war anthems ever written, came from the pen of the genteel Julia Ward Howe, the wife of a well-known asylum reformer and abolitionist, Samuel Gridley Howe of Boston. The daughter of a New York banker, Howe enjoyed an excellent education, wrote poetry, and helped her husband edit a reform newspaper. She later related how she came to write this remarkable verse:

> I awoke in the gray of the morning twilight, and as I lay waiting for the dawn, the long lines of the desired poem began to twine themselves in my mind. Having thought out all the stanzas, I said to myself, "I must get up and write these verses down, lest I fall asleep again and forget them." So with a sudden effort I sprang out of bed . . . and scrawled the verses almost without looking at the paper. . . . Having completed my writing, I returned to bed and fell asleep, saying to myself, "I like this better than most things that I have written."

Her melody came from an 1861 camp song by William Steffe of South Carolina. Soldiers had begun to sing "John Brown's body lies a-mouldering in the grave" to this tune when Howe wrote her hymn. "Battle Hymn of the Republic" first appeared in *The Atlantic Monthly*. Howe was paid four dollars for her great work; her name did not appear on the poem.

Questions to Consider. What common features do you find in the language and imagery of these two songs? To what extent were the messages similar or different? Given what you know about the Civil War, do these two songs seem to be reasonable representations of the ideals of the two sides of the conflict? Did "liberty" and "freedom" mean the same thing for these authors?

Maryland My Maryland (1861)

JAMES RYDER RANDALL

The despot's heel is on thy shore,
  Maryland!
His torch is at thy temple door,
  Maryland!
Avenge the patriotic gore
That flecked the streets of Baltimore,
And be the battle queen of yore,
  Maryland! My Maryland!

Hark to an exiled son's appeal,
  Maryland!
My mother State! to thee I kneel,
  Maryland!
For life and death, for woe and weal,
Thy peerless chivalry reveal,
And gird thy beauteous limbs with steel,
  Maryland! My Maryland!

. . . .

Come! for thy shield is bright and strong,
  Maryland!
Come! for thy dalliance does thee wrong,
  Maryland!
Come to thine own heroic throng,
Stalking with Liberty along,
And chaunt thy dauntless slogan song,
Maryland! My Maryland!

Dear Mother! burst the tyrant's chain,
  Maryland!
Virginia should not call in vain,
  Maryland!
She meets her sisters on the plain—
"Sic semper!" 'tis the proud refrain
That baffles minions back again,
  Maryland! My Maryland!

I hear the distant thunder-hum,
  Maryland!
The Old Line's bugle, fife, and drum,
  Maryland!

H. M. Wharton, ed., *War Songs and Poems of the Southern Confederacy, 1861–1865* (Philadelphia, 1904), 95–98.

She is not dead, nor deaf, nor dumb—
Huzza! she spurns the Northern scum!
She breathes! she burns! she'll come! she'll come!
　　Maryland! My Maryland!

★━━★━━★

Battle Hymn of the Republic (1862)

JULIA WARD HOWE

Mine eyes have seen the glory of the coming of the Lord:
He is trampling out the vintage where the grapes of wrath are stored;
He hath loosed the fateful lightning of his terrible swift sword:
　　His truth is marching on.

I have seen Him in the watch fires of a hundred circling camps;
They have builded Him an altar in the evening dews and damps;
I can read His righteous sentence by the dim and flaring lamps.
　　His day is marching on.

I have read a fiery gospel writ in burnished rows of steel:
"As ye deal with my contemners, so with you my grace shall deal;
Let the Hero, born of woman, crush the serpent with his heel,
　　Since God is marching on."

He has sounded forth the trumpet that shall never call retreat;
He is sifting out the hearts of men before his judgment seat:
Oh! be swift, my soul, to answer Him! be jubilant, my feet!
　　Our God is marching on.

In the beauty of the lilies Christ was born across the sea,
With a glory in His bosom that transfigures you and me:
As He died to make men holy, let us die to make men free,
　　While God is marching on.

[Chorus]
Glory, Glory, hallelujah!
Glory, glory, hallelujah!
Glory, glory, hallelujah!
　　His truth is marching on.

The Atlantic Monthly, February 1862.

40

SINEWS OF WAR

The Civil War was the first large-scale, long-term modern war in North America, and to wage it both the United States and Confederate governments required what countries everywhere have required for modern warfare: large armies, big contracts to equip and maintain them, revenue to pay for the armies and the contracts, and, nearly always, some form of rationing. Of these conventional war measures, the armies were paramount, and in this respect the Rebels were initially in reasonably good shape, with a steady flow of volunteers drawn by martial fervor, frontier habits of hunting and Indian fighting, and the desire to defend their homeland against both military invasion and political interference with slavery and white supremacy.

By early 1862, however, this reliance on volunteer forces looked increasingly inadequate to the Confederate government in Richmond—uneven, not wholly reliable, and especially under too much control by the individual states, some of which were not even willing to release their own militia units for national service. There was also growing regional resistance to the entire war effort, especially in the mountainous interior districts with relatively few slaves.

In March 1862 Confederate President Jefferson Davis sent a message to Congress (excerpted below) urging a formal draft and explaining why it was needed. A conscription act, the first in North American history, followed shortly. The measure was not altogether successful. Resistance to conscription continued, and it remained hard for field commanders to maintain full-strength forces. Confederate army strength peaked in mid-1863 at about five hundred thousand men and declined thereafter. Even so, nearly a million men—out of a white male draft-age population between the ages of eighteen and thirty-nine that numbered only slightly more—did in fact serve. Only a hundred thousand or so of these were actual conscripts, but many of the rest served in part because of the pressure of possible conscription. In this sense conscription, which eventually took everyone under the age of fifty who did not own at least twenty slaves, may be said to have constituted the single most important Confederate government initiative of the war.

The United States did not conscript soldiers until mid-1863, a year later than the Rebels, concentrating initially on training, outfitting, equipping, and deploying its hordes of volunteers. Congressional attention turned instead to measures to pay for the war and especially to promote the interests of the remaining states of the Union—building a transcontinental railroad, for example, establishing a national banking system, and, especially, expanding the existing system of higher education. Congressman Justin Morrill had first sponsored a bill to fund new "land grant colleges" in 1857, only to see President James Buchanan, a Democrat under Southern influence, veto the legislation. In 1862, with the Southerners gone from Congress, Morrill reintroduced his bill, which passed handily. Abraham Lincoln eagerly signed it.

With the possible exception of the Northwest Ordinance of 1785, the Morrill Land Grant College Act was the most important federal education measure ever passed. It gave thirteen million acres of federal land to the states, which formed the basis of the far-flung American state university system. No legislation of this kind was ever proposed in the Confederacy, but the rebellious states, initially excluded, were made a part of the system in 1890. The universities that arose under the impetus of the Morrill Act eventually educated hundreds of thousands who would not otherwise have attended college. The act was therefore one of the most far-reaching pieces of reform legislation ever enacted in any country.

Born in Kentucky in 1808, the young Jefferson Davis moved to the frontier state of Mississippi with his parents, who accumulated great wealth in cotton land and slaves. Davis attended the U.S. Military Academy at West Point, served in the army, became a Mississippi planter himself, was an officer in the Mexican War, and was elected to the United States Senate in 1847. He was secretary of war in the 1850s, then went to the Senate again until 1861, when Mississippi withdrew from the Union. Having aggressively urged the expansion of slavery through absorption of territory in the Caribbean and the American West and now one of the wealthiest slaveholders in the South, it was natural for him to be chosen president of the Confederacy in February 1862, shortly before calling for conscription. Lacking Abraham Lincoln's political skills, Davis's oversensitive and reserved nature made for poor relations with important state governors, while his military expertise led him to interfere with field command decisions, again producing friction. But Robert E. Lee said after the war, "Few people could have done better. I know of none that could have done as well." Davis served two years in prison for treason after the war, but was never brought to trial. He died in Mississippi in 1889, a relic of the "lost cause."

Justin Morrill was born in Strafford, Vermont, in 1810. He left school at age fifteen to work in a store, became a partner, and made enough money to retire to politics. He was elected to Congress in 1854 as a

Whig, but soon helped organize the Republican Party in Vermont. He remained in the House until 1867, serving at one point as chairman of the Ways and Means Committee; he then entered the Senate, where he served for thirty years. Morrill supported high tariffs to raise revenue and protect industry and also, as a fiscal conservative, high taxes to maintain a balanced budget. He was a key figure in the landscaping of the Capitol grounds and the building of the Washington Monument and the Library of Congress. But his chief contribution to the United States was the Land Grant College Act, which he viewed as both a war measure and a peace and progress measure. He died in Washington in 1898.

Questions to Consider. Conscription is invariably an exercise of power by the central government of a country. Did Davis's call for a Confederate draft undermine the states' rights ideology of the South? How persuasive do you find his arguments on behalf of conscription? Does the message suggest that he expected resistance to the measure? If so, from what quarters? Davis proposed to draft all men between ages eighteen and thirty-five. Why did he choose this age cohort? The measure would in fact apply only to white Southerners. What phrase in Davis's message enabled him to indicate that without actually saying so?

Education is not normally thought of as a war measure. But Justin Morrill did think of his bill as in part a war measure. In what ways might it have served the war interests of the United States? Given the goals of the act, who would benefit most from its passage? To what extent might this explain why there was no such initiative in the Confederacy? To what extent might this have been a vote-buying scheme for the Republican Party and Abraham Lincoln? Did Morrill intend land grant college education to be wholly utilitarian and technical in nature? If not, why not?

★━━★━━★

Message on Conscription (1862)

JEFFERSON DAVIS

March 28, 1862. To the Senate and House of Representatives of the Confederate States.

The operation of the various laws now in force for raising armies has exhibited the necessity for reform. The frequent changes and amendments which have been made have rendered the system so complicated as to make

James D. Richardson, ed., *The Messages and Papers of Jefferson Davis and the Confederacy* (Chelsea House–Robert Hector, New York, 1966), I: 205–206.

it often quite difficult to determine what the law really is, and to what extent prior enactments are modified by more recent legislation. There is also embarrassment from conflict between State and Confederate legislation. I am happy to assure you of the entire harmony of purpose and cordiality of feeling which have continued to exist between myself and the Executives of the several States; and it is to this cause that our success in keeping adequate forces in the field is to be attributed. These reasons would suffice for inviting your earnest attention to the necessity of some simple and general system for exercising the power of raising armies, which is vested in the Congress by the Constitution.

But there is another and more important consideration. The vast preparations made by the enemy for a combined assault at numerous points on our frontier and seacoast have produced the result that might have been expected. They have animated the people with a spirit of resistance so general, so resolute, and so self-sacrificing that it requires rather to be regulated than to be stimulated. The right of the State to demand, and the duty of each citizen to render, military service, need only to be stated to be admitted. It is not, however, wise or judicious policy to place in active service that portion of the force of a people which experience has shown to be necessary as a reserve. Youths under the age of eighteen years require further instruction; men of matured experience are needed for maintaining order and good government at home and in supervising preparations for rendering efficient the armies in the field. These two classes constitute the proper reserve for home defense, ready to be called out in case of emergency, and to be kept in the field only while the emergency exists. But in order to maintain this reserve intact it is necessary that in a great war like that in which we are now engaged all persons of intermediate age not legally exempt for good cause should pay their debt of military service to the country, that the burdens should not fall exclusively on the most ardent and patriotic. I therefore recommend the passage of a law declaring that all persons residing within the Confederate States, between the ages of eighteen and thirty-five years, and rightfully subject to military duty, shall be held to be in the military service of the Confederate States, and that some plain and simple method be adopted for their prompt enrollment and organization, repealing all the legislation heretofore enacted which would conflict with the system proposed.

Land Grant College Act (1862)

JUSTIN MORRILL

Be it enacted by the Senate and House of Representatives of the United States of America in Congress assembled, That there be granted to the several States, for the purposes hereinafter mentioned, an amount of public land, to be apportioned to each State a quantity equal to thirty thousand acres for each senator and representative in Congress to which the States are respectively entitled. . . .

And be it further enacted, That all moneys derived from the sale of the lands aforesaid by the States to which the lands are apportioned, and from the sale of land scrip hereinbefore provided for, shall be invested in stocks of the United States, or of the States, or some other safe stocks, yielding not less than five per centum upon the par value of said stocks; and that the moneys so invested shall constitute a perpetual fund, the capital of which shall remain forever undiminished, (except so far as may be provided in section fifth of this act,) and the interest of which shall be inviolably appropriated, by each State which may take and claim the benefit of this act, to the endowment, support, and maintenance of at least one college where the leading object shall be, without excluding other scientific and classical studies, and including military tactics, to teach such branches of learning as are related to agriculture and mechanic arts, in such manner as the legislatures of the State may respectively prescribe, in order to promote the liberal and practical education of the industrial classes in the several pursuits and professions in life. . . .

No State while in a condition of rebellion or insurrection against the government of the United States shall be entitled to the benefit of this Act.

U.S. Statutes at Large XII: 503.

41

A DECLARATION OF FREEDOM

From the outset, the abolitionists urged Abraham Lincoln to make freeing the slaves the major objective of the war. But Lincoln declared: "My paramount object in this struggle is to save the Union." The Republican platform had promised to check the extension of slavery, but it also pledged not to interfere with slavery where it legally existed. Four border slave states—Maryland, Kentucky, Missouri, and Delaware—had remained in the Union, and Lincoln was afraid that an abolitionist policy would drive them into the Confederacy, with disastrous results for the Union cause. He was not convinced at first, moreover, that the majority of Northerners favored abolition.

As the Civil War progressed, Northern public opinion moved slowly in the direction of emancipation. At the same time it was becoming clear that a Union victory would mean the end of slavery. Whenever Union troops occupied any part of the Confederacy, the slaves promptly left the plantations and became camp followers of the Northern armies. Union generals began asking what policy to adopt toward slavery in the occupied parts of the South. In addition, the European public was becoming critical of the North for its failure to emancipate the slaves. Lincoln finally decided that the time had come to take action.

At a secret cabinet meeting on July 22, 1862, Lincoln presented a proclamation abolishing slavery, on which he had been working nearly a month. Secretary of State William H. Seward urged him not to issue it until after a Union victory. Then, on September 17, came the battle of Antietam, at which the Union armies of General George M. McClellan halted the advance of General Robert E. Lee's troops. On September 22, Lincoln officially proclaimed emancipation. In his capacity as commander in chief he announced that, "on the 1st day of January, A.D. 1863, all persons held as slaves within any State or designated part of a State the people whereof shall then be in rebellion against the United States shall be then, thenceforward, and forever free."

The Emancipation Proclamation did not immediately end slavery.

It did not apply to the border states because they were not in rebellion. Nor did it apply to those parts of the Confederacy then held by Union troops. Nevertheless, in all Confederate territories subsequently occupied by Northern troops, the slaves became free by the terms of Lincoln's proclamation. Furthermore, the proclamation led to the voluntary freeing of slaves in many places where it did not apply; Missouri and Maryland freed their slaves in 1863 and 1864. But it was the Thirteenth Amendment that ended slavery everywhere in the United States for all time. Introduced in Congress in December 1863 and adopted with Lincoln's energetic support in January 1865, it became part of the Constitution the following December when the necessary three-fourths of the states had ratified it.

Questions to Consider. The Emancipation Proclamation has been called as prosaic as a bill of lading. Do you think this is a fair appraisal? Do you think a statement more like the preamble to the Declaration of Independence would have been better? Why do you think Lincoln, a great prose master, avoided exalted language in writing the proclamation? On what constitutional powers as president did he depend in announcing his policy? In what ways does the proclamation demonstrate that Lincoln was a practical man? Reactions to the proclamation were varied. The London *Spectator* made fun of it. "The principle," sneered the editor, "is not that a human being cannot justly own another, but that he cannot own him unless he is loyal to the United States." Was the editor's comment justified? Not everyone agreed with the *Spectator.* Many abolitionists and most Southern blacks hailed the proclamation as a giant step on the road to freedom. Were they correct?

The Emancipation Proclamation (1863)

ABRAHAM LINCOLN

Whereas on the 22d day of September, A.D. 1862, a proclamation was issued by the President of the United States, containing among other things, the following, to wit:

John Nicolay and John Hay, eds., *Complete Works of Abraham Lincoln* (12 v., Lincoln Memorial University, n.p., 1894), VIII: 161–164.

"That on the 1st day of January, A.D. 1863, all persons held as slaves within any State or designated part of a State the people whereof shall then be in rebellion against the United States shall be then, thenceforward, and forever free; and the executive government of the United States, including the military and naval authority thereof, will recognize and maintain the freedom of such persons and will do no act or acts to repress such persons, or any of them, in any efforts they may make for their actual freedom.

"That the executive will on the 1st day of January aforesaid, by proclamation, designate the States and parts of States, if any, in which the people thereof, respectively, shall then be in rebellion against the United States; and the fact that any State or the people thereof shall on that day be in good faith represented in the Congress of the United States by members chosen thereto at elections wherein a majority of the qualified voters of such States shall have participated shall, in the absence of strong countervailing testimony, be deemed conclusive evidence that such State and the people thereof are not then in rebellion against the United States."

Now, therefore, I, Abraham Lincoln, President of the United States, by virtue of the power in me vested as Commander-in-Chief of the Army and Navy of the United States in time of actual armed rebellion against the authority and government of the United States, and as a fit and necessary war measure for suppressing said rebellion, do, on this 1st day of January, A.D. 1863, and in accordance with my purpose so to do, publicly proclaimed for the full period of one hundred days from the first day above mentioned, order and designate as the States and parts of States wherein the people thereof, respectively, are this day in rebellion against the United States the following, to wit:

Arkansas, Texas, Louisiana (except the parishes of St. Bernard, Plaquemines, Jefferson, St. John, St. Charles, St. James, Ascension, Assumption, Terrebonne, Lafourche, St. Mary, St. Martin, and Orleans, including the city of New Orleans), Mississippi, Alabama, Florida, Georgia, South Carolina, North Carolina, and Virginia (except the forty-eight counties designated as West Virginia, and also the counties of Berkeley, Accomac, Northhampton, Elizabeth City, York, Princess Anne, and Norfolk, including the cities of Norfolk and Portsmouth), and which excepted parts are for the present left precisely as if this proclamation were not issued.

And by virtue of the power and for the purpose aforesaid, I do order and declare that all persons held as slaves within said designated States and parts of States are, and henceforward shall be, free; and that the Executive Government of the United States, including the military and naval authorities thereof, will recognize and maintain the freedom of said persons.

And I hereby enjoin upon the people so declared to be free to abstain from all violence, unless in necessary self-defense; and I recommend to them that, in all cases when allowed, they labor faithfully for reasonable wages.

And I further declare and make known that such persons of suitable condition will be received into the armed service of the United States to garrison forts, positions, stations, and other places, and to man vessels of all sorts in said service.

And upon this act, sincerely believed to be an act of justice, warranted by the Constitution upon military necessity, I invoke the considerate judgment of mankind and the gracious favor of Almighty God.

42

PEOPLE'S GOVERNMENT

Late in June 1863, General Robert E. Lee crossed the Potomac River and moved his Confederate army rapidly through Maryland into Pennsylvania. On July 1 his troops met the Union army, commanded by General George G. Meade, at Gettysburg, Pennsylvania. After three days of fierce fighting, with thousands of casualties, Lee's greatly weakened army began to retreat. Lincoln was disappointed that Lee's army was able to escape, but he realized that the Confederates had suffered a decisive defeat. "I am very grateful to Meade," he said, "for the great service he did at Gettysburg." The Gettysburg battle marked the peak of the Confederate effort. Never again were the Confederates able to invade the North, and they never came close to winning the war after that time.

Four months after the bloody encounter—on November 19, 1863—when a national cemetery was dedicated on the Gettysburg battlefield, Lincoln delivered perhaps his most famous address. Edward Everett, famed for his oratory, spoke first, talking for almost two hours. Lincoln's address lasted only a couple of minutes. Afterward, it is said, Everett took Lincoln's hand and told him, "My speech will soon be forgotten; yours never will be. How gladly I would exchange my hundred pages for your twenty lines!" Everett was right. His own speech was soon forgotten, whereas Lincoln's brief address came to be regarded as one of the most powerful statements of the democratic outlook ever made.

Questions to Consider. Why was Everett so impressed with Lincoln's address? Lincoln once said that his basic political ideas came from the Declaration of Independence. Do you think this influence appears in the Gettysburg Address? What in Lincoln's opinion was the basic meaning of the Civil War? To what extent was style, as well as substance, important in the address Lincoln wrote for the Gettysburg dedication?

Abraham Lincoln. Lincoln grew his beard after he became president in order to lend himself dignity and, perhaps, to disguise what he feared was a "homely" face. (Library of Congress)

★━━★━━★

The Gettysburg Address (1863)

ABRAHAM LINCOLN

Fourscore and seven years ago our fathers brought forth on this continent a new nation, conceived in liberty, and dedicated to the proposition that all men are created equal.

John Nicolay and John Hay, eds., *Complete Works of Abraham Lincoln* (12 v., Lincoln Memorial University, n.p., 1894), IX: 209–210.

Now we are engaged in a great civil war, testing whether that nation, or any nation so conceived and so dedicated, can long endure. We are met on a great battle-field of that war. We have come to dedicate a portion of that field as a final resting-place for those who here gave their lives that that nation might live. It is altogether fitting and proper that we should do this.

But, in a larger sense, we cannot dedicate—we cannot consecrate—we cannot hallow—this ground. The brave men, living and dead, who struggled here, have consecrated it far above our poor power to add or detract. The world will little note nor long remember what we say here, but it can never forget what they did here. It is for us, the living, rather, to be dedicated here to the unfinished work which they who fought here have thus far so nobly advanced. It is rather for us to be here dedicated to the great task remaining before us—that from these honored dead we take increased devotion to that cause for which they gave the last full measure of devotion; that we here highly resolve that these dead shall not have died in vain; that this nation, under God, shall have a new birth of freedom; and that government of the people, by the people, for the people, shall not perish from the earth.

43

FACES OF WAR

Northerners believed the war that broke out with the Southern bombardment of Fort Sumter in April 1861 would be over in months. But the Confederate army, led by officers whose military prowess far exceeded that of the Union command, proved to be a wily and formidable adversary, and to the dismay of President Lincoln, in the early years of the war—until the Battle of Gettysburg in 1863—decisive victory eluded the Union.

In 1864 Lincoln placed the strong-willed Ulysses S. Grant at the head of all Union forces. Late that same year, as Grant advanced toward Richmond with the Army of the Potomac, the forty-four-year-old General William Tecumseh Sherman drove the western army through three hundred miles of Georgia, cutting a thirty- to sixty-mile wide path of destruction from Atlanta to the sea. To avoid extended supply lines, he ordered his soldiers—nearly sixty thousand men—to "forage liberally on the country" for provisions, supplies, pack animals, and wagons. His commanders were to "enforce a devastation more or less relentless" wherever there was resistance of any kind. Demolitions engineers tore up railroad tracks, heated them, and hung them from trees, and wherever it was "necessary," troops put houses, mills, cotton gins, plantations, and entire towns to the torch. Sherman was determined not only to destroy the South's capacity to wage war but to break its will to resist.

It was as a result of such thinking that he burned Atlanta. In September the mayor of Atlanta had petitioned Sherman to reconsider his order that Atlanta be evacuated because of the "extraordinary hardship" and "inconvenience" it would entail:

> How is it possible for the . . . women and children to find any shelter? And how can they live through the winter in the woods [with] no shelter or subsistence. . . . You know the woe, the horrors, and the suffering, cannot be described by words; imagination can only conceive of it, and we ask you to take these things into consideration. . . . What has this helpless people done, that they should be driven from their homes, to wander strangers and outcasts, and exiles, and to subsist on charity?

As the first document shows, Sherman did not revoke his order. After the evacuation was complete, he ordered the city, already partially burned by retreating rebels, destroyed.

Yet Sherman was not a brutal man. In 1879, eleven years before his death, he addressed the graduating class of a military academy:

> I am tired and sick of war. Its glory is all moonshine. It is only those who have neither fired a shot nor heard the shrieks and groans of the wounded who cry aloud for blood, more vengeance, more desolation. War is hell.

Perhaps as well as any soldier of his generation, Sherman understood the nature of modern warfare and refused to be sentimental about it. Georgia reeled from the destruction he had brought upon it, but his scorched-earth policies worked. So awful, however, was the devastation of his "March to the Sea" that the physical and psychological wounds inflicted on the South took generations to heal.

The destruction is vividly described by Eliza Andrews in *The War-Time Diary of a Georgia Girl,* a portion of which is reproduced in the second document. In 1864 Andrews was twenty-four and living at a relative's plantation in southwest Georgia, where her father had sent her for safety. Observing the terrible effects of Sherman's march, she recorded how she felt about the destruction, the collapse of the Confederacy, and the impact of the war on women. "The exigencies of the times did away with many conventions," Andrews observed, and her diary provides insights into the plight of Southern women during the war and Reconstruction.

Her own life exemplified how the war had indeed wiped out "many conventions." Having lost her father's substantial estate (Garnett Andrews, although a Unionist, had owned two hundred slaves), she was forced to rely on her own resources to survive, and did so by teaching and by writing novels, serial fiction for periodicals, books on botany, and articles on socialism. In 1931 Andrews died in Rome, Georgia, at the age of ninety. Convinced that for the North the Civil War had been not a moral crusade but a fight to promote the interests of capitalism, she went to her grave a Marxist.

Questions to Consider. How persuasive do you find Sherman's reasoning in his message to the Atlantans? Would his arguments justify the unlimited destruction of hostile cities? In contrast to the North, where during the war women had opportunities to work in the Sanitary Commission or the Nursing Corps, in the Confederacy there were no government-sponsored wartime organizations that employed women. They had to cope on their own. Do you think Eliza Andrews's response might have been typical? What was the specific nature of the destruction she witnessed?

Message to the Atlanta City Council (1864)

WILLIAM TECUMSEH SHERMAN

Gentlemen: I have your letter of the 11th, in the nature of a petition to revoke my orders removing all the inhabitants from Atlanta. I have read it carefully, and give full credit to your statements of the distress that will be occasioned, and yet shall not revoke my orders, because they were not designed to meet the humanities of the case, but to prepare for the future struggles in which millions of good people outside of Atlanta have a deep interest. We must have peace, not only at Atlanta, but in all America. To secure this, we must stop the war that now desolates our once happy and favored country. To stop war, we must defeat the rebel armies which are arrayed against the laws and Constitution that all must respect and obey. To defeat those armies, we must prepare the way to reach them in their recesses, provided with the arms and instruments which enable us to accomplish our purpose. Now, I know the vindictive nature of our enemy, that we may have many years of military operations from this quarter; and, therefore, deem it wise and prudent to prepare in time. The use of Atlanta for warlike purposes is inconsistent with its character as a home for families. There will be no manufactures, commerce, or agriculture here, for the maintenance of families, and sooner or later want will compel the inhabitants to go. Why not go now, when all the arrangements are completed for the transfer, instead of waiting till the plunging shot of contending armies will renew the scenes of the past month? Of course, I do not apprehend any such thing at this moment, but you do not suppose this army will be here until the war is over. I cannot discuss this subject with you fairly, because I cannot impart to you what we propose to do, but I assert that our military plans make it necessary for the inhabitants to go away, and I can only renew my offer of services to make their exodus in any direction as easy and comfortable as possible.

You cannot qualify war in harsher terms than I will. War is cruelty, and you cannot refine it; and those who brought war into our country deserve all the curses and maledictions a people can pour out. I know I had no hand in making this war, and I know I will make more sacrifices to-day than any of you to secure peace. But you cannot have peace and a division of our country. If the United States submits to a division now, it will not stop, but will go on until we reap the fate of Mexico, which is eternal war. The United States does and must assert its authority, wherever it once had power; for, if it relaxes one bit to pressure, it is gone, and I believe that such is the national feeling. This feeling assumes various shapes, but always comes back to that of

William T. Sherman, *Memoirs of General William T. Sherman* (Appleton, New York, 1875).

A devastated land. In this painting by David English Henderson, a Virginia family returns to a home shattered by the bloody battle of Fredericksburg. Significantly, no men of military age remain. (Gettysburg National Military Park)

Union. Once admit the Union, once more acknowledge the authority of the national Government, and, instead of devoting your houses and streets and roads to the dread uses of war, I and this army become at once your protectors and supporters, shielding you from danger, let it come from what quarter it may. I know that a few individuals cannot resist a torrent of error and passion, such as swept the South into rebellion, but you can point out, so that we may know those who desire a government, and those who insist on war and its desolation.

You might as well appeal against the thunder-storm as against these terrible hardships of war. They are inevitable, and the only way the people of Atlanta can hope once more to live in peace and quiet at home, is to stop the war, which can only be done by admitting that it began in error and is perpetuated in pride.

We don't want your Negroes, or your horses, or your houses, or your lands, or any thing you have, but we do want and will have a just obedience to the laws of the United States. That we will have, and if it involves the destruction of your improvements, we cannot help it.

You have heretofore read public sentiment in your newspapers, that live by falsehood and excitement; and the quicker you seek for truth in other quarters, the better. I repeat then that, by the original compact of government, the United States had certain rights in Georgia, which have never been relinquished and never will be; that the South began war by seizing forts, arsenals, mints, custom-houses, etc., etc., long before Mr. Lincoln was installed, and before the South had one jot or tittle of provocation. I myself have seen in Missouri, Kentucky, Tennessee, and Mississippi, hundreds and thousands of women and children fleeing from your armies and desperadoes, hungry and with bleeding feet. In Memphis, Vicksburg, and Mississippi, we fed thousands upon thousands of the families of rebel soldiers left on our hands, and whom we could not see starve. Now that war comes home to you, you feel very different. You deprecate its horrors, but did not feel them when you sent car-loads of soldiers and ammunition, and moulded shells and shot, to carry war into Kentucky and Tennessee, to desolate the homes of hundreds and thousands of good people who only asked to live in peace at their old homes, and under the Government of their inheritance. But these comparisons are idle. I want peace, and believe it can only be reached through union and war, and I will ever conduct war with a view to perfect an early success.

But, my dear sirs, when peace does come, you may call on me for any thing. Then will I share with you the last cracker, and watch with you to shield your homes and families against danger from every quarter.

Now you must go, and take with you the old and feeble, feed and nurse them, and build for them, in more quiet places, proper habitations to shield them against the weather until the mad passions of men cool down, and allow the Union and peace once more to settle over your old homes at Atlanta.

★═══★═══★

Diary of a Georgia Girl (1864)

ELIZA ANDREWS

December 24, 1864.—About three miles from Sparta we struck the "burnt country," as it is well named by the natives, and then I could better understand the wrath and desperation of these poor people. I almost felt as if I should like to hang a Yankee myself. There was hardly a fence left standing all the way from Sparta to Gordon. The fields were trampled down and the road was lined with carcasses of horses, hogs, and cattle that the invaders, unable either to consume or to carry away with them, had wantonly shot down, to starve out the people and prevent them from making their crops.

Eliza Andrews, *The War-Time Diary of a Georgia Girl* (Appleton, New York, 1908).

The stench in some places was unbearable; every few hundred yards we had to hold our noses or stop them with the cologne Mrs. Elzey had given us, and it proved a great boon. The dwellings that were standing all showed signs of pillage, and on every plantation we saw the charred remains of the ginhouse and packing screw, while here and there lone chimney stacks, "Sherman's sentinels," told of homes laid in ashes. The infamous wretches! I couldn't wonder now that these poor people should want to put a rope round the neck of every red-handed "devil of them" they could lay their hands on. Hayricks and fodder stacks were demolished, corncribs were empty, and every bale of cotton that could be found was burnt by the savages. I saw no grain of any sort except little patches they had spilled when feeding their horses and which there was not even a chicken left in the country to eat. A bag of oats might have lain anywhere along the road without danger from the beasts of the field, though I cannot say it would have been safe from the assaults of hungry man.

Crowds of soldiers were tramping over the road in both directions; it was like traveling through the streets of a populous town all day. They were mostly on foot, and I saw numbers seated on the roadside greedily eating raw turnips, meat skins, parched corn—anything they could find, even picking up the loose grains that Sherman's horses had left. I felt tempted to stop and empty the contents of our provision baskets into their laps, but the dreadful accounts that were given of the state of the country before us made prudence get the better of our generosity.

Before crossing the Oconee at Milledgeville we ascended an immense hill, from which there was a fine view of the town, with Governor Brown's fortifications in the foreground and the river rolling at our feet. The Yankees had burnt the bridge; so we had to cross on a ferry. There was a long train of vehicles ahead of us, and it was nearly an hour before our turn came; so we had ample time to look about us. On our left was a field where thirty thousand Yankees had camped hardly three weeks before. It was strewn with the debris they had left behind, and the poor people of the neighborhood were wandering over it, seeking for anything they could find to eat, even picking up grains of corn that were scattered around where the Yankees had fed their horses. We were told that a great many valuables were found there at first, plunder that the invaders had left behind, but the place had been picked over so often by this time that little now remained except tufts of loose cotton, piles of half-rotted grain, and the carcasses of slaughtered animals, which raised a horrible stench. Some men were plowing in one part of the field, making ready for next year's crop.

44

Binding Wounds

In June 1864, when the Republicans nominated Abraham Lincoln for a second term, the end of the war seemed as far away as ever. Northerners were shocked at the heavy casualties reported from battlefields in Virginia, and criticism of the administration had become so harsh that in mid-August Lincoln was convinced he would not be reelected. The Radical Republicans, who spoke for the antislavery faction of the party, condemned him as "politically, militarily, and financially a failure" and for a time backed John C. Frémont for the presidency. The Northern Democrats nominated General George B. McClellan, a former federal commander, and adopted a platform calling for the immediate cessation of hostilities and the restoration of the Union by a negotiated peace. Lincoln was so sure McClellan would defeat him that he wrote a secret memorandum explaining how he would cooperate with the new president after the election in order to save the Union.

But a series of federal victories—the closing of Mobile Bay, the capture of Atlanta, and the routing of Southern forces in the Shenandoah Valley—led public opinion to swing back rapidly to Lincoln. Republican newspapers began ridiculing the "war-is-a-failure" platform of the Democrats, and Frémont decided to drop out of the campaign. Lincoln's prediction that he would not be reelected proved wrong. On election day he won a plurality of nearly half a million votes and carried every state in the Union except Kentucky, Delaware, and New Jersey.

In his second inaugural address on March 4, 1865, Lincoln singled out slavery as the cause of the Civil War and stated that its eradication was inevitable. He expressed hope for a speedy end to the conflict, called for "malice toward none" and "charity for all," and looked forward to the day when Americans would achieve a "just and lasting peace" among themselves and with all nations. On April 9, Lee surrendered to Grant at Appomattox; two days later Lincoln made his last public address, outlining his reconstruction policy. He had never considered the South to be outside of the Union and hoped for a speedy reconciliation. On April 14, at his last cabinet meeting, he urged the cabinet members to put aside all thoughts of hatred and revenge. That evening he was shot.

Questions to Consider. Lincoln's second inaugural address is commonly regarded as one of the greatest addresses ever made by an American president. Why do you think this is so? What did he regard as the basic issue of the Civil War? What irony did he see in the attitude of the contestants? What use of the Bible did he make? Do you think this was likely to appeal to Americans in 1865?

★══★══★

Second Inaugural Address (1865)

ABRAHAM LINCOLN

FELLOW-COUNTRYMEN:—At this second appearing to take the oath of the presidential office there is less occasion for an extended address than there was at the first. Then a statement somewhat in detail of a course to be pursued seemed fitting and proper. Now, at the expiration of four years, during which public declarations have been constantly called forth on every point and phase of the great contest which still absorbs the attention and engrosses the energies of the nation, little that is new could be presented. The progress of our arms, upon which all else chiefly depends, is as well known to the public as to myself, and it is, I trust, reasonably satisfactory and encouraging to all. With high hope for the future, no prediction in regard to it is ventured.

On the occasion corresponding to this four years ago all thoughts were anxiously directed to an impending civil war. All dreaded it, all sought to avert it. While the inaugural address was being delivered from this place, devoted altogether to *saving* the Union without war, insurgent agents were in the city seeking to *destroy* it without war—seeking to dissolve the Union and divide effects by negotiation. Both parties deprecated war, but one of them would *make* war rather than let the nation survive, and the other would *accept* war rather than let it perish, and the war came.

One eighth of the whole population was colored slaves, not distributed generally over the Union, but localized in the southern part of it. These slaves constituted a peculiar and powerful interest. All knew that this interest was somehow the cause of the war. To strengthen, perpetuate, and extend this interest was the object for which the insurgents would rend the Union even by war, while the Government claimed no right to do more than to restrict the territorial enlargement of it. Neither party expected for the war the magnitude nor the duration which it has already attained. Neither anticipated that the *cause* of the conflict might cease with or even before the conflict itself

James D. Richardson, ed., *A Compilation of the Messages and Papers of the Presidents* (Government Printing Office, Washington, D.C., 1897–1907), VIII: 3477–3478.

should cease. Each looked for an easier triumph, and a result less fundamental and astounding. Both read the same Bible and pray to the same God, and each invokes His aid against the other. It may seem strange that any men should dare to ask a just God's assistance in wringing their bread from the sweat of other men's faces, but let us judge not, that we be not judged. The prayers of both could not be answered. That of neither has been answered fully. The Almighty has His own purposes. "Woe unto the world because of offenses; for it must needs be that offenses come, but woe to that man by whom the offense cometh." If we shall suppose that American slavery is one of those offenses which, in the providence of God, must needs come, but which, having continued through His appointed time, He now wills to remove, and that He gives to both North and South this terrible war as the woe due to those by whom the offense came, shall we discern therein any departure from those divine attributes which the believers in a living God always ascribe to Him? Fondly do we hope, fervently do we pray, that this mighty scourge of war may speedily pass away. Yet, if God wills that it continue until all the wealth piled by the bondsman's two hundred and fifty years of unrequited toil shall be sunk, and until every drop of blood drawn with the lash shall be paid by another drawn with the sword, as was said three thousand years ago, so still it must be said, "The judgments of the Lord are true and righteous altogether."

With malice toward none, with charity for all, with firmness in the right as God gives us to see the right, let us strive on to finish the work we are in, to bind up the nation's wounds, to care for him who shall have borne the battle and for his widow and his orphan, to do all which may achieve and cherish a just and lasting peace among ourselves and with all nations.

Freedwoman in cotton field at harvest. No part of the labor on a cotton plantation was more terrible than picking. At harvest, when time was of the essence to
avoid spoiling rains, the hands of the "hands" became bloody and twisted from
pulling fluffy cotton bolls from the stiff, spiny, pointed husks, and their backs
ached from morning to night—from "kin see to cain't see"—from pulling the heavy
bags of pulled cotton behind in the furrows. Emancipation changed all this very
little. This woman, photographed in a Georgia field in the late nineteenth century,
has a strong face and level gaze, but by day's end, never mind life's end, she
would feel little but pain. (Georgia Division of Archives & History, Office of Secretary of State)

CHAPTER SIX

The Agony of Reconstruction

45

KLANSMEN OF THE CAROLINAS

Reconstruction developed in a series of moves and countermoves. In a white Southern backlash to Union victory and emancipation came the "black codes" for coercing black laborers and President Andrew Johnson's pardon of Confederate landowners. Then in a Northern backlash to these codes and pardons came the Civil Rights bills, the sweeping Reconstruction Acts of 1867, and the Fourteenth and Fifteenth Amendments, all designed to guarantee black political rights. White Southerners reacted to these impositions in turn with secret night-time terrorist or "night rider" organizations designed to shatter Republican political power. Congress tried to protect Republican voters and the freedmen with the Force Acts of 1870 allowing the use of the army to prevent physical assaults, but Northern willingness to commit troops and resources to the struggle was waning. By the mid-1870s only three Southern states remained in Republican hands, and within three years racist Democrats controlled these, too. The night riders had turned the tide.

Although numerous secret societies for whites appeared in the Reconstruction South—including the Order of the White Camelia (Louisiana), the Pale Faces (Tennessee), the White Brotherhood (North Carolina), and the Invisible Circle (South Carolina)—the largest and most influential society, and the one that spawned these imitators, was the Ku Klux Klan, the so-called Invisible Empire. The Klan began in Tennessee in 1866 as a young men's social club with secret costumes and rituals similar to those of the Masons, the Odd-Fellows, and other popular societies. In 1867, however, following passage of the Reconstruction Acts, anti-Republican racists began to see the usefulness of such a spookily secret order, and the Klan was reorganized to provide for "dens," "provinces" (counties), and "realms" (states), all under the authority of a "Grand Wizard," who in 1867 was believed to have been Nathan B. Forrest, a former slave trader and Confederate general.

The Klan structure was probably never fully established because of the disorganized conditions of the postwar South. Other societies with different names emerged, and the Reconstruction-era "Ku-Klux" may

have disbanded as a formal entity in the early 1870s. But it clearly survived in spirit and in loosely formed groups, continuing to terrorize Republicans and their allies among the newly enfranchised freedmen
into the 1870s and sowing fear among the black families who composed, after all, the labor force on which the white planters still depended. The excerpt reprinted below includes congressional testimony
by David Schenck, a member of the North Carolina Klan seeking to
portray it in the best possible light, followed by testimony from Elias
Hill, a South Carolina black man victimized by a local "den" of the
Klan. Schenck and Hill were testifying before a joint Senate-House
committee concerned with antiblack terrorism.

Questions to Consider. The oath taken by David Schenck emphasizes
the Klan's religious, constitutional, and benevolent qualities, whereas
Elias Hill's story reveals its terrorist features. Are there elements in the
Klan oath that seem to hint at or justify the use of violence? Why does
the oath contain the phrases "original purity," "pecuniary embarrass-
ments," and "traitor's doom"? What "secrets of this order" could deserve death? Klansmen later claimed that because they could terrorize
the superstitious freedmen simply by using masks, odd voices, and
ghostly sheets, no real violence was necessary. Opponents have claimed,
on the other hand, that Klansmen were basically sadists acting out sex-
ual phobias and deep paranoia. What light does Elias Hill's testimony
shed on these conflicting claims? What position did Hill hold in the
black community? Did the Klansmen seem to be assaulting him because of his condition or because of his position in the black community?
Why did they ask Hill to pray for them? Would it be fair or accurate to
call the Ku Klux Klan a terrorist organization that succeeded?

Report of the Joint Committee
on Reconstruction (1872)

A select committee of the Senate, upon the 10th of March, 1871, made a report
of the result of their investigation into the security of person and property
in the State of North Carolina. . . . A sub-committee of their number proceeded to the State of South Carolina, and examined witnesses in that State
until July 29. . . .

*Report of the Joint Select Committee to Inquire into the Condition of Affairs in the Late Insurrec-
tionary States* (Government Printing Office, Washington, D.C., 1872), 25–27, 44–47.

A North Carolina Ku Klux Klan meeting to plan the murder of a black Republican, from an 1871 engraving in a New York publication. Although the artist imagined the scene, he managed to convey both the bizarre and spooky garb of the Klan members and the defenselessness and terror of the lone kneeling freedman. The Klan victimized not only former slaves suspected of supporting the Republican Party but also freedmen who obtained land or learned to read and write. (Library of Congress)

David Schenck, esq., a member of the bar of Lincoln County, North Carolina . . . was initiated in October, 1868, as a member of the Invisible Empire. . . . In his own words: "We were in favor of constitutional liberty as handed down to us by our forefathers. I think the idea incorporated was that we were opposed to the [fourteenth and fifteenth] amendments to the Constitution. I desire to explain in regard to that that it was not to be—at least, I did not intend by that that it should be—forcible resistance, but a political principle."

The oath itself is as follows:

> I, (name,) before the great immaculate Judge of heaven and earth, and upon the Holy Evangelist of Almighty God, do, of my own free will and accord, subscribe to the following sacred, binding obligation:
>
> I. I am on the side of justice and humanity and constitutional liberty, as bequeathed to us by our forefathers in its original purity.
>
> II. I reject and oppose the principles of the radical [Republican] party.
>
> III. I pledge aid to a brother of the Ku-Klux Klan in sickness, distress, or pecuniary embarrassments. Females, friends, widows, and their households shall be the special objects of my care and protection.
>
> IV. Should I ever divulge, or cause to be divulged, any of the secrets of this order, or any of the foregoing obligations, I must meet with the fearful punishment of death and traitor's doom, which is death, death, death, at the hands of the brethren. . . .

Elias Hill of York County, South Carolina, is a remarkable character. He is crippled in both legs and arms, which are shriveled by rheumatism; he cannot walk, cannot help himself . . . ; was in early life a slave, whose freedom was purchased by his father. . . . He learned his letters and to read by calling the school children into the cabin as they passed, and also learned to write. He became a Baptist preacher, and after the war engaged in teaching colored children, and conducted the business correspondence of many of his colored neighbors. . . . We put the story of his wrongs in his own language:

"On the night of the 5th of May, after I had heard a great deal of what they had done in that neighborhood, they came . . . to my brother's door, which is in the same yard, and broke open the door and attacked his wife, and I heard her screaming and mourning. I could not understand what they said, for they were talking in an outlandish and unnatural tone, which I had heard they generally used at a negro's house. They said, 'Where's Elias?' She said, 'He doesn't stay here; yon is his house.' I had heard them strike her five or six licks. Someone then hit my door. . . .

"They carried me into the yard between the houses, my brother's and mine, and put me on the ground. . . . 'Who did that burning? Who burned our houses?' I told them it was not me. I could not burn houses. Then they hit me with their fists, and said I did it, I ordered it. They went on asking me didn't I tell the black men to ravish all the white women. No, I answered them. They struck me again. . . . 'Haven't you been preaching and praying about the Ku-Klux? Haven't you been preaching political sermons? Doesn't a [Republican Party newspaper] come to your house? Haven't you written letters?' Generally one asked me all the questions, but the rest were squatting over me—some six men I counted as I lay there. . . . I told them if they would take me back into the house, and lay me in the bed, which was close adjoining my books and papers, I would try and get it. They said I would never go back to that bed, for they were going to kill me. . . . They caught my leg and pulled me over the yard, and then left me there, knowing I could not walk nor crawl. . . .

"After they had stayed in the house for a considerable time, they came back to where I lay and asked if I wasn't afraid at all. They pointed pistols at me all around my head once or twice, as if they were going to shoot me. . . . One caught me by the leg and hurt me, for my leg for forty years has been drawn each year, more and more, and I made moan when it hurt so. One said, 'G–d d—n it, hush!' He had a horsewhip, [and] I reckon he struck me eight cuts right on the hip bone; it was almost the only place he could hit my body, my legs are so short. They all had disguises. . . . One of them then took a strap, and buckled it around my neck and said, 'Let's take him to the river and drown him.' . . .

"Then they said, 'Look here! Will you put a card in the paper to renounce all republicanism? Will you quit preaching?' I told them I did not know. I said that to save my life. . . . They said if I did not they would come back the next week and kill me. [After more licks with the strap] one of them went into the house where my brother and sister-in-law lived, and brought her to pick me up. As she stooped down to pick me up one of them struck her, and as she was carrying me into the house another struck her with a strap. . . . They said, 'Don't you pray against Ku-Klux, but pray that God may forgive Ku-Klux. Pray that God may bless and save us.' I was so chilled with cold lying out of doors so long and in such pain I could not speak to pray, but I tried to, and they said that would do very well, and all went out of the house. . . ."

Satisfied that he could no longer live in that community, Hill wrote to make inquiry about the means of going to Liberia. Hearing this, many of his neighbors desired to go also. . . . Others are still hoping for relief, through the means of this sub-committee.

46

A Kind of Unity

Despite Congress's seizure of control over Reconstruction policy and Ulysses S. Grant's defeat of Andrew Johnson for the presidency in 1868, Radical Reconstruction—the garrisoning of the South, the disfranchisement of former rebels, and the control of Southern state governments by Republican votes—did not last long in most places. During President Grant's first term of office, the white-dominated Democratic Party gained control of North Carolina, Tennessee, and Virginia, the three ex-Confederate states with the lowest percentage of black population. During Grant's second term, Democrats seized control of Alabama, Arkansas, Georgia, Mississippi, and Texas. That left Republican governments (and federal troops) in Florida, Louisiana, and South Carolina, three states with large black populations.

Those states mattered greatly in national politics. During the election of 1876 both parties resorted to fraud. Two sets of electoral returns came in from the three states, and it was necessary for Congress to set up an electoral commission to decide whether Rutherford B. Hayes, the Republican candidate, or Samuel J. Tilden, the Democratic standard bearer, had won. By a strict party vote of 8 to 7, the commission awarded all 20 disputed electoral votes to the Republicans. Hayes became president, with 185 votes to Tilden's 184. In the end, Southern Democrats reached a compromise with Northern Republicans. The Democrats agreed to accept the commission's decision and the Republicans promised to withdraw the remaining federal troops from the South. In April 1877, the last federal soldiers left the South. Solid Democratic control—and stepped-up measures to disfranchise black voters—quickly followed.

Although political maneuvering was important in finally killing Republican Reconstruction, the underlying reason it died was simply that Northerners were losing the will to suppress an increasingly violent white South. The nation's approaching centennial celebration in 1876 triggered an especially strong outpouring of sentiment in favor of improving sectional feelings by withdrawing the troops, even if withdrawal meant the resurgence of the Democratic Party. That, in turn, would permit an overdue rebonding of the century-old republic. The following unsigned editorial ran in the August 1875 issue of *Scribner's Monthly,* an influential, generally Republican, New York magazine. It expressed, with unusual eloquence, this emotional yearning for peace.

Questions to Consider. What was the occasion of the *Scribner's* editorial? Was this a natural time to consider troop withdrawals? What, in the view of the editor, was the major accomplishment of the Civil War? What specific political theory had been tested and defeated? When addressing the "men of the South," was the editor speaking to all Southern men? What did the phrase "brotherly sympathy" mean? Was it naive or was it realistic for the writer to think that the upcoming centennial could "heal all the old wounds" and "reconcile all the old differences"? Would Abraham Lincoln have agreed with the spirit of this editorial?

★━━★━━★

What the Centennial Ought to Accomplish (1875)

SCRIBNER'S MONTHLY

We are to have grand doings next year. There is to be an Exposition. There are to be speeches, and songs, and processions, and elaborate ceremonies and general rejoicings. Cannon are to be fired, flags are to be floated, and the eagle is expected to scream while he dips the tip of either pinion in the Atlantic and the Pacific, and sprinkles the land with a new baptism of freedom. The national oratory will exhaust the figures of speech in patriotic glorification, while the effete civilizations of the Old World, and the despots of the East, tottering upon their tumbling thrones, will rub their eyes and sleepily inquire, "What's the row?" The Centennial is expected to celebrate in a fitting way—somewhat dimly apprehended, it is true—the birth of a nation.

Well, the object is a good one. When the old colonies declared themselves free, they took a grand step in the march of progress; but now, before we begin our celebration of this event, would it not be well for us to inquire whether we have a nation? In a large number of the States of this country there exists not only a belief that the United States do not constitute a nation, but a theory of State rights which forbids that they ever shall become one. We hear about the perturbed condition of the Southern mind. We hear it said that multitudes there are just as disloyal as they were during the civil war. This, we believe, we are justified in denying. Before the war they had a theory of State rights. They fought to establish that theory, and they now speak of the

Miss Liberty's torch. A display at the great 1876 Centennial Exposition, Philadelphia. (Library of Congress)

result as "the lost cause." They are not actively in rebellion, and they do not propose to be. They do not hope for the re-establishment of slavery. They fought bravely and well to establish their theory, but the majority was against them; and if the result of the war emphasized any fact, it was that *en masse* the people of the United States constitute a nation—indivisible in constituents, in interest, in destiny. The result of the war was without significance, if it did not mean that the United States constitute a nation which cannot be divided; which will not permit itself to be divided; which is integral, indissoluble, indestructible. We do not care what theories of State rights are entertained outside of this. State rights, in all the States, should be jealously guarded, and, by all legitimate means, defended. New York should be as jealous of her State prerogatives as South Carolina or Louisiana; but this theory which makes of the Union a rope of sand, and of the States a collection of petty nationalities that can at liberty drop the bands which hold them together, is forever exploded. It has been tested at the point of the bayonet. It went down in blood, and went down for all time. Its adherents may mourn over the fact, as we can never cease to mourn over the events which accompanied it, over the sad, incalculable cost to them and to those who opposed them. The great point with them is to recognize the fact that, for richer or poorer, in sickness and health, until death do us part, these United States constitute a nation; that we are to live, grow, prosper, and suffer together, united by bands that cannot be sundered.

Unless this fact is fully recognized throughout the Union, our Centennial will be but a hollow mockery. If we are to celebrate anything worth celebrating, it is the birth of a nation. If we are to celebrate anything worth celebrating, it should be by the whole heart and united voice of the nation. If we can make the Centennial an occasion for emphasizing the great lesson of the war, and universally assenting to the results of the war, it will, indeed, be worth all the money expended upon and the time devoted to it. If around the old Altars of Liberty we cannot rejoin our hands in brotherly affection and national loyalty, let us spike the cannon that will only proclaim our weakness, put our flags at half-mast, smother our eagles, eat our ashes, and wait for our American aloe to give us a better blossoming.

A few weeks ago, Mr. Jefferson Davis, the ex-President of the Confederacy, was reported to have exhorted an audience to which he was speaking to be as loyal to the old flag of the Union now as they were during the Mexican War. If the South could know what music there was in these words to Northern ears—how grateful we were to their old chief for them—it would appreciate the strength of our longing for a complete restoration of the national feeling that existed when Northern and Southern blood mingled in common sacrifice on Mexican soil. This national feeling, this national pride, this brotherly sympathy *must be restored*; and accursed be any Northern or Southern man, whether in power or out of power, whether politician, theorizer, carpetbagger, president-maker or plunderer, who puts obstacles in the way of such a restoration. Men of the South, we want you. Men of the South, we long for the restoration of your peace and your prosperity. We would see your cities thriving, your homes happy, your plantations teeming with plenteous harvests, your schools overflowing, your wisest statesmen leading you, and all causes and all memories of discord wiped out forever. You do not believe this? Then you do not know the heart of the North. Have you cause of complaint against the politicians? Alas! so have we. Help us, as loving and loyal

American citizens, to make our politicians better. Only remember and believe that there is nothing that the North wants so much to-day, as your recognition of the fact that the old relations between you and us are forever restored—that your hope, your pride, your policy, and your destiny are one with ours. Our children will grow up to despise our childishness, if we cannot do away with our personal hates so far, that in the cause of an established nationality we may join hands under the old flag.

To bring about this reunion of the two sections of the country in the old fellowship, should be the leading object of the approaching Centennial. A celebration of the national birth, begun, carried on, and finished by a section, would be a mockery and a shame. The nations of the world might well point at it the finger of scorn. The money expended upon it were better sunk in the sea, or devoted to repairing the waste places of the war. Men of the South, it is for you to say whether your magnanimity is equal to your valor—whether you are as reasonable as you are brave, and whether, like your old chief, you accept that definite and irreversible result of the war which makes you and yours forever members of the great American nation with us. Let us see to it, North and South, that the Centennial heals all the old wounds, reconciles all the old differences, and furnishes the occasion for such a reunion of the great American nationality, as shall make our celebration an expression of fraternal good-will among all sections and all States, and a corner-stone over which shall be reared a new temple to national freedom, concord, peace, and prosperity.

47

AFTERMATH

Frederick Douglass regarded the Declaration of Independence as a "watchword of freedom." But he was tempted to turn it to the wall, he said, because its human rights principles were so shamelessly violated. A former slave himself, Douglass knew what he was talking about. Douglass thought that enslaving blacks fettered whites as well and that the United States would never be truly free until it ended chattel slavery. During the Civil War, he had several conversations with Lincoln, urging him to make emancipation his major aim. He also put unremitting pressure on the Union army to accept black volunteers, and after resistance to admitting blacks into the army gave way, he toured the country encouraging blacks to enlist and imploring the government to treat black and white soldiers equally in matters of pay and promotion.

Douglass had great hopes for his fellow blacks after the Civil War. He demanded they be given full rights—political, legal, educational, and economic—as citizens. He also wanted to see the wall of separation between the races crumble and see "the colored people of this country, enjoying the same freedom [as whites], voting at the same ballot-box, using the same cartridge-box, going to the same schools, attending the same churches, travelling in the same street cars, in the same railroad cars, on the same steam-boats, proud of the same country, fighting the same war, and enjoying the same peace and all its advantages." He regarded the Republican Party as the "party of progress, justice and freedom" and at election time took to the stump and rallied black votes for the party. He was rewarded for these services by appointment as marshal of the District of Columbia in 1877, as recorder of deeds for the District in 1881, and as minister to Haiti in 1889. But he was also asked by Republican leaders to keep a low profile, was omitted from White House guest lists, and was excluded from presidential receptions even though one duty of the District marshal was to introduce the guests at White House state occasions.

Douglass was puzzled and then upset by the increasing indifference of Republican leaders to conditions among blacks after the Civil War. In 1883 he attended a convention of blacks in Louisville, Kentucky, which met to discuss their plight and reaffirm their demand for full civil rights. In his keynote address, which is reprinted here, Douglass vividly portrayed the discrimination and persecution his people encountered, but he continued to believe that "prejudice, with all its malign accomplishments, may yet be removed by peaceful means."

Born into slavery in Maryland in 1817, Frederick Augustus Washington Bailey learned to read and write despite efforts to keep him illiterate. In 1838 he managed to escape to freedom and adopted the name Frederick Douglass. Shortly afterward he became associated with William Lloyd Garrison and developed into such an articulate spokesman for the antislavery cause that people doubted he had ever been a slave. In 1845 he published his *Narrative of the Life of Frederick Douglass, an American Slave,* naming names, places, dates, and precise events to convince people he had been born in bondage. Douglass continued to be an articulate spokesman for the black cause throughout his life. Shortly before his death in 1895 a college student asked him what a young black could do to help the cause. Douglass is supposed to have told him, "Agitate! Agitate! Agitate!"

Questions to Consider. In the following address Douglass was speaking to a convention of blacks in Louisville, but his appeal was primarily to American whites. How did he try to convince them that blacks deserved the same rights and opportunities as all Americans? How powerful did he think the color line was? What outrages against his people did he report? What was his attitude toward the Republican Party, which he had so faithfully served? Were the grievances he cited largely economic or were they social and political in nature?

★══★══★

Address to the Louisville Convention (1883)

FREDERICK DOUGLASS

Born on American soil in common with yourselves, deriving our bodies and our minds from its dust, centuries having passed away since our ancestors were torn from the shores of Africa, we, like yourselves, hold ourselves to be in every sense Americans, and that we may, therefore, venture to speak to you in a tone not lower than that which becomes earnest men and American citizens. Having watered your soil with our tears, enriched it with our blood, performed its roughest labor in time of peace, defended it against enemies in time of war, and at all times been loyal and true to its best interests, we deem

Philip Foner, ed., *The Life and Writings of Frederick Douglass* (4 v., International Publishers, New York, 1955), IV: 373–392. Reprinted by permission.

Frederick Douglass. Douglass's greatest work came before and during the Civil War. One of the most eloquent and magnetic of all the abolitionist leaders, he contributed enormously to the antislavery cause. During the Civil War he pressed hard for the enlistment of blacks to fight in the Union armies on an equal footing with whites. After the war he continued his efforts for civil rights, including black suffrage. For his services to the Republican Party he received appointments as secretary to the Santo Domingo commission, marshal and recorder of deeds for the District of Columbia, and U.S. minister to Haiti. (National Portrait Gallery, Smithsonian Institution/Art Resource, NY)

it no arrogance or presumption to manifest now a common concern with you for its welfare, prosperity, honor and glory. . . .

It is our lot to live among a people whose laws, traditions, and prejudices have been against us for centuries, and from these they are not yet free. To assume that they are free from these evils simply because they have changed their laws is to assume what is utterly unreasonable and contrary to facts. Large bodies move slowly. Individuals may be converted on the instant and change their whole course of life. Nations never. Time and events are required for the conversion of nations. Not even the character of a great political organization can be changed by a new platform. It will be the same old snake though in a new skin. Though we have had war, reconstruction and abolition as a nation, we still linger in the shadow and blight of an extinct institution. Though the colored man is no longer subject to be bought and sold, he is still surrounded by an adverse sentiment which fetters all his movements. In his downward course he meets with no resistance, but his course upward is resented and resisted at every step of his progress. If he comes in ignorance, rags, and wretchedness, he conforms to the popular belief of his character, and in that character he is welcome. But if he shall come as a gentleman, a scholar, and a statesman, he is hailed as a contradiction to the national faith concerning his race, and his coming is resented as impudence. In the one case he may provoke contempt and derision, but in the other he is an affront to pride, and provokes malice. Let him do what he will, there is at present, therefore, no escape for him. The color line meets him everywhere, and in a measure shuts him out from all respectable and profitable trades and callings. In spite of all your religion and laws he is a rejected man.

He is rejected by trade unions, of every trade, and refused work while he lives, and burial when he dies, and yet he is asked to forget his color, and forget that which everybody else remembers. If he offers himself to a builder as a mechanic, to a client as a lawyer, to a patient as a physician, to a college as a professor, to a firm as a clerk, to a Government Department as an agent, or an officer, he is sternly met on the color line, and his claim to consideration in some way is disputed on the ground of color.

Not even our churches, whose members profess to follow the despised Nazarene, whose home, when on earth, was among the lowly and despised, have yet conquered this feeling of color madness, and what is true of our churches is also true of our courts of law. Neither is free from this all-pervading atmosphere of color hate. The one describes the Deity as impartial, no respecter of persons, and the other the Goddess of Justice as blindfolded, with sword by her side and scales in her hand held evenly between high and low, rich and low, white and black, but both are the images of American imagination, rather than American practices.

Taking advantage of the general disposition in this country to impute crime to color, white men *color* their faces to commit crime and wash off the hated color to escape punishment. In many places where the commission of crime is alleged against one of our color, the ordinary processes of law are set aside as too slow for the impetuous justice of the infuriated populace. They take the law into their own bloody hands and proceed to whip, stab, shoot, hang, or burn the alleged culprit, without the intervention of courts, counsel, judges, juries, or witnesses. In such cases it is not the business of the accusers to prove guilt, but it is for the accused to prove his innocence, a thing hard for him to do in these infernal Lynch courts. A man accused, surprised, frightened, and captured by a motley crowd, dragged with a rope about his neck in midnight-darkness to the nearest tree, and told in the coarsest terms of profanity to prepare for death, would be more than human if he did not, in his terror-stricken appearance, more confirm suspicion of guilt than the contrary. Worse still, in the presence of such hell-black outrages, the pulpit is usually dumb, and the press in the neighborhood is silent or openly takes side with the mob. There are occasional cases in which white men are lynched, but one sparrow does not make a summer. Every one knows that what is called Lynch law is peculiarly the law for colored people and for nobody else. If there were no other grievance than this horrible and barbarous Lynch law custom, we should be justified in assembling, as we have now done, to expose and denounce it. But this is not all. Even now, after twenty years of so-called emancipation, we are subject to lawless raids of midnight riders, who, with blackened faces, invade our homes and perpetrate the foulest of crimes upon us and our families. This condition of things is too flagrant and notorious to require specifications or proof. Thus in all the relations of life and death we are met by the color line.

While we recognize the color line as a hurtful force, a mountain barrier to our progress, wounding our bleeding feet with its flinty rocks at every step, we do not despair. We are a hopeful people. This convention is a proof of our faith in you, in reason, in truth and justice—our belief that prejudice, with all its malign accomplishments, may yet be removed by peaceful means; that, assisted by time and events and the growing enlightenment of both races, the color line will ultimately become harmless. When this shall come it will then only be used, as it should be, to distinguish one variety of the human family from another. It will cease to have any civil, political, or moral significance, and colored conventions will then be dispensed with as anachronisms, wholly out of place, but not till then. Do not marvel that we are discouraged. The faith within us has a rational basis, and is confirmed by facts. When we consider how deep-seated this feeling against us is; the long centuries it has been forming; the forces of avarice which have been marshaled to sustain it; how the language and literature of the country have been pervaded with it; how the church, the press, the play-house, and other influences of the country have been arrayed in its support, the progress toward its extinction must be considered vast and wonderful. . . .

We do not believe, as we are often told, that the Negro is the ugly child of the national family, and the more he is kept out of sight the better it will be for him. You know that liberty given is never so precious as liberty sought for and fought for. The man outraged is the man to make the outcry. Depend upon it, men will not care much for a people who do not care for themselves.

Our meeting here was opposed by some of our members, because it would disturb the peace of the Republican party. The suggestion came from coward lips and misapprehended the character of that party. If the Republican party cannot stand a demand for justice and fair play, it ought to go down. We were men before that party was born, and our manhood is more sacred than any party can be. Parties were made for men, not men for parties.

The colored people of the South are the laboring people of the South. The labor of a country is the source of its wealth; without the colored laborer to-day the South would be a howling wilderness, given up to bats, owls, wolves, and bears. He was the source of its wealth before the war, and has been the source of its prosperity since the war. He almost alone is visible in her fields, with implements of toil in his hands, and laboriously using them to-day.

Let us look candidly at the matter. While we see and hear that the South is more prosperous than it ever was before and rapidly recovering from the waste of war, while we read that it raises more cotton, sugar, rice, tobacco, corn, and other valuable products than it ever produced before, how happens it, we sternly ask, that the houses of its laborers are miserable huts, that their clothes are rags, and their food the coarsest and scantiest? How happens it that the land-owner is becoming richer and the laborer poorer?

The implication is irresistible—that where the landlord is prosperous the laborer ought to share his prosperity, and whenever and wherever we find this is not the case there is manifestly wrong somewhere. . . .

Flagrant as have been the outrages committed upon colored citizens in respect to their civil rights, more flagrant, shocking, and scandalous still have been the outrages committed upon our political rights by means of bulldozing and Kukluxing, Mississippi plans, fraudulent courts, tissue ballots, and the like devices. Three States in which the colored people outnumber the white population are without colored representation and their political voice suppressed. The colored citizens in those States are virtually disfranchised, the Constitution held in utter contempt and its provisions nullified. This has been done in the face of the Republican party and successive Republican administrations. . . .

This is no question of party. It is a question of law and government. It is a question whether men shall be protected by law, or be left to the mercy of cyclones of anarchy and bloodshed. It is whether the Government or the mob shall rule this land; whether the promises solemnly made to us in the constitution be manfully kept or meanly and flagrantly broken. Upon this vital point we ask the whole people of the United States to take notice that whatever of political power we have shall be exerted for no man of any party who will not, in advance of election, promise to use every power given him by the Government, State or National, to make the black man's path to the ballot-box as straight, smooth and safe as that of any other American citizen. . . .

We hold it to be self-evident that no class or color should be the exclusive rulers of this country. If there is such a ruling class, there must of course be a subject class, and when this condition is once established this Government of the people, by the people, and for the people, will have perished from the earth.